COMMANDO COUNTRY

Stuart Allan

Published by
NMS Enterprises Limited – Publishing
a division of NMS Enterprises Limited
National Museums Scotland
Chambers Street
Edinburgh EH1 1JF

Text © Trustees of the National Museums
of Scotland 2007
except for quotations from other works or
where noted to the contrary.

Images © Trustees of the National
Museums of Scotland
except where noted to the contrary.

No reproduction permitted without written
permission.

ISBN 978-1-905267-14-9

*No part of this publication may be reproduced,
stored in a retrieval system or transmitted, in
any form or by any means, electronic, mechan-
ical, photocopying, recording or otherwise,
without the prior permission of the publisher.*

The right of Stuart Allan to be identified as the
author of this book has been asserted by him in
accordance with the Copyright, Designs and
Patents Act 1988.

**British Library Cataloguing in
Publication Data**
A catalogue record of this book
is available from the British Library.

Published with the support of National
Museums Scotland.

Cover design by Mark Blackadder.
Cover photographs: © The Scotsman
Publications Ltd. Licensor www.scran.ac.uk
© The Trustees of the National Museums
of Scotland.
Cover photography by NMS Photography.

Internal text design by NMSE – Publishing,
NMS Enterprises Limited.
Printed and bound in Great Britain by
Athenaeum Press Ltd, Gateshead,
Tyne & Wear.

For a full listing of NMS Enterprises Limited –
Publishing titles and related merchandise:
www.nms.ac.uk/books

Contents

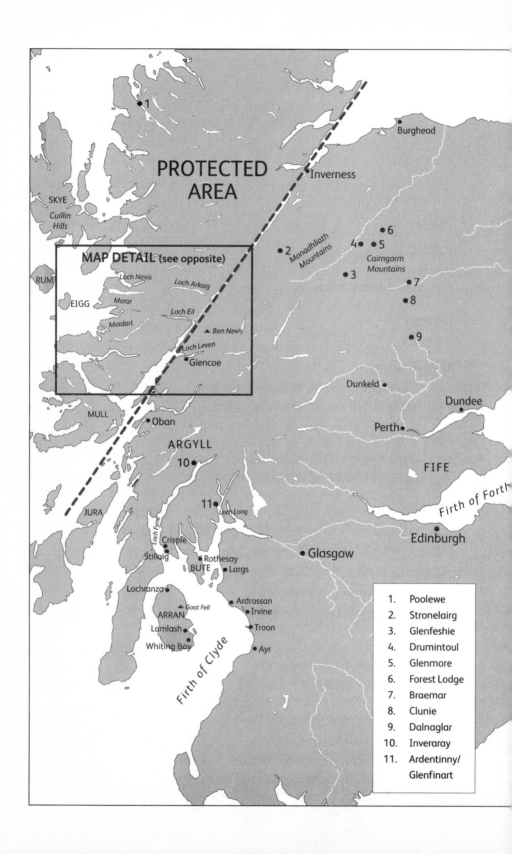

PROTECTED AREA

SKYE
Cuillin Hills

RUM

EIGG

MAP DETAIL (see opposite)

Loch Nevis
Loch Arkaig
Morar
Loch Eil
Moidart
▲ Ben Nevis
Loch Leven
Glencoe

Burghead

Inverness

● 2
Monadhliath Mountains

● 6
● 4 ● 5
Cairngorm Mountains
● 3
● 7
● 8

● 9

Dunkeld ●

Dundee

Perth ●

FIFE

Firth of Forth

MULL
● Oban

ARGYLL

10 ●

11 ●
Loch Long

Loch Fyne

Crispie

Stillaig
● Rothesay
BUTE ● Largs

Lochranza ●

ARRAN
▲ Goat Fell

Lamlash ●

Whiting Bay

Firth of Clyde

Ardrossan
● Irvine

● Troon

● Ayr

● Glasgow

Edinburgh ●

JURA

1. Poolewe
2. Stronelairg
3. Glenfeshie
4. Drumintoul
5. Glenmore
6. Forest Lodge
7. Braemar
8. Clunie
9. Dalnaglar
10. Inveraray
11. Ardentinny/
    Glenfinart

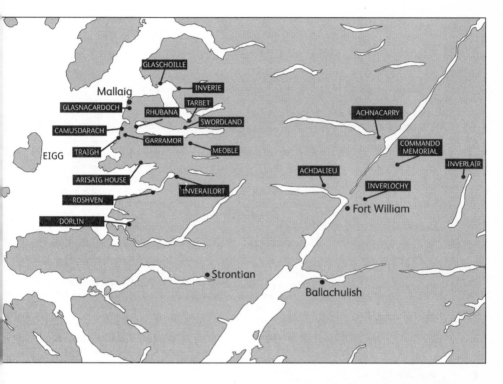

SPECIAL TRAINING CENTRES
Detail of main map opposite

Image and text credits

No reproduction of material in copyright is permitted without prior contact with the publisher. Acknowledgements for use of source material and photographs within this publication are as follows:

IMAGES/PHOTOGRAPHS

THE HONOURABLE
IAN CHANT-SEMPILL
art sections 1(7), 3(2)

CLAN CAMERON MUSEUM
art sections 1(6), 3(10), 3(11)

MRS ANNE CLUNAS
art section 2(14)

CZECH NEWS AGENCY
art section 4(4), 4(5)

THE HONOURABLE HUGH FRASER
art sections 1(4), 4(18), 4(19)

MR A. FYFFE
art section 1(13)

HEADQUARTERS SCOTS GUARDS
art section 2(2), 2(3)

IMPERIAL WAR MUSEUM
art sections 3(1), 3(4), 3(5),
3(8), 3(12), 4(1), 4(7), 4(15)

MS A. M. KEENAN AND
MR R. MUNGIN, ROSHVEN
art section 2(7)

MR STANISŁAW KORZENIOWSKI
art section 4(3)

LIDDELL HART CENTRE
FOR MILITARY ARCHIVES
art sections 2(8), 2(9), 2(11),
3(6)

E. H. VAN MAURIK
art section 4(2)

MR PETER MILES
art section 3(7)

THE NATIONAL ARMY MUSEUM
art section 1(9)

NATIONAL MUSEUMS SCOTLAND
art sections 1(1), 1(2), 1(3),
1(10), 1(11), 1(12), 1(14),
2(6), 2(10), 2(12), 2(13),
3(3), 3(9), 4(8), 4(16), 4(17);
cover; maps

NORWAY'S RESISTANCE
MUSEUM, OSLO
art sections 4(9), 4(11), 4(12),
4(13)

TIM O'DONOVAN
art sections 2(5), 4(6)

ROYAL NAVAL
COMMANDO ASSOCIATION
(Licensed with permission of
Greenhill Books)
art section 3(13)

ROYAL SCOTS
REGIMENTAL MUSEUM
art sections 1(8), 1(4), 4(18),
4(19)

SCOTT POLAR RESEARCH
INSTITUTE, UNIVERSITY OF
CAMBRIDGE
art section 2(1)

SCRAN (www.scran.ac.uk)
© The Scotsman
Publications Limited
cover

FRANK SMYTHE ESTATE
art section 3(14), 3(15)

SOE ADVISOR, FOREIGN &
COMMONWEALTH OFFICE
art section 4(14)

COLLECTION OF THE
STIRLINGS OF KEIR
art section 2(4)

MR JAMES U. THOMSON/
MAJOR A. A. FYFFE
art section 4(10)

JOSA YOUNG
art section 1(5)

TEXT

THE ORION PUBLISHING GROUP LTD
all attempts at tracing the copyright holder of *No Colours or Crest* by P. Kemp (London: Cassell, 1958) and *Spies and Saboteurs* by W. Morgan (London: Gollancz, 1955) were unsuccessful.

PENGUIN BOOKS LTD
Extract from *The Moon's a Balloon* by D. Niven (Copyright © David Niven, 1971) is reproduced by permission of Penguin Books Ltd (*see p. 42*).

RUSI JOURNAL
for permission to reproduce excerpts from *Journal of the Royal United Service Institution.*

PFD
for permission to reproduce an excerpt from *Officers and Gentlemen* by Evelyn Waugh (London: Chapman and Hall, 1955). Permission granted by PFD on behalf of the Estate of Evelyn Waugh (*see pp. 103-104*).

The publisher would like to thank staff at NMS Photography who supplied images for this publication.

Every attempt has been made to contact copyright holders to use the material in this publication. If any image or quote has been inadvertently missed, please contact the publisher.

Acknowledgements

WITH THANKS TO: Kate Adie, Eric Allan, Pat Allardice, Stella Ancell, H. Lynne Arnott, Mrs A. F. Austen, Stewart Austin, Krystof Barbarski, Col. Christopher Bates, David Blair, Holly Booth, Douglas Botting, Henry Brown, David Browne, Hutchison Burt, Sir Donald Cameron of Lochiel, Donald Cameron of Lochiel, Max Cameron, Major R. A. C. Cameron, Simon Cameron, Robin Campbell, Toni Carver, the Hon. Ian Chant-Sempill, Tony Chew, Malcolm Churchill, Rosamund Churchill, Harry and Joan Clyne, Anne Clunas, Pip Dodd, Eric Dove, James Dunning, Frode Færøy, Prof. John Forfar, Gjermund Fjeld, the Hon. Hugh and Drusilla Fraser, Alasdair Fyffe, John S. Gibson, Jim Gillies, Kevin Gorman, Bill Grant, Rear Admiral Edward Gueritz, Jean Guiet, Col. Tony Guinan, David Harrison, Peter Higgins, Knut Haugland, Lieut.-Col. Rob Heatley, Diana Henderson, Lieut.-Col. Grenville Johnston, Magdalena Kanik, Bridget Kellas, Hilary King, Margaret King, Stanisław Korzeniowski, Ivar Kraglund, Andrew Lappin, Jimmy Lappin, Heather Lane, Col. Oliver Lindsay, Neil Livingstone, Hayden Lorimer, Francis Mackay, Donald Mackenzie, Margaret Mackenzie, Anne Maclean, Paul Marquet, Walter Marshall, Alastair Massie, Lieut.-Col. Richard Mayfield, Peter Miles, Paul Millar, John Morrison, Denis Muir, May D. Murray, Dick Mungin, Rear Admiral J. A. L. Myres, Barbara Niven, Ken Oakley, Tim O'Donovan, Stan Paget, Emma Parker, Malcolm Poole, Fergus Read, Alastair Ross, Lord Rowallan, Barbara Salmon, Sydney Scroggie, Mark Seaman, Margaret Short, Tony Smythe, Gunnar Sønsteby, David Stafford, Maisie Steven, Archie Stirling of Keir, Duncan Stuart, Andrej Suchitz, Col. David Sutherland, Heather Thomson, Iain Thornber, Mick Tighe, John Warwicker, Paal Wergeland, Barbara Wigley, Ronnie Williamson, Lord Wilson of Tillyhorn, Brigadier J. S. Wilson, Josa Young, Ron Youngman, Alpine Club, British Schools Exploring Society, Clan Cameron Museum, Commando Association, Forestry Commission Scotland, Gordonstoun, Guards Museum, Highland Council Archives, Highland Fieldcraft Training

Centre Association, Headquarters Scots Guards, Imperial War Museum, Liddell Hart Centre for Military Archives, Lingeklubben, National Archives, National Archives of Scotland, National Army Museum, National Library of Scotland, Norway's Resistance Museum, Norwegian Armed Forces Museum, Oban War and Peace Museum, Polish Institute and Sikorski Museum, Royal Marines Museum, Royal Marines Reserve Scotland, Royal Naval Commando Association, Royal Scots Regimental Museum, SAS Regimental Association, Scottish Mountaineering Club, Scott Polar Research Institute, Special Forces Club.

The author is particularly indebted to Allan Carswell, Richard Baxter, Sir Thomas Macpherson of Biallid, John S. Mackay, Angus MacKinnon, A. Struan Robertson and E. H. Van Maurik. It was his privilege to enjoy the assistance of the late Dallas Allardice, John Downton, Aonghais Fyffe, Ronald 'Henry' Hall, Sydney Hudson, Arthur Kellas and Campbell Steven.

Editing and design was by Lesley Ann Taylor, Marián Sumega of NMS Enterprises Limited – Publishing. Photography by Duncan Anderson, Joyce Smith and Leslie Florence. The *Commando Country* Exhibition project team were Jacqueline Austin, Jonathan Ferguson, Charlotte Hirst, Kimberley Baxter, Rosalyn Clancey, Jen Simpson, Hannah Dolby, Sarah Foskett, Vicki Hanley, Charles Stable, Brian Melville, Mike Kidd, Steven Anderson, Stuart Jack, Grant MacRae, Chris Dawson, Wayne Johnston.

Foreword

ALLAN CARSWELL

ON A WET, windswept, winter's day in November 2004, I and few hundred other spectators waited, huddled under umbrellas, on a small hill just outside the village of Spean Bridge in the west highlands of Scotland. Above us loomed the three giant bronze figures of the Commando Memorial, their impassive gaze fixed on the distant snow-topped mountains.

The occasion was the annual Service of Remembrance of the wartime Commando Association, an event held at the memorial since it was first unveiled in 1952. This year, however, was special. The Association, its membership dwindling, was to be wound up, and this was to be their last pilgrimage to the memorial and to the country where they had trained.

Soon they came, marching to the sound of the pipes, up the road from the village, just as they would have done more than 60 years before en route from the railway station at Spean Bridge to the Commando Basic Training Centre at nearby Achnacarry. There were probably around 50 of them, nearly all now in their eighties, each proudly wearing the green beret – the symbol of their special status. They had come from all over the United Kingdom, and beyond, to be there that day for one last time.

Behind the veterans came younger men in uniform, representatives from the special forces of half a dozen nations. Besides being a service of remembrance for those Commandos who died during the Second World War, the occasion was also an acknowledgement that these very special soldiers, and the circumstances and manner in which they were created, had redefined much in the nature of military service across the world. It was also an affirmation that they have their strongest roots in the highlands of Scotland.

What follows in this book, the culmination of six years' research, is an examination not only of the origins of the Commandos but of the other related branches of 'irregular' or 'special' forces that grew up in the highlands during the darkest days of the Second World War. However, it began with the Commandos as the theme for an exhibition at the National War Museum, and that idea owed much to a powerful personal memory of an early visit to the Spean Bridge memorial.

Memorials like that at Spean Bridge exist both to spur the memory and to inspire questions – who, what, why? The men on parade for that last time in 2004 were there to remember. This book, to a large extent, tells the story of what they were recalling. In doing so it goes a long way to answering the questions posed by those three bronze giants on the hill.

Allan Carswell, *Curator*
NATIONAL WAR MUSEUM SCOTLAND
2000-05

Men bred in the Rough Bounds
THE BRITISH ARMY IN THE HIGHLANDS

DURING THE SPRING of 1940 a remote property in the west highlands of Scotland was taken over by a small group of British Army officers working for Military Intelligence. Their task was to create a school of irregular warfare, a training centre where soldiers and civilians could be taught the techniques of guerrilla fighting, skills that were suddenly much in demand. As retreating British forces were evacuated from Norway and France, continental Europe fell under enemy occupation and the British mainland itself came under threat of invasion. Throughout the United Kingdom, efforts began in earnest to prepare small military units and individuals for sea-borne raids against enemy-held coastlines, for sabotage missions against targets deeper inside enemy-occupied territory, and even to resist an invader on British soil should the situation deteriorate further. In this time of great danger and urgent need, the mountain terrain, sea lochs and challenging weather of the highland environment made the north-west of Scotland the perfect place to train for warfare of this kind.

War was no stranger to the Scottish highlands. Known and cherished for grandeur and atmosphere, regard for the stern beauty of the landscape had long been nourished by popular memory of its warlike past, by traditional conceptions of a warrior society that bred clan conflict and tragic rebellion. The British Army had been far from immune to the attractions and romance of highland martial culture, at least since the late eighteenth century, but tended through immediate necessity to take a more utilitarian view of the landscape itself. Professional military men were among the first to view and reflect upon Scotland's mountainous north-west as outsiders. They preceded the tourists who were later to seek out and see the shape of the land rather differently through eyes trained by the Romantic Movement in art, literature and music. To the soldiers of the eighteenth-century army, the mountain fastnesses and furthest reaches of this remotest part of the kingdom appeared above all as a practical problem, a place where they were vulnerable. Sent in 1724 with a Royal Commission to report on the state of the highlands, General George Wade first recommended the construction of his celebrated system of road-linked fortifications with an assessment of

> ... the great disadvantages which regular troops are under when they
> engage with those who inhabit mountain situations. The Savennes
> in France, the Catalans in Spain, have in all times been instances of
> this truth. The Highlands in Scotland are still more impractical, from
> the want of Roads and Bridges, and from the excessive rains that
> almost continually fall in those parts; which, by nature and constant
> use, becomes habitual to the Natives, but very difficultly supported
> by the regular troops. They are unacquainted with the passages
> by which the mountains are traversed; exposed to frequent ambus-
> cades, and shot from the tops of the hills, which they return without
> effect ....[1]

Even setting professional military considerations aside, the aesthetics of the scenery did little to fire the imagination among government emissaries to the north. No hint of the sublime coloured the view of official men of Wade's day, sent to exert royal authority over this intractable and inaccessible portion of the realm. Edward Burt, government contractor and agent for Wade, found time to essay an early account of highland topography for the benefit of a metropolitan readership, expressing little by way of sentiment for anything other than home:

> Now let us go among the hills, and see if we can find something more
> agreeable than their outward appearance .... But before I begin the
> particular account of my progress, I shall venture at a general descrip-
> tion of one of the mountain spaces, between glen and glen: and when
> that is done, you may make the comparison with one of our southern
> rambles; in which, without any previous route, we used to wander
> from place to place, just so as the beauty of the country invited.
> How have we been pleased with the easy ascent of an eminence,
> which almost imperceptibly brought us to the beautiful prospects seen,
> from its summit! What a delightful variety of fields, and meadows of
> various tints of green, adorned with trees and blooming hedges: and
> the whole embellished with woods, groves, waters, flocks, herds, and

magnificent seats of the happy (at least seemingly so); and every other rising ground opening a new a lovely landscape!

But in one of these monts (as the Highlanders call them), soon after your entrance on the first hill, you lose, for good and all, the sight of the plain from whence you parted; and nothing follows but the view of rocks and heath, both beneath and on every side, with high and barren mountains round about.

Thus you creep slowly on, between the hills in rocky ways, sometimes over these eminences, and often on their declivities, continually hoping the next ridge before you will be the summit of the highest, and so often deceived in that hope, as almost to despair of ever reaching the top. And thus you are still rising by long ascents, and again descending by shorter, till you arrive at the highest ground; from whence you go down in much the same manner, reversed, and never have the glen in view that you wish to see, as the end of your present trouble, till you are just upon it. And when you are there, the inconveniences (though not the hazards) are almost as great as in the tedious passage to it ....[2]

To the British soldier, the inconveniences and hazards of this strange mountain country were compounded by the warlike abilities and proclivities of some of its inhabitants. Wade's concerns about the vulnerability of regular troops in such an environment were based on recent experiences in confronting highland armies. In the wake of the 1715 Rebellion, the natural barriers of the west highlands frustrated attempts to disarm the Jacobite clans. In 1719 another highland army, supported by Spanish troops, had to be sought out and defeated on the steep slopes of Glenshiel, well beyond the comfort zone of British regular troops. Attempting to prevent such crises before they developed, Crown policy over generations had been to scatter garrisons and otherwise police the highlanders with men of their own kind, employing independent companies of 'Highland Watch' who knew the local political situations and, crucially, the ground itself. In the summer of 1745 this approach once again proved inadequate to the scale of the task when another Jacobite army began to gather in the west. Tasked to respond with an army of regular troops, the British Commander-in-Chief in Scotland, Lieutenant-General Sir John Cope, was initially reluctant to search out the small but growing highland insurrection too far into its own mountains, leaving the Jacobite army free to gather strength and march south, using indeed the very road network that had been constructed on Wade's recommendation. Subsequent Jacobite victories in the lowlands, at Prestonpans and Falkirk, spiced the customary contempt expressed for the 'savage' highlanders with a fear of their military prowess, primitive as it was held to be.

When the Jacobite threat was extinguished at Culloden outside Inverness in 1746, the victorious British Army might finally have felt itself vindicated in its earlier dismissals of the Jacobite army as a rabble. Even then, the furthest reaches of the west highlands were not fully, cruelly pacified until after the back of the Jacobite army had been broken.

And in the wake of the troops that laid waste to the seats of rebellion came the mapmakers. Between 1747 and 1751 military surveyors mapped the whole of northern Scotland, including those wilder parts where British troops had hitherto been loath to march. The Military Survey of Scotland was the first national cartographic survey, the progenitor of the Ordnance Survey; and, as a 'political instrument' to neutralise the possibility of future insurrection, was every bit as powerful a measure as the building of forts and roads that preceded and accompanied it.[3]

The lie of the land delineated in this way, the British government meanwhile sought to monopolise the military labour of its inhabitants. Mass recruitment of highlanders into the regular British Army was a practice that stopped them being recruited by anyone else and, more significantly, was a phenomenon that served the British state well in its global wars over the following decades. Prime Minister William Pitt took credit in the matter before Parliament in 1766, making an explicit connection between the success of the new highland regiments and the terrain that made them:

> I sought for merit wherever it could be found. It is my boast that I was the first Minister who looked for it and found it in the mountains of the north. I called it forth and drew into your service a hardy and intrepid race of men .... These men in the last war were brought to combat on your side; they served with fidelity as they fought with valour, and conquered for you in every part of the world ....[4]

Although by the opening decade of the nineteenth century the flood of recruits had slowed, the success of highland regiments in the wars against Napoleon's France established their reputation for valour. Their emergence corresponded to growing literary and popular fascination with all things Gaelic, in light of which the common highland soldier appeared a noble and hardy product of the culture and environment from which he was perceived to come. These were the 'Men bred in the rough bounds' (*sliochd altram nan Garbhchrioch*) of Gaelic poet Duncan Ban Macintyre, 'Men of *élan* and mettle .... Descendants of noble clans'.[5] Marked out by their picturesque appearance in tartan and bonnet, military success saw the highland regiments become a permanent fixture in the British Army, setting off towards their apogee in the Victorian era as a widely celebrated symbol of Scotland itself.

But with the de-population of the highlands, and the drawing of the region into the economy and society of the United Kingdom as a whole, the connection between the highland soldier and the environment and life that made him became less marked. Highlanders had initially been thought well-suited for dedicated use as light troops against irregular forces in the forests of British North America, both in the Seven Years' War and the American War of Independence. General Wolfe, hero of the storming of Quebec in 1759, had made the connection between the highlands and the backwoods of America as early as 1751. Writing while on garrison duty 'in the midst of Popery and Jacobitism' in northern Scotland, still harrying the highlands in the aftermath of Culloden, he displayed a notably unsympathetic view of the potential utility of the locals in such far-flung places as Nova Scotia: 'I should imagine that two or three independent Highland Companies might be of use; they are hardy, intrepid, accustomed to a rough country, and no great mischief if they fall.'[6]

Away from the North American theatre of war it was, however, their distinctive dress and other outward manifestations of culture that were to distinguish highland regiments from the rest of the regular infantry, more than any proclivity for a particular fighting role. The territory and topography of the highlands essentially ceased to be of particular concern or application for military purposes. For the officer class of the army, the Scottish highlands was no longer a place to be feared or scoured for recruits, but rather a place for recreation. In the 1750s Wolfe himself had taken time out from searching for French recruiters to go shooting game in the Scottish hills. By the middle of the nineteenth century the great highland estates were widely cleared of their tenants and many turned over to field sports. While the fighting exploits of highland regiments were hailed across the British empire, it was as a place for hunting, shooting and fishing that the well-connected British Army officer would likely have known the highlands best. Their sporting endeavour relied on a new way of life that emerged for highland countrymen in the employ of the estates, the skills of the ghillie, the stalker and the keeper.

In December 1899, amidst public anxiety over British reverses and casualties suffered during the disastrous opening phase of the second Boer War in South Africa, the military potential of those who professed the highland sporting life, the men with skills in fieldcraft, marksmanship and observation, were brought to the attention of the War Office. British forces in South Africa were struggling to contend with an enemy of locally raised irregulars, Boer farmers who were highly mobile, proficient in horsemanship and long-range marksmanship, and who were fighting on their own ground. One response was to assemble and organise volunteers, principally from the part-time, partially-trained units of home defence cavalry already existing throughout the United Kingdom, and despatch them to South Africa. This new 'Imperial Yeomanry' was intended directly to counter the mobility and irregular tactics of the Boer units that were proving so discomfiting to large formations of British regular troops operating over great expanses of testing terrain. Even before this great effort was put in hand, one highland landowner came up with an innovative variant of the idea. Simon Fraser, 16th Lord Lovat, was a clan chief, former soldier, and owner of some 250,000 acres of Scottish highland ground. He believed that the abilities of the men he employed to watch and stalk deer across his land could readily be applied in South Africa to the observation and hunting down of the enemy.[7]

Lovat's offer to raise 150 stalkers and ghillies from his own and neighbouring properties initially met with scepticism at the War Office, but, as the Imperial Yeomanry scheme took off, Lovat's call for volunteers was answered from across the highlands. A new mounted infantry unit, the Lovat Scouts, was created and accepted for service. Three contingents of Lovat Scouts served in South Africa, scouting, patrolling and fighting, and the regiment was to become a lasting feature of the Army thereafter. During the Great War, while the Scottish highlands offered up men in their thousands to serve in orthodox infantry battalions on the Western Front, in Gallipoli, Macedonia, Salonika, Palestine and Italy, the Lovat Scouts managed to retain their specialist function and make their own contribution in observation, fieldcraft and sharp-shooting.

The idea of the Scottish highlands as a place of challenge, as a scene of manly sporting endeavour, as an environment with something to offer therefore in time of war, was something that pre-existed the development of the Second World War special training centres that form the subject of this book. These training schools were tasked with a new and urgent mission, with innovation and free thinking in the face of a desperate military situation, and it was not the job of those who created and ran them to ruminate on the traditions of that part of the world in which they were set to work. And yet the name of Lord Lovat is just one of many threads that unite this story of the 1940s with the highland warfare of earlier times. His son, the 17th Lord Lovat, was a prime mover in the first of the highland special training centres created at Lochailort in 1940, and from there went on to become one of the most celebrated of all Commando officers.

Achnacarry, initially an adjunct of the Lochailort school but from early 1942 the main centre of Commando training, legendary for its toughness, was the ancestral home of the Camerons of Lochiel. To their cost the family had brought out their clan in 1745 to fight in the Jacobite army of Prince Charles Edward Stuart and to shield their prince after his defeat. The late Sir Donald Cameron of Lochiel, a serving Lovat Scouts officer when the Commandos took over his father's house, used to recall that the British Army had burnt Achnacarry twice: once in 1746 and again in 1943.[8] On the second occasion the destruction wrought by the Commandos at least was not complete and, unlike the earlier conflagration set by troops harrying Lochaber in the weeks after Culloden, the fire was not started deliberately.

Other houses requisitioned for training in Lochaber and the 'Rough Bounds' of Knoydart, Morar, Arisaig and Moidart had their own traditions of strife. Close by Achdalieu, temporary home of prototype commando Independent Companies in 1940, another Cameron chief of yore had bitten the throat from an officer of General Monk's occupying army in 1652 and later declared it 'the sweetest bite ever he had in his lifetime'.[9] Further south, at Inverary on the shores of Loch Fyne, Combined Operations Command set up a shore establishment in September 1940. This training centre, where Commandos and others learnt the skills and hazards of sea-borne assault, was named HMS *Quebec*, a nod towards the exploits of the aforementioned James Wolfe who, complete with a contingent of highland soldiers, took Quebec City, the capital of New France, by amphibious landing in 1759.

Stories still abound about shady military goings-on in secluded highland properties during the Second World War. Information about their conception and operation is not so mysterious as to be so very hard to come by, but the sources are disconnected, scattered through the histories and records of different military organisations, and the memoirs, published and unpublished, of those who were there in different capacities. The *Commando Country* exhibition at Scotland's National War Museum drew together material evidence and memories of irregular warfare training in the Scottish highlands from a variety of sources and collections, public and private.[10] It sought to explore the principles and methods of the individual training centres, to show how they shared expertise and developed common approaches, and to suggest that their innovations and improvisations shaped the way special forces, and indeed regular forces, were to be trained thereafter. This was not to suggest that special service training was the preserve of the Scottish highlands alone, or that Scotsmen were disproportionately prominent in its development. For the Independent Companies, the Commandos, Special Operations Executive and the other irregular formations that will be encountered in what follows, the test of Lochaber and the 'Rough Bounds' was one important element in a varied and complex diet of training that could be conducted in locations throughout the United Kingdom and beyond. Training amidst Scottish mountains and lochs was not an experience necessarily encountered by every exponent of special operations during the Second World War. But the Scottish highlands nevertheless put a stamp on the whole enterprise. It was the place where theory was first tested in practice, the place where topography and remote location combined with unique efficacy to the purpose, and where a way of thinking about the land and the character of man it was held to breed gave a cultural grounding to the deadly and dangerous work at hand.

NOTES TO INTRODUCTION

1. General George Wade: Manuscript report of 10 December 1724, transcribed as an appendix in R. Jamieson (ed.) *Letters from a Gentleman in the North of Scotland to his Friend in London* .... (5th edition) (London: 1818), pp. 289-316.
2. R. Jamieson (ed.): op. cit., pp. 266-89.

3. Charles W. J. Withers: *Geography, Science and National Identity* (Cambridge: Cambridge University Press, 2001), pp. 149-53.

4. Parliamentary record quoted in W. Notestein: *The Scot in History* (Cape, 1946), p. 192.

5. Duncan Ban Macintyre: 'Oran Do 'N T-Seann Fhreiceadan Ghaidhealach' ('Song to the Old Highland Watch') in A. MacLeod (ed.) *The Songs of Duncan Ban Macintyre*, Scottish Gaelic Texts Society (Edinburgh: Oliver and Boyd, 1952), pp. 255-63.

6. Both quotations from Wolfe's letter of June 1751 to Lieutenant-Colonel William Rickson, quoted in J. T. Finlay: *Wolfe in Scotland* (London: Longmans, Green & Co., 1928), p. 226.

7. The Rt. Hon. Sir Francis Lindley: *Lord Lovat KT, KCMG, KCVO, CB, DSO A Biography* (London: Hutchinson & Co, 1935), p. 80.

8. Recounted in person to the author, September 2001. See also Records of the Ministry of Defence, National Archives, Kew, DEFE2/1134 where a historical summary attributes the fire at Achnacarry on 5 November 1943 to a faulty boiler.

9. [John Drummond]: *Memoirs of Sir Ewen Cameron of Locheill, Chief of Clan Cameron, with an introductory account of the history and antiquities of that family and the neighbouring clans* (Edinburgh: Abbotsford Club, 1842).

10. A special exhibition at the National War Museum Scotland, Edinburgh Castle, October 2006 to February 2008.

PART ONE

The Big House

SPECIAL TRAINING CENTRE LOCHAILORT

Later that summer, David was sent on a course in the remote highlands. A long way on beyond the railhead at Fort William, the students
gathered in a very ugly, Victorian-Gothic Castle where it never
stopped raining, or so it seemed to David, for whom rain had long
ceased to be important as a cause of discomfort, remaining only as a
factor, sometimes helpful and at other times adverse, in the planning
and prosecution of Commando warfare. This and its subsidiary
crafts were the subject of the course.

SO BEGINS AN account of the course at the Special Training Centre
Lochailort, from Robert Henriques' *The Commander*, an autobiographical novel of one Commando officer's service during the early years of the
Second World War.[1] Henriques was perhaps a little unkind in delineating
Inverailort House (or Castle) 'very ugly', but it can still appear gloomy and
a little foreboding on the wrong day. So it must have seemed to many who
arrived there from 1940 to 1945, full of anticipation and uncertainty, for
all the military and naval activity they would have found underway
around and about it. Without question the setting is spectacular. This
former home of the Cameron-Head family, distinguished scions of the
Chiefs of Lochiel, sits close to the shore of Loch Ailort, just beyond where
the road south-west into Moidart turns off from the 'Road to the Isles' that
runs from Fort William by Glenfinnan, Arisaig and up to the fishing port
of Mallaig. In the 1940s the turn-off south led nowhere but Inverailort,
which was the end of the made-up road. Immediately behind the house lies
the deer forest of Inverailort whence rise the hills of Seann Cruach, and An
Stac, outliers of the Rois-Bheinn ridge popular today with hillwalkers for
its airy, twisting progress and, on clear days, its commanding views north-
wards across the Sound of Arisaig. If its beauty is stark and rugged, this is
nonetheless one of the most tranquil and atmospheric portions of the west

coast of Scotland. North-east of the house, between a modern fish farm and Glenshian Lodge, one-time medical accommodation of the Special Training Centre, some surviving brick huts and the remnants of a parade ground betray something of the intense military occupation that took place here during the early years of Second World War. From June 1940 tranquillity was rarely a feature of the local scene, as the area round Inverailort resounded with words of command, gunfire and explosions.

In late May 1940 Mrs Pauline Cameron-Head was not at home at Inverailort. On the 30th, on the point of returning home from London, she received an unexpected letter from the British Army's Highland Area headquarters in Perth. Its content sent her on her way back north in understandable consternation. Scottish Command in Edinburgh had received notice that her properties at Inverailort and Glenshian were urgently required by the War Office for unspecified military purposes. Requisition papers were enclosed and, by the time she received the letter, an advance party of the military unit occupying the house would already have arrived. Mrs Cameron-Head headed rapidly to the scene of the action and soon conveyed her sorry story in a letter to her friend Sir Donald Cameron of Lochiel. Unbeknown to either correspondent, Lochiel was about to undergo an equivalent experience at the hands of the War Office over his nearby properties at Achnacarry and Achdalieu Lodge. Mrs Cameron-Head wrote from the inn at Lochailort where, barred from her house, she was forced to take a room:

> ... when I arrived at Lochailort station there were only two officers who said the Castle was half emptied and that they had no accommodation for me and I could not go to it. They have taken my three garages and planted tents everywhere, even in the middle of the farmyard without any permission from me or anyone representing me. The whole of the furniture has gone to store in Fort William. There seems to be no one really in command here except a nice Captain Stacy who can do nothing except order the man to proceed with the clearing of the two houses. The officers are going to live in the Castle and there are some 70/80 tents for the men as well as Glenshian House.

She went on to express her willingness to contribute what she could to the war effort, but to bemoan the 'wholesale destruction' of her property:

They are planting their tents all over my ground and breaking down fences and walls and leaving gates open so that the beasts get out and all the Hotel cattle will get in and have a good feed on growing crops. Surely there is some redress for this, or can we claim for fresh crops for those which are destroyed?

As matters turned out, the 81-year-old Mrs Cameron-Head was not fated to reside again at Inverailort. She spent the last months of her life at her sister's house at Dunain Park near Inverness, corresponding with the staff she retained on part of her estate and occasionally visiting Lochailort in person ruefully to survey further depredations to her patrimony. She died four years before Inverailort was returned to the family in May 1945. It came instead to her son Francis and the woman he had met and married while she was serving as an ambulance driver in support of the training centre that Inverailort had become. In 1944 the Cameron-Heads received a payment of £200 from the War Office in compensation for damage to surfaces, dykes, fences and buildings caused by military training and War Department contractors' operations between 1940 and 1942. In 1948, under the Compensation (Defence) Act of 1939, they received a lump sum of £6300 in settlement of their claim against the Admiralty. The Admiralty had taken over the requisition from the War Office in 1943, and with it liability for damage to the house. The 1948 settlement took into account the Cameron-Head's purchase of certain huts erected during the occupation, and also the requirement to dismantle a pier that had been built out into Loch Ailort and to restore the family's own jetty.[2]

On her first, dispossessed night at the Lochailort Inn, it might be hoped the elder Mrs Cameron-Head found at least one understanding listener for her woes. Another guest at the Inn was a man a little closer to her in years than the young officers busy with the emptying and reorganisation of her house, and one who knew something about resilience in face of adversity. Although he could not have divulged it, he would also have known a little more about what was happening at Inverailort than Mrs Cameron-Head could have guessed herself. Beneath her signature in the Lochailort Inn guest book for 1 June 1940 is that of Surgeon Commander George Murray Levick RN. Murray Levick was a polar explorer of some repute, veteran of Captain Robert Falcon Scott's ill-fated *Terra Nova* Expedition to the South Pole of 1910-13.[3] As Medical Officer to the expedition's Northern Party, Murray Levick had endured an epic winter in an ice-cave on Inexpressible Island, a feature in Antarctica's Terra Nova Bay where the name gives a clue to its nature. Returning in 1940 to the Royal Navy out of retirement, Murray Levick was by then a man in his early 60s with much still to give to the war effort. His long acquaintance with survival in extreme environments had recommended him to the organisation that was about to transform Mrs Cameron-Head's house into the first British school of irregular warfare.

Murray Levick was just one of an extraordinary group of specialists that was to form the original teaching staff of the Special Training Centre Lochailort. Three other holders of the prestigious Polar Medal joined Murray Levick to teach survival skills, which until then were little understood or practised by regular military forces. Their teaching colleagues included some of the leading mountaineers of the day, marksmen, weapons and demolitions experts, stalkers from highland estates, experienced guerrilla fighters, seamen, policemen and thieves. To understand how and to what purpose this eclectic mixture of military and civilian practitioners came to be assembling at remote Lochailort in June 1940, it is necessary to look back to the years immediately before the outbreak of the Second World War and into the machinations of clandestine organisations operating within the War Office in Whitehall.

* * *

It was as late as autumn 1938, in the weeks after the Munich Crisis, that the War Office took steps to make a formal study of the possibilities for irregular warfare in coming conflict. What might today be called a 'think tank' was set up ostensibly to look at recent guerrilla campaigns in China and Spain with a view to possible operations in colonial theatres. Its secret brief, however, was to consider how British support might be provided to resistance efforts in Europe should the German Army march and conquer east.[4] By March 1939, with German forces already gathering in Czechoslovakia and this grim scenario looking increasingly likely, the research team had grown and was operating under the Directorate of Military Intelligence with the designation Military Intelligence (Research), or 'MI(R)' as it was invariably rendered.[5] With its initial recommendations as to the potential value of guerrilla operations accepted in principle by the War Office and the Foreign Office, MI(R) was allowed to develop and consider how its ideas might be put into practice.

MI(R) was headed by Lieutenant-Colonel J. F. C. (Joe) Holland, an officer whose First World War service included a period operating as a pilot supporting the irregular campaign waged in the Middle East by T. E. Lawrence 'of Arabia'. Holland also had post-war experience in Ireland where the Irish Republican Army's successful guerrilla campaign against British forces from 1919-21 made effective use of bombings, assassinations, raiding and ambushes. The IRA had presented officers such as Holland, who was seriously wounded there, with a demonstration of the extent to which a small number of irregulars enjoying a network of local support could cause serious difficulties for an occupying army, as the British were perceived. Before their departure the British security forces, both military and police, had responded with measures of a similar stamp, leaving specially recruited paramilitary auxiliaries to execute the uglier elements of counter-insurgency warfare on their behalf.[6]

One of Holland's first MI(R) recruits had also seen service in Ireland in the early 1920s. Lieutenant-Colonel Colin McVean Gubbins was a career soldier who followed his distinguished First World War record on the Western Front, with spells serving in support of anti-Bolshevik forces in Russia, in security operations in Ireland, and on postings in India. His early experience and understanding of irregular warfare was to see him emerge as one of the central figures in Allied special operations during the Second World War, propel him to the rank of Major-General, a knighthood, and the accolades and awards of numerous nations towards whose liberation he worked. Significantly perhaps, in relation to what was to unfold under his direction in the war years in Scotland, Gubbins' family background had a highland flavour. In childhood, while his father worked in the Diplomatic Service in Japan, Gubbins and his brother spent long periods in the care of his mother's family on the Isle of Mull, a place Gubbins later recalled as idyllic:

> Mull offered my brother and me everything that healthy and active young boys could possibly wish for, the sea ... at our door, the mountains behind rising over three thousand feet to their peak in Ben More, small burns for brown trout, a river where the sea-trout ran, and game on the hills when we were old enough to shoot, grouse, snipe, and woodcock and blue hares ... there it all was – a physical paradise ....

From my years in Mull too came a very special attachment and faith in all things Scottish and particularly Highlanders being superior to anything the rest of the world could show! This was carried to the point of irrationality but persisted for many years in certain aspects.[7]

Gubbins' particular concern at MI(R) was with the practicalities of tactics and training, guerrilla methods being entirely outside the compass of orthodox British Army tactical doctrine at this period. Holland initially set Gubbins to the production of a series of training manuals. The fruits of study at home and abroad, three pamphlets were duly produced, a collaboration between Gubbins and a demolitions expert, M. R. Jefferis, under the titles 'The Art of Guerilla Warfare', 'The Partisan Leader's Handbook' and 'How to Use High Explosives'.[8]

The first of these set out general principles in a 'Guerilla's Creed', with guidance for small units seeking to harass the movement and operation of superior enemy forces. It stressed the importance of surprise attacks and the need, on the hit and run principle, to avoid any prolonged engagement. It also made much of the quality of leadership in guerrilla groups, a point picked up and amplified in the second pamphlet which offered more practical instruction in methods of organisation and attack in such endeavours as road or rail sabotage, and the care and concealment of explosives. The final pamphlet was a straightforward technical manual, which owed much to the expertise of Jefferis.

With the benefit of hindsight some theoretical elements of the first pamphlets can at first appear to today's reader somewhat as statements of the obvious. But even so, they are a reminder that as late as 1939, and despite centuries of varied experiences of small-scale conflict on the edges of the British empire, British forces, in the shape of MI(R), were more or less starting from scratch in their approach to the subject. The general principles needed to be delineated, understood and expounded. These slim volumes in plain cover, printed on edible rice paper, were originally intended to be translated into several languages. Albeit still in English, they were in demand from British backed operatives as far afield as China and as late as May 1941.[9] Closer to home they gave a first point of reference for the earliest practical attempts at designing a scheme of training, as would be realised at Lochailort, and they were also distributed to the aid of a secret network of would-be guerrilla fighters within the United Kingdom.

While the guides were being compiled, Gubbins and his colleagues were quietly recruiting and retaining personnel with aptitude or experience, language skills and business experience of other countries, that might prove useful to MI(R) in the future. For advice on training, the first approaches into such specialist circles as that of the British polar explorers were made at this stage. MI(R) were also looking for individuals with the potential to be operational officers, men with relevant experience or who were otherwise thought suitable to be trained for missions overseas to make first contact with incipient resistance movements in occupied or threatened territory. These individuals were identified and approached through what might be called the 'Old Boys' Network' of personal acquaintance and recommendation, quiet approaches to military units and university recruiting boards, building up a card-index of some 1000 potential operatives. A number of civilians among them were sent on a brief course of Regular Army officer training and quickly received officer commissions.[10]

Among the select group who came under the auspices of MI(R) in the early summer of 1939 was Captain W. J. (Bill) Stirling, a former Scots Guards regular officer, still on the Regular Army Reserve of Officers. William Stirling of Keir was the young head of one of Scotland's venerable landowning families, and the owner of a mansion house and sizeable estate at Keir in Perthshire. After leaving the Army he had been pursuing a business career as a public works and engineering contractor. In addition to the Keir estate, the Stirlings owned substantial lands in Morar in the 'Rough Bounds' of the west highlands, not far from Lochailort. Stirling's connections – family, social and professional – were to bring MI(R) to Lochailort a year later.

*   *   *

During the first half of 1939 MI(R) made overtures to intelligence services in eastern Europe, initiatives that took Colin Gubbins to Estonia, Latvia, Lithuania, Romania and Poland. The missions to Poland yielded the most tangible results, although it has been asserted that the most valuable outcome related not to guerrilla warfare but to information about the German 'Enigma' coding system.[11] MI(R) deserves great credit for its early appreciation of the situation likely to unfold in eastern Europe, but its attempts to prepare meaningful British support for guerrilla activity were rather overtaken by events. Gubbins' last visit to Poland was as part of a British Military Mission that actually crossed into the country after German military aggression against its eastern neighbour had commenced. The speed and success of the German invasion of Poland in September 1939 left little scope for MI(R) to make much progress at all in co-operation with Polish authorities towards the organisation of resistance behind enemy lines. As Poland succumbed to German invaders from the west, and Soviet incursion from the east, the British Military Mission was in the end hard pressed merely to escape south across the border into Romania. Meanwhile, on 3 September 1939, the British government had responded formally to the German invasion of Poland by declaring war on Germany, but there was little of practical value that Britain could advance to Poland's aid. In these first months of the Second World War, MI(R) naturally worked towards supporting resistance within the occupied territory of Poland and Czechoslovakia. But this small unit, set up with a brief to research and to plan, found itself struggling to carry out its own recommendations, lacking the capacity and resources to make much impression.

While eastern Europe was proving difficult ground for MI(R), and while the Regular and Territorial Army soldiers of the British Expeditionary Force sat out in France awaiting a possible German invasion in the west, the eyes of Allied military strategists turned north towards Scandinavia and Finland. The Non-Aggression Pact of August 1939 between Germany and the Soviet Union afforded Stalin an opportunity to counter Germany's power and likely hostile intentions by occupying eastern Poland, the Baltic states and, in December 1939, by invading Finland. When the Finns gallantly and unexpectedly held the Soviet advance, Britain agreed to co-operate with France in sending an Allied force to their aid. Thoughts of supporting Finland were not entirely altruistic; the British viewed the situation in light of their wish to establish a military presence in strategic locations in the region that could help prevent vital resources of iron ore reaching Germany from Sweden. In the event, MI(R)'s limited involvement in the purported Finnish expedition was frustrated by the difficulties of passing forces through neutral Norway and Sweden. But another, highly unusual force created for dispatch to Finland was to prove extremely useful to MI(R) in the months that followed; not in Finland, as matters turned out, but in Scotland. This was the 5th (Supplementary Reserve) Battalion Scots Guards, the British

Army's first unit of ski troops. It was from among this strange creation that the nucleus of staff for MI(R)'s special training centre at Lochailort was to be drawn.

* * *

An air of amateur endeavour pervades the curious and brief history of the 5th Scots Guards ski battalion, perhaps hindered by the fact that its ski training was conducted during March 1940 in the less than bellicose atmosphere of Chamonix, a fashionable ski resort in the French Alps. But the *ad hoc* nature of this enterprise was little different to the atmosphere of improvisation in which the whole question of special operations would be approached during 1940 and 1941. In early 1940 Britain entirely lacked any trained mountain troops that could operate in a mobile role in a winter theatre such as northern Finland. The solution applied was a call for volunteers from throughout the Army and directly from civilian life, individuals with experience of skiing, sledging and mountaineering. These were then, even more than today, rather expensive and exclusive pursuits, and ones with a small but highly dedicated following. It was little surprise then that there was a healthy response, with a preponderance of officers among the hundreds of eager recruits. The imbalance was such that, in order to join the Battalion, numerous commissioned and non-commissioned officers agreed to accept temporary demotion and served in the ranks.

Officers or otherwise, the call for ski specialists for an undisclosed mission brought forth a kind of individual who was tired of waiting for the real business of fighting a war to come to him. This impatience with the monotony of much of day-to-day war service, the desire for action and impulse to 'get on with it', was to be characteristic of those who volunteered for irregular warfare training and special service units in the future. In a British Army that was struggling to emerge from a general state of unreadiness for a European war, the creation of this single ski battalion appears rather an unlikely development. More surprising still was the decision to base it upon the Brigade of Guards, a bastion of tradition and orthodoxy within that Army. The state of the British Army of the 'Phoney War' phase of late 1939 and early 1940 has been much criticised, but if it was unprepared and under-resourced for a major war it was an organisation that had nonetheless retained some of the best qualities of a small, professional, highly-disciplined force. The 5th Scots Guards episode represented an attempt to meld the enthusiasm of the gentlemen skiers and mountaineers with a dose of sound military experience and doctrine. The volunteer enthusiasts were leavened by a sprinkling of non-commissioned officers from the Guards regiments, and a proportion of conventional Scots Guardsmen with no experience of, or particular interest in, skiing, but who knew how to be soldiers. This was the kind of combination that, when applied properly and allowed to develop, was to make for the most successful of special operations endeavours during the rest of the war.

The 5th Scots Guards commanding officer, Lieutenant-Colonel J. S. Coats, was a Coldstream Guards officer who was also a skilled winter sports exponent (and who was to represent Great Britain in the 1948 Olympic bobsleigh event). Second in command was Major Bryan Mayfield, an experienced skier who had years of regular service behind him as a Scots Guards officer. The 'Assistant Adjutant and Officer in Command Ski Equipment' was Captain Martin Lindsay. Lindsay's responsibilities in fitting and kitting the battalion derived from his distinguished service on two important polar expeditions: the British Arctic Air Route Expedition in east Greenland in 1930-31, and the British Trans-Greenland Expedition of 1934. Lindsay was a holder of the Polar Medal, and had been further honoured by the Geographical Societies of France, Sweden and Belgium. His 1934 endeavours included discovery of the highest ice plateau and highest peak within the Arctic Circle, and completion of a record-breaking 1900-kilometre sledge journey.[12]

Assisting Lindsay was another pre-war polar explorer, Freddy Spencer Chapman, a schoolmaster at Gordonstoun whose military experience was limited to brief service with a Territorial Army battalion of the Seaforth Highlanders. Both men were known to the public for their association with the celebrated polar expedition leader Gino Watkins who lost his life in Greenland in 1932. But Lindsay and Spencer Chapman were expedition celebrities and popular authors in their own right. As a mountaineer as well as explorer, Spencer Chapman perhaps led in this field. While serving with 5th Scots Guards, his fourth book was awaiting publication, an account of his first ascent of the 24,000-feet Himalayan peak Chomolhari.[13] He later recalled his part in the pre-Chamonix preparations of the 5th Scots Guards:

The month of January was spent in hectically equipping a battalion on the specialised lines of a polar expedition with skis (flown over from Zurich) and special winter bindings, Nansen sledges (made at an aircraft factory at Heston) and man-hauling gear, eiderdown sleeping-bags, double pyramid tents, Grenfell-cloth wind-jackets, white on one side and fawn on the other, sealskin boots (to be flown over by the Hudson Bay Company), snow-glasses, sledging rations and many other peculiar items of equipment much of which had to be specially made in the shortest time possible .... I, having designed the equipment, had the elevated rank of staff-sergeant and was helped by J. M. Scott and Quintin Riley while our department was taken over by Martin Lindsay who, as regular officer, had retained his commission. The four of us had all been members of Gino Watkins' Greenland Expeditions and spent our time either giving dress rehearsals of polar camping technique in the gymnasium, or fitting winter bindings to skis, and packing up our incredibly varied and fragile assortment of equipment in the goods-sheds at Aldershot.[14]

Following organisation and initial training at the Guards Brigade depot at Pirbright, the Battalion was despatched to the Alps and to the attention of instructors from the French Army's élite mountain corps, the *Chasseurs Alpins*. The Chamonix training sessions were recalled by 5th Scots Guardsman Campbell Steven, a young Scottish mountaineer and Alpinist, one of those who had been interviewed and selected for training from among the many volunteers for the unit.

As we formed up on the iron-hard snow, the biting frost banished the last traces of sleep, for although the sun was already touching the topmost spires of the aiguilles, it would be long enough before it reached the valley. Then we would move off across the fields, skis crunching on the crisp snow-furrows, till we had reached one of the tracks that slanted upwards through the woods. For the rest of the morning and again after lunch-break we would be kept busy on nursery slopes. These were glorious hours, warm and carefree after the sun had thawed us out, and our only complaint was that time passed too quickly. The experts, of course, protested loudly that such practice was unworthy of their skill, but it was strange all the same how thoroughly they always seemed to be enjoying themselves.

For my part I found the snow frozen much too hard, and at times it was difficult to believe that I had ever been on skis before.

We were given various tests, always down slalom courses of such steepness that I inevitably came to grief at turn after turn. I felt the threat of being returned to my unit hanging horribly close above my head, and tried in vain to console myself that at least I must be better than another Guardsman, who boasted that his whole claim to skiing proficiency was that he could ride a horse.[15]

Steven's anxieties about failing to impress in training are here expressed in terms that will be familiar to anyone acquainted with the lore of British special service training. Since the trainees were all volunteers, usually drawn from more conventional military units, the sanction for individual shortfall was to be returned to one's unit of origin. This entailed a resumption of the less exciting manner of military employment from which the volunteer had wished to escape in the first place, together with the knowledge that one had failed to make the grade considered necessary for 'special employment'. This uncomfortable concept was later to become immediately and universally understood among trainee Commandos, always expressed through the acronym 'RTU' – 'Returned to Unit'.[16]

Agreeable as it must have been, the overall experience in Chamonix was one of frustration, a marker for the Battalion's existence overall. There was no opportunity to train alongside the *Chasseurs Alpins* stationed at Chamonix since, due to heightened avalanche risk, these potential mentors had been confined to the valley by their commanding officer. It was also found easier to train soldiers to ski and sledge than it was to train skiers and sledge-haulers to be soldiers, and all were novices in the infantry tactics required for arctic warfare. Martin Lindsay's own report on the experience at Chamonix concluded that, undermined by haste and a lack of preliminary preparations, the Battalion returned unfit to fight under the special conditions for which it was formed.[17]

It was perhaps as well that the hasty preparations of 5th Scots Guards came to naught, at least in terms of deployment on active operations. After only a week on the French snows the skiers returned to the United Kingdom and were actually embarked on a liner at Glasgow docks before the whole Anglo-French expedition to Finland was called off. With little prospect of timely or substantial aid from the western Allies, the Finns had sought terms from the Soviet Union and the 'Winter War' in Finland was at an end. An earlier departure, or a prolonging of the campaign, and the Battalion might easily have been lost to capture or worse and for little purpose. The regimental history of the Scots Guards reflects that 'it cannot be judged wise to have concentrated in one poorly equipped and untrained unit so many leaders and potential leaders'.[18] Certainly, from the roll of 5th Scots Guards came several of the individuals who were to be pioneers in the new field of special operations.

It was nevertheless with dismay that, back at their base, the volunteers of the 5th Scots Guards received the news that the unit was to be disbanded. The ski battalion's disappointment was compounded by the realisation that a British military expedition was on the point of leaving for another Scandinavian destination, and that 5th Scots Guards were to have no part in the coming operations in Norway. The officers and men would not have been aware of the army politics surrounding their progress thus far and were in no position to realise that they had been fortunate to get as far as they did. In certain quarters of the War Office, the idea of a ski battalion had received short shrift from the outset.[19] A subsequent assessment of the whole exercise saw the concept being shelved, much to the satisfaction of the doubters.

* * *

For MI(R) the war in Finland had proved beyond reach, but the planned expedition to Norway now appeared to offer fresh opportunities. Still at stake for British interests was the supply of Swedish iron ore, essential to the German war effort, which passed through Norwegian territory en route to Germany. After 9 April 1940 there was also the pressing matter of the German invasion of Norway, which began on that day with sea-borne landings and parachute assaults at Oslo and Stavanger. The strategic potential of naval bases along the coast meant that German control of Norway threatened much greater harm than any longstanding worries about the continuing supply of minerals to Germany. Once again, and on this occasion with the reach to do something about it, the British had not moved swiftly enough to counter German aggression. As Norway fought for its freedom, a significant Allied expeditionary force of British, French and Polish troops, originally brought together towards the support of Finland, was reassembled and set sail to seize objectives in Norway originally targeted before the German invasion began.

1. George Murray Levick (centre) photographed after surviving the Antarctic winter of 1911-12 in an ice-cave on Inexpressible Island.

(LICENSED WITH PERMISSION OF THE SCOTT POLAR RESEARCH INSTITUTE, UNIVERSITY OF CAMBRIDGE)

2. Captain Martin Lindsay (centre) with 5th Scots Guards ski troops in the French Alps, 1940.

(HEADQUARTERS SCOTS GUARDS)

3. Sergeant Freddy Spencer Chapman, serving with 5th Scots Guards in 1940, sports a French *chasseurs alpins* beret with Scots Guards cap badge.

(HEADQUARTERS SCOTS GUARDS)

4. William Stirling of Keir (seated) with the Operation *Knife* team, training on the Keir estate, spring 1940.

(IN THE COLLECTION OF THE STIRLINGS OF KEIR)

5. Buildings constructed at the Special Training Centre Lochailort, north-east of Inverailort, 1941.

(TIM O'DONOVAN)

6. Arthur Kellas (right) with a fellow officer of No.10 Independent Company during training in Lochaber, 1940.

(NMS)

7. Detail from the guest book of the Lochailort Inn for spring and summer 1940 recording the visits of Colonel Joe Holland, head of MI(R), and film star and Commando volunteer Captain David Niven.

(COURTESY OF MS A. M. KEENAN AND MR R. MUNGIN, ROSHVEN)

8. Craft and personnel at the small boat training station at Dorlin, overlooked by Castle Tioram, 1941.

(TRUSTEES OF THE LIDDELL HART CENTRE FOR MILITARY ARCHIVES)

9. Assault landing exercise on the shore of Loch Ailort, 1941.

(TRUSTEES OF THE LIDDELL HART CENTRE FOR MILITARY ARCHIVES)

10. 'Blows, No.4, Knee', a figure from William Fairbairn's illustrated manual *All-In Fighting*, 1942.

(NMS)

11. Staff at STC Lochailort, April 1941, including third from left Captain William Fairbairn, ninth from left Lieutenant-Colonel Hugh Stockwell, seventh from right Major J. C. M. T. O'Donovan, sixth from right Captain Eric Sykes.

(TRUSTEES OF THE LIDDELL HART CENTRE FOR MILITARY ARCHIVES)

12. Instructors outside Inverailort, July 1942. Sergeant Angus MacKinnon is third from right of the back row. Sergeant A. F. Austen is second from left of the front row.

(NMS)

13. Officers on the staff of STC Lochailort, July 1942. Lieutenant-Colonel C. S. Howard is seated centre. Beside him, fourth from right, is the padre Captain W. E. Gladstone-Millar, who preserved this photograph.

(NMS)

14. Ronald Hall, a student at STC Lochailort: 'They said, "If you think our methods are not cricket, remember that Hitler does not play this game".'

(MRS ANNE CLUNAS)

MI(R)'s main contribution was to raise, in great haste, special guerrilla companies for operations in Norway formed by volunteers drawn from the Territorial Army. Three of these 'Independent Companies', of which more later, sailed from the River Clyde and arrived behind the main Norwegian expedition. They were briefly to see action in the confused withdrawal that presaged the evacuation of the whole British force. However, MI(R) had also despatched a number of small teams in advance of the main expeditionary force to initiate and co-ordinate guerrilla operations, principally aimed against vulnerable points along the sea and land routes of the iron ore traffic. The teams had little luck or success, as once again the speed of the German advance overtook them and overwhelmed the home forces with which they were attempting to liaise.

One MI(R) mission was especially ambitious, but failed even to reach Norwegian coastal waters. This was Operation *Knife*, a six-man team that was directed to land by submarine in the Sognefjord in central Norway and co-operate with local Norwegian forces in destroying the rail and road bridges that linked Oslo with the north of the country. The intention was to hamper any German land advance north and simultaneously disrupt the iron ore supply in the opposite direction. No such thing was achieved. On 23 April 1940 Operation *Knife* was borne from the depot ship *Forth* at Rosyth in the Firth of Forth by the 'T' class submarine HMS *Truant*. Not far into the voyage from Scotland to Norway, *Truant* was attacked by an enemy U-Boat and damaged by the explosions of two magnetic torpedoes. It was a near thing, and the crippled *Truant* was fortunate merely to be able to return to the Forth in safety.

One of the six-strong MI(R) team that disembarked at Rosyth hoping for and expecting a second opportunity to launch Operation *Knife*, was Captain Peter Kemp. Kemp was among many British volunteers who, in the late 1930s, had gone to fight in the Spanish Civil War. Motivated by a sense of adventure and a profound concern about the threat of international communism, he had the distinction of being one of the very few who had fought not on the Republican side but for Franco's Nationalists. It was this experience of guerrilla fighting in Spain that brought Kemp to the attentions of MI(R). His war memoir recalls the formation of the *Knife* team:

Lieutenant-Colonel Bryan Mayfield, Scots Guards, who was to command the expedition, was a regular soldier who had left the Army before the war to go into business. An experienced skier, he had recently been Second in Command to Colonel Jimmy Coats in the '5th Scots Guards' ....

Easily the most junior of our party, I was delighted to find myself promoted overnight to the rank of Captain, which seemed to be the lowest rank on our Establishment. After me the most junior was Bill Stirling, at this time a captain in the Scots Guards; a man of six foot five and proportionately broad, he would, I thought, find a submarine uncomfortably cramped. Our demolitions officer was Jim Gavin, a regular Sapper and skilled mountaineer who had found time off from his duties to take part in one of the Everest expeditions. The remaining two members of the party were Ralph Farrant, a regular officer in a Line regiment, and David Stacey who in civilian life had been a stockbroker. Not only was I the most junior, but also I had the least skiing experience – apart from Bill Stirling, who had never been on skis in his life. The others had all served in the '5th Scots Guards'.[20]

From its beginning there had been a connection between 5th Scots Guards and MI(R); furthermore as brother officers in the Scots Guards during the 1930s, Bryan Mayfield and William Stirling of Keir were old comrades and sometime shooting partners.[21] It was Stirling who suggested that the *Knife* team await further instructions not at Rosyth, but at his ancestral home at Keir some 30 miles west. Although hospitality and country pursuits were on hand to be enjoyed on the Keir estate, photographic evidence shows that the *Knife* team also busied themselves with shooting of a different kind. They had brought with them from Rosyth the weapons, explosives and equipment assembled for the Norway mission and, explosives aside, they proceeded to experiment with these and train themselves further in their use. Meanwhile, as the Allied expedition and Norwegian forces wilted under German pressure in the south and centre of Norway, word was received that there would be no second attempt at Operation *Knife*.

Faced with the unhappy prospect of the *Knife* team being dispersed, Stirling and Mayfield took action to follow up the group's discussions about irregular warfare training and operations reflecting on their unfulfilled experiences with MI(R) and the 5th Scots Guards. Kemp records in his memoir that it was Stirling's idea to create a training school that would teach the theory and practice of irregular warfare, giving greater structure to the preparation of future missions that might be better realised than their own recent anti-climactic adventure.[22] Stirling and Mayfield took the proposal in person to MI(R) headquarters in London where their idea met with immediate approval. The positive reception reflected the fact that MI(R) was thinking ahead of them. Holland and Gubbins had themselves identified the need for a formal training branch of Military Intelligence that could be developed to instruct small teams like *Knife*, larger formations like the Independent Companies lately despatched to Norway, and, in theory, resistance operatives extracted from enemy-occupied countries. Funds were already in place.[23]

What Stirling and Mayfield could offer to MI(R) was the services of themselves and their *Knife* colleagues as instructors, plus clear proposals about where such a school could and should be created. Stirling's home at Keir was on the point of conversion into a military hospital and, being in a populated area of central Scotland on the southern edge of the highlands, it was not quite what they had in mind. But Stirling knew the shooting estates of the west highlands, with their wild, rugged country and abundance of Victorian and Edwardian era shooting lodges; secluded, substantial buildings, many of them empty for much of the year, that would make for suitable military accommodation. The north-west of Scotland offered another advantage for such secretive undertakings. The whole of Scotland north-west of the Great Glen, a vast area of Inverness-shire, Ross and Cromarty and Sutherland, and including much of the Hebrides and the Northern Isles, was one of those parts of the United Kingdom that had been designated a 'Protected Area' by order of the Home Secretary. Through a Defence Regulation empowered by the Emergency Powers (Defence) Act of 1939, this special status was enacted to enhance the security of military and naval installations – in the case of northern Scotland principally the strategically sensitive coastline and the naval base at Scapa Flow in Orkney.[24] The measures imposed controls on access, with permits required to enter the area. Thanks to the topography, entry by land could be controlled by a string of checkpoints at road crossings along the line of the natural water barrier of Lochs Linnhe, Lochy, Oich and Ness, and the Caledonian Canal that connected them. Even permanent residents of the area required extra certification, additional to the national identity card, to pass through the checkpoints.

Such a huge area offered a great number of properties which, with War Office backing for a military requirement of some urgency, the *Knife* party were almost entirely free to select from without reference to the feelings of the proprietors. Although Stirling knew the Morar and Moidart area well enough, it is not certain that it was he who specifically identified the Inverailort estate as the ideal spot for the new training school. While in London, Stirling and Mayfield had enlisted into their aid another from that rich seam of pre-war Scots Guards officers, Simon Fraser, Lord Lovat. Lovat was Stirling's cousin and an old university friend of Peter Kemp. He had earlier bumped into Kemp and Mayfield, pre-Operation *Knife*, at White's club in London, and he knew something of their present occupation.

At the time Lord Lovat was seeking active military employment, having recently parted company from his family regiment, the Lovat Scouts. This had been something of an acrimonious split. Lovat, serving as an officer in the regiment created by his father, had been dismayed to discover that his commanding officer had apparently failed to grasp approaches from the War Office towards a special role for the Scouts in the planned Norway expedition. What Lovat likely did not know was that MI(R) was behind this proposal, and indeed that MI(R) had earlier identified and approached the Lovat Scouts with a view to using their skills in fieldcraft to develop a system of guerrilla warfare training.[25] Neither suggestion came to fruition. While Lovat and some of his fellows saw only an opportunity missed, it is perhaps understandable that the officer in command of the Lovat Scouts chose not to take up a sketchy proposal from quarters unclear, offering a new role on foot in the snows of Norway when operations elsewhere, in the mounted observation role for which the regiment had been trained, might well have been close at hand. When, shortly afterwards, the Lovat Scouts were directed to the exacting but less than glamorous job of garrisoning the Faroe Islands, dismounted, Holland noted in MI(R) records that 'the Lovat Scouts went to the Faroes and lost the opportunity of stalking, sniping and surprising the Germans in Norway!'[26] Lord Lovat had already fashioned his departure. When he again met up at White's with his cousin Bill Stirling and Bryan Mayfield during their trip to MI(R) headquarters, Lovat was all set to take up duties as a Divisional sniping instructor based in Northern Ireland. He needed little encouragement to throw in his lot instead with the as yet homeless *Knife* team: 'It is difficult to describe my elation. White's is a charitable spot, and if I had stood on my head nobody would have been in the least surprised.'[27]

When Lovat arrived at Keir he brought his characteristic dash and directness to the team, a hint of ruthlessness that was to serve the Commandos well in the ensuing years. To the immediate purpose he brought personal know-how in highland fieldcraft, honed by years of sport and management on the estates to which he was born. Contemplating likely locations for an irregular warfare school, Lovat knew the territory inside the Protected Area as well as anyone; he himself owned a good deal of it. According to Peter Kemp, it was Stirling and Mayfield who identified the area along the Road to the Isles through Morar as the training ground and set the requisitioning process in motion.[28] Local tradition has it, however, that it was Lord Lovat who personally selected Inverailort and a number of other, smaller houses for the purpose.[29] Whoever made the final choice, the team had settled on an area with all the natural advantages of rugged country and broken coastline suitable for fieldcraft and survival training, and for learning small-boat work and assault landing techniques. It offered isolation and low population density conducive to security and indeed to public safety when live firing was brought to bear, and it had the important asset of proximity to the west highland railway whereby trainees and supplies could be delivered and despatched. The railway offered additional benefit as an ideal practice target for dummy demolitions.

This then was the situation that presented itself to Mrs Cameron-Head at Inverailort at the end of May 1940. The 'nice Captain Stacy' she found supervising the overturn of her house was David Stacey, one of the Operation *Knife* raiding team freshly arrived from his sojourn at Keir, and a former skiing Scots Guardsman. Surgeon-Commander George Murray Levick, whose acquaintance it seems likely she made at the Lochailort Inn, was one of those specialists identified by MI(R) as being of value in formulating a training course for those engaged in guerrilla warfare. Murray Levick was an early arrival. Mayfield and Stirling had been appointed Commanding Officer and Chief Instructor respectively, and at this point were away recruiting further staff and instructors through their own and MI(R)'s connections. The specialist teaching staff soon to assemble represented one of the most extraordinary combinations of talent and personality that the British war effort was to produce.

* * *

The new MI(R) irregular warfare school was designated the Special Training Centre Lochailort, commonly abbreviated to STC Lochailort. The MI(R) connection was never referred to. Technically, the administration and running of the Centre came under the authority of the War Office's Director of Military Training while, for the time being, Military Intelligence determined its function. In the early months none of this was terribly clear to those in situ, be they students or staff. One of the original instructors, Himalayan climber Captain J. M. L. (Jim) Gavin, later recalled that at the time he himself had no clear understanding of what specific authorities lay behind the Centre's establishment, despite being there from the beginning and having been a member of the *Knife* team.[30] For the same security reasons, the Centre's students certainly were not expected to have any knowledge of what powers lay behind the experience they were undergoing.

STC headquarters was Inverailort itself, habitually referred to as 'the Big House' in the manner traditional in the localities of large estates. Inverailort served for officers' accommodation and lecture rooms. Non-commissioned officers occupied nearby Glenshian Lodge and other estate buildings, leaving the trainees themselves to tents and huts erected close to Inverailort. Huts were also erected on islets in the River Ailort. These were used for lectures where a physical challenge was added to the theoretical work by the need to wade through the river to get there, and then absorb such information as was possible while sitting in wet clothes. One Lochailort student, 2nd Lieutenant R. F. (Ronald) Hall of the Dorsetshire Regiment, recalled hearing lectures, 'either wet up to the ankles, the knees, the waist or perhaps even the chest, depending on how high the water was'.[31]

The area behind the house soon bristled with obstacle courses and shooting ranges, some conventional, others less so. The challenge of the assault courses stuck in the mind of another student, 2nd Lieutenant Norman Craig:

> The pride of the place was its obstacle course. Considerable ingenuity had gone into the construction of these obstacles and every conceivable device, natural and artificial, was included. Over these you had to double with full equipment and a rifle. The courses were constantly

waterlogged so that, having successfully negotiated one fiendish obstacle, you arrived exhausted on the ground, only to sink up to your knees in a bog on the way to the next. At the end of one of the courses was a cliff-face that had to be climbed by rope. The rope was always shiny from the boots of those who had gone before, your own clothing saturated and your hands slippery.[32]

Of the shooting ranges, one, a small defile between the hill of Tom Odhar and the slopes of Seann Cruach, was christened 'Sniper Valley', and here demolitions drill as well as live firing was carried out. Over time the weapons training infrastructure developed to a considerable degree of sophistication. One construction, recalled as 'a sinister revolver range' by one instructor, was an elaborate test of reflex shooting.[33] Students armed with pistols proceeded through this 'Mystery House' created from a derelict building, wherein were activated metal pop-up targets fashioned in the image of enemy soldiers, all of which had to be hit. This exercise was extended and elaborated in time, both at Lochailort and at the many training schools that followed its example. The range would include decoy targets in the image of innocent civilians where the quick-thinking student could demonstrate the split-second discrimination not to fire at them. Close by, another house was also the scene of live firing, the evidence of which remained for many years in accumulations of spent small arms cartridges dug into the ground. A sheet of iron uncovered in the vicinity during the 1990s was found to be punctured by the impact of larger projectiles, possibly rounds fired from weapons such as the Boyes rifle (an anti-tank weapon with which special service units experimented from 1940-42) and with larger holes created by a weapon of considerably greater calibre.[34]

The core complex around Inverailort include an area of shoreline just west of the house where small-scale assault landing from the loch was practised, and also Mrs Cameron-Head's boat-house, from where four of her dinghies were requisitioned for training use.[35] Over to the north the railway line to Mallaig ran above the River Ailort. Here, as well as at the viaduct at Glenfinnan a few miles to the east, students learned to lay demolition charges. The railway halt at Lochailort itself was on the doorstep of the new training complex. New student intakes arriving by train were put straight into the regime without warning or warm-up of any kind:

We were sitting comfortably there in the train and all of a sudden it came to an abrupt halt. We were all thrown forward and kit bags came off the luggage racks and the place was a shambles. Then we realised that the train was under fire and there were explosions going off all around us. Then instructors leapt out of holes in the ground and shouted at us, 'Get out of the train, get out of the train, grab your kit and follow us!' And so of course we all scrambled out, grabbed everything we had, and we were doubled, and ran from there all the way to the Big House clutching our belongings.[36]

Away from the Inverailort estate buildings, STC Lochailort had the use of Roshven House five miles further down the shore of Lochailort, requisitioned from Peter Blackburn of Roshven. A further 25 miles south, on the south shore of Loch Moidart, the mansion house at Dorlin was requisitioned and run under STC Lochailort's direction as a specialist boat training school. Six miles north-west of Lochailort, along the Road to the Isles, stood Arisaig House, the imposing home of Miss Charlotte G. Astley-Nicolson, the principal landowner in the area. This sizeable property was also requisitioned for MI(R).[37] Unlike Mrs Cameron-Head, Miss Astley-Nicolson had the relative convenience of being able to remain nearby in one of her numerous properties, several of which, but not all, were to be taken over for military purposes before the year was out. Further properties in the wider area were requisitioned for MI(R) as auxiliary establishments where troops could be accommodated to await training or for other purposes. These included Achnacarry, ancestral home of the Camerons of Lochiel, which lies between Loch Arkaig and Loch Lochy some 35 miles distant by road from Lochailort, and, much nearer, Achdalieu Lodge on the shore of Loch Eil, another piece of the Cameron patrimony. North of Fort William, Torcastle Lodge and Inverlochy Castle were identified as suitable for future use and placed under the sway of the Special Training Centre. In the case of Inverlochy Castle, an 1860s extravagance built close to the ruin of the ancient fortress of Inverlochy, members of owner Lord Abinger's family remained in occupation of part of the house even after it was brought into temporary use by military personnel.[38]

Inverailort House and its environs was the centre of activity. The original establishment of STC Lochailort numbered 203 personnel, this set at a level that allowed 100 officers and 500 other ranks to be trained at one time. There were 55 instructors, a number that quickly increased and which, by the end of June, included six civilians, three identified in the documentation as 'ghillies', sportsmen's attendants recruited from nearby highland estates. Mules and ponies to the number 30 were also provided for, with staff to look after them. By the end of June the establishment had been augmented by a further 27 instructors, with additional administrative staff, capable of training 150 officers and up to 2500 other ranks. In addition to the permanent staff, use was made of Local Defence Volunteers (later the Home Guard) from the Morar and Moidart areas, and from the Small Isles of Rum, Eigg and Muck. These part-time volunteer soldiers, too old or otherwise unsuitable for full military service, tasked with local home defence and deadly serious in that responsibility, provided 'demonstration troops' to show Lochailort students what was required. They frequently acted the part of 'the enemy' in guarding targets or pursuing students across the hills.[39]

Much sweat was lost on the hills immediately behind Inverailort, where a steep initial climb up a rock wall led onto the slopes of the 2670 feet (814 metres) of An Stac, a staple ascent for the students under all conditions and one frequently ordered with little warning. While Lochailort was the base, training schemes and exercises ranged across the wider area of the Rough Bounds, using the challenging hill country of South Morar to the north and Moidart to the south, and such natural obstacles as the waters of Loch Shiel to test the students' mettle day and night. Training exercises from Lochailort reached as far afield as Fort Augustus to the north-east, and north-west out to the Isle of Skye:

> We were taken at dusk one evening in assault boats from Inverailort across to Skye. We landed on the west coast of Skye, blew a gap in barbed wire with Bangalore torpedoes, and then crossed and attacked Portree, it raining all the time. Having attacked Portree we advanced down Skye attacking various places along the way, eventually attacking Broadford and ending up near the Kyle where we got on a destroyer and were brought back to Inverailort and landed on the jetty.[40]

An unofficial but important part of the infrastructure, for the officers and staff at least, was the local hotel and its bar which stood above the bridge over the River Ailort close to the railway station. The Lochailort

Inn was the domain of Miss McCrae, something of a local character, wrapped in Gaelic mysticism, claiming kinship to the king of the fairies and given to reminding her military guests of the area's Jacobite past. The reduction in private visitors consequent upon the Restricted Area status of the west highlands inevitably put a serious dent in her takings, as it did on other businesses in the area reliant on tourism, but she and the nephew who looked after the hotel could count instead on a steady traffic of visitors to the Special Training Centre. These included observers from the Admiralty and the War Office, concert parties sent to entertain STC personnel, and the wives and friends of officers on the staff. This was the closest to comfort most of those serving at Lochailort could enjoy, with the exception of Lord Lovat and the promoted and newly-married Major Stirling who both enjoyed the luxury of having houses of their own in the vicinity to which family and friends could be invited.

The Inn saw some carousing courtesy of the Special Training Centre, and not all of its visitors were of interest by dint of their military distinction. In July 1940 the Inn welcomed a party hosted by Lochailort student and screen idol Captain David Niven. Niven had suspended an accelerating Hollywood career in 1939 to rejoin the Army (he had been a commissioned officer in the Highland Light Infantry in the early 1930s), and arrived for special training at Lochailort as one of 'the restless who will volunteer for anything in order to escape the boredom of what they are presently doing'. Niven's published recollections of his time in the west highlands are characteristically entertaining, and are much concerned with conquests of a romantic rather than military nature.[41] Another special service volunteer going through the course in July 1940, 2nd Lieutenant David Sutherland, remembered something of Niven's impact on one local of an impressionable age:

> The food was not particularly good, so on the last evening of the course David Niven booked a large table at the local pub. We had spinach soup, grilled salmon, raspberries and cream. The owner had an attractive daughter who kept peeping at David Niven through the kitchen door. He could take this no longer. He stormed into the kitchen and kissed her: she fainted. I remember David Niven saying to the flabbergasted proprietor, 'Sir, you will have to put some backbone into this pretty girl before I take her on as a leading lady'.[42]

* * *

With little more to work from than the Gubbins' three MI(R) pamphlets on guerrilla warfare, the scheme of training that evolved at Lochailort owed a great deal to the individual expertise of the instructing staff put together by Mayfield and Stirling. The principal asset of the area chosen for the Centre was, of course, the rugged country in which it was situated, and instruction in highland fieldcraft was a fundamental feature of the course. The senior instructor in fieldcraft was Lord Lovat. His first assistant was Peter Kemp, who described Lovat as 'a brilliant instructor as well as a superb fighting soldier, he taught me in the three weeks I was with him all I know about movement across country and the principles of natural camouflage'.[43] David Sutherland's recollection was that the whole place was 'Lord Lovat's brainchild':

> ... I remember what a romantic figure he was, standing on the lawn in front of the lodge with Lovat Scouts bonnet, battle dress, hill-walking boots and stick, with a stalker's telescope in a leather case slung over his shoulder.[44]

To promulgate the sportsman's wisdom, Lovat called on the assistance of three civilian stalkers from his own estates, Messrs McFarlane, Ormiston and Chisholm. The know-how and marksmanship of the highland deerstalker was reinforced by military men of similar highland estate background, three non-commissioned officers from the Lovat Scouts, Sergeants MacLennan, Chisholm and Davidson. Knowledge was imparted through lecturing and demonstration in the field, with games and competitive exercises to reinforce the messages. Fieldcraft competitions in use by 1941 included a manhunt, a stalking version of 'Hide and Seek' known as the 'Spider and Fly Competition', and a duel fought by two men stalking each other in a limited area.[45]

Stalking day and night, and the skills of living off the land, were lessons that had to be absorbed and understood by all the students at Lochailort. As one recalled, initiation into the latter involved ' ... learning to live off fruits and berries so that you could exist with perhaps the killing of a rabbit, skinning and gutting it and so forth and the fact that you could have a very small fire with just a couple of sticks and cook without pots and pans'.[46]

The stalkers could work with animals and knew how to kill, prepare and cook quarry much larger than a rabbit. From the hill men, students learned a new word and the skill it described, the 'gralloch', or disembowelling of deer.[47] One former stalker and shepherd who served as an instructor at Lochailort a little later (1941-42) was Sergeant Angus MacKinnon:

> We showed them how to stalk deer and skin deer, kill a sheep and
> if they were in enemy country and they were stuck for transport and
> there was a horse in a field, you had a rope or two, you would catch
> the horse and yoke it into a cart, or whatever is handy, just with
> ropes ....
>
> And after that we took them to the hill, and we would put flags at
> maybe about 150-200 yards apart, and they had to stalk us, we were
> the enemy, and they had to stalk us. And we put them on a bit of
> ground where they were bound to be seen. They had to use the ground
> to get across the ground without being seen, and of course when they
> came in and had a talk about it they would say 'No man could cross
> there'. So I was sent to go across this bit of ground, showing how to
> do it .... And then they were coming across that ground and heads
> bobbing up in the air and we were firing live ammunition across their
> heads. And you wouldn't see them for a while and when they did
> come up there again, they were first class. It fairly helped them, the
> live ammunition, but you needed to watch and no shoot them, and
> watch and no kill them.[48]

The use of live ammunition to heighten the realism of training conditions, and not just for target shooting, was one innovation that STC Lochailort helped to introduce into battle training. Naturally this practice was not without considerable risk. There were fatalities at Lochailort, and in the training centres that followed its lead, but apparently no more than a handful; with every precaution taken the casualty rate was considered acceptable. Shooting and explosives were not the only danger, since the test of water, hard country and inclement weather also made the students vulnerable to drowning, exposure and mountain accidents, like one remembered by Angus MacKinnon:

That only happened once when I was at Lochailort, it only happened once. This officer discharged him o'er the back of that high hill between Lochailort and Roshven .... But to discharge him o'er the back of that hill is a death trap ye ken, because they just made o'er the top of it, and of course a lot of them didn't know what snow was, and of course they skited off doon there. They were kicking them off seemingly as they were passing. And this fellow was killed and we got the pony and put him on like a stag. Terrible.[49]

Students were not the only ones at risk. Weapons instructor Captain P. A. Walbridge was seriously wounded during a practice assault landing early in 1941, when a grenade he had thrown malfunctioned and then exploded after a long delay.[50]

Lord Lovat's fellow officers in the fieldcraft wing were recruited from the lists of specially qualified personnel earlier compiled by MI(R). Two, the polar explorers Freddy Spencer Chapman and Martin Lindsay, had been leading lights in the 5th Scots Guards. The first summer at Lochailort did not offer the ideal climate to impart their experiences of survival in Greenland and the Himalayas, but they had much more to teach from their knowledge of the natural world, their understanding of meteorological patterns and hazards, their skills of navigation by the stars, and their familiarity with the equipping and provisioning of small teams for survival in any country. Of Spencer Chapman, fellow Lochailort instructor Captain Jim Gavin recorded:

> ... his special qualities were that he was a very great naturalist and he knew all about plants and which ones you could eat and which ones you couldn't and so on. He was a very good fisherman. He could tickle trout in a stream as a boy so he knew all about catching fish. He knew all about birds, a great ornithologist .... He had all those qualities, apart from other qualities which he had like being a very great mountaineer. He climbed Chomolhari by himself, a great peak, one of the great ascents I think, and a very good writer, a bit of a poet. He had marvellous qualities. But this particular thing, one thing he knew about: plants and birds and fish.[51]

Spencer Chapman's own memoir highlights his interest in specialist equipment, which he had already put to use advising the War Office and equipping 5th Scots Guards. Students at Lochailort usually trained in standard British Army boots, battle dress and personal equipment, or denim fatigues, but this he was able to supplement:

> The fieldcraft training was based on the lore of the Lovat Scouts, with plenty of practical map reading and direction finding, especially at night, stalking – the enthusiasm of students being first aroused with deer stalking – long-range observation with the telescope, and a minute study of the techniques of ambush assisted by lively demonstrations. The standard army equipment we found too cumbersome, and our patrols were given rubber footwear, the mountaineer's rucksack and lightweight tent, and the Polar explorer's concentrated rations. Each course ended up with a most arduous and realistic two-day-and-night scheme over rough and difficult country around Lochs Beoraid and Morar.[52]

In total the fieldcraft wing of STC Lochailort could boast five holders of the prestigious Polar Medal. One of these was another early MI(R) recruit, Captain J. M. (Jimmy) Scott, a member of Gino Watkins' British Arctic Air Route Expedition of 1930-31, who had also served in 5th Scots Guards. Another was Andrew Croft, an expedition comrade of Martin Lindsay. Croft arrived at Lochailort after narrowly escaping from German forces while operating independently for MI(R) in Norway, and then returning to the Norwegian fjords for further service in the closing days of the campaign. His stay at Lochailort was short, but advanced him into a distinguished war career in special operations. King of them all was George Murray Levick. On top of a distinguished career in naval medicine, Murray Levick carried the aura of having served with Scott of the Antarctic, albeit that his relations with the great man were not always the most cordial. Like Spencer Chapman and Lindsay, he had enjoyed some popularity in print, his contribution a classic study of Antarctic penguins.[53] He could even claim an Antarctic mountain named after him, the 2390-metre Mount Levick in the Deep Freeze Range of Victoria Land which was first charted by the Northern Party of Scott's expedition with Murray Levick as the medical officer. In retirement from the Royal Navy, Murray Levick had already sought to disseminate the skills and attractions of polar exploration to younger students. In 1932 he founded the Public Schools Exploring Society (later the British Schools Exploring

Society, still functioning today), which took parties from boys' schools to Arctic Scandinavia and Canada.

Murray Levick applied medical and scientific principle to the challenges of fitness, diet and survival for special service troops, and he used his time at Lochailort, and later at other highland training centres, to hone the theories published in his 1944 training manual *Hardening of Commando Troops for Warfare*. This official guide covered the 'hardening of the body' inculcating resistance to exposure and fatigue, 'pack marching', 'the bivouac', 'seasickness and immersion in water' and 'the science of rationing'.[54] Murray Levick's contribution at Lochailort was by no means limited to lecturing and demonstration, as confirmed by a member of the signals instruction wing:

> Most of the students who did the STC course would probably remember him as their 'Most Unforgettable Character' …. For a man of his age his endurance was almost unbelievable and he always took part in the three day exercise which came at the end of the course. It included two nights under the stars, winter and summer, and one could get very wet in the first twelve hours of the exercise.[55]

The 'Three Day Venture' was the final test, an exercise which put together elements of all that had been taught in a gruelling exercise meant to simulate a real guerrilla operation. It might take place around Lochailort, Morar and out to the Glenfinnan railway viaduct, or with a different scenario could range as far afield as the environs of Achnacarry further into Lochaber. The exercise was also known as the 'Captain Blood Attack', after the name given to the leader of the guerrilla force in the imaginative narratives that supported the scheme. Captain Jimmy Scott took the time to set out one Captain Blood scenario with a literary flourish, apparently for the added amusement of his fellow instructors. It began:

> This happened at a time when the towns and valleys of the Scottish mainland were overrun by a powerful, well disciplined and excellently equipped Lowland Army. A few free Highlanders still roamed the mountains as they did in the days that followed the '45, for the invaders were no hill-men, that was their only weakness. But the industries, roads and railways were in their hands: only the Hebrides

were free and the seat of the Free Scottish Government had moved to the Isle of Skye.

In this desperate situation, Captain Blood, 'a bold and ingenious officer who commanded a company of hill-men in the Isle of Eigg', leads his party to arsenals and hiding places at precise locations through Morar, to conduct simultaneous attacks along 20 miles of the Fort William to Mallaig railway.[56]

On 9 June 1940 the fieldcraft wing welcomed a new recruit, by way of a replacement for Peter Kemp who was required for special duties elsewhere. The new arrival was Chief Instructor Stirling's younger brother, 2nd Lieutenant A. D. (David) Stirling.[57] David Stirling had been one of those who dropped to a sergeant's rank to serve in 5th Scots Guards and was disappointed thereafter to find himself back in the routine of regular soldiering as an officer with the Scots Guards, minus the skis. Brought up to country pursuits like his elder brother, the young Stirling harboured a precocious ambition to be the first man to climb Mount Everest and had amassed mountaineering experience to that end in Scotland, the Swiss Alps and the Canadian Rockies. But under the principle applied to all new instructors, Stirling was required to have taken and passed the whole of the Lochailort course before he was allowed to teach any of it. He in fact arrived with one of the very first intakes of students. David Stirling's brief stint as an instructor at Lochailort, where he quarrelled with his cousin Lord Lovat, set him on the path to Commando service in the Middle East and to subsequent exploits at the head of the famous desert raiding unit which he created, the Special Air Service.

David Stirling was only one of a number of mountaineers who applied what they knew of Alpine ranges to direct Lochailort students in scaling the lesser crags and ridges of the west highlands. They also climbed for recreation. At the foot of the sheer north face of Ben Nevis stood (and still stands) the Charles Inglis Clark Memorial Hut, the property of the Scottish Mountaineering Club. The climbing and visitors books for the hut for 1940 show more than one party from STC Lochailort busy on the cliff faces above. An early trip is recorded on 22 June, with a party of J. M. L. Gavin, F. S. Chapman, A. Greenwood and A. D. Stirling listed as guests of club member E. A. M. Wedderburn. All five of the party were ex-5th Scots Guards and describe themselves as such in the Hut record, wherein Wedderburn recorded their epic day, and night, on the Ben:

Arrived at hut for late tea after day's work. Left 6.30 for Tower
Ridge. Over Douglas Boulder direct and up Tower by Pigott's route.
Summit 9.30. Lovely evening. Left 10.30 to descend by Carn Mor
Dearg Arête. Meal at hut & away again at midnight. Back at
Lochailort, 3.00 a.m.![58]

E. A. M. (Sandy) Wedderburn had been a leading young Scottish
climber of the 1930s with an impressive record of ascents in Norway and
the Alps. A war service commissioned officer in the Royal Scots, he was to
be a climbing mentor for special service troops in different capacities over
the next four years, until proceeding on active service in Italy with the
Lovat Scouts where he met his death in an accident.[59] Working from an
administrative base at Lochailort, Wedderburn developed a four-week
course of intensive instruction in mountaineering and sea-cliff assault that
took students to prime climbing country in Glencoe and the Isle of Skye.
The teaching covered cliff-base boat-landings and the haulage of weapons
and equipment, as well as the conventional techniques of crag-climbing
and rope-work. Wedderburn operated a ratio of one instructor to seven
students, a high level of supervision which was made possible by enlisting
the best of the students from one course as assistant instructors for the
next. Testimony to Wedderburn's methods came from well-qualified
quarters in the shape of a War Office report submitted by one of Britain's
leading pre-war mountaineers N. E. (Noel) Odell, a Captain in the Royal
Engineers:

> Personal experience of being led up a well-known severe climb by
> a student of two weeks' experience only, brought home forcibly the
> excellence of the system of training which has been adopted.[60]

Supporting the innovations of the fieldcraft wing and the balletic
exertions of the climbers was more straightforward teaching in the essential skills of map-reading and use of the compass. This was taught in a
classroom by a Warrant Officer of the Army Education Corps, with
follow-up practical instruction and testing in the field. The original map-
reading instructor was fully at home in the west highland environment:

> ... possessed of a near-perfect Inverness-shire accent he delighted
> in telling his students that the purest English in the British Isles was

spoken in Inverness-shire. He was also very well versed in Scots history, particularly the '45, always getting a bit of fun by informing his students how lucky they were to be given a free walk over this historic countryside.[61]

For the students this subject offered some of the quieter moments in the training regime, always assuming that no surprises had been laid on to shake them from any complacency.

Nasty surprises were certainly a feature even of classroom sessions in another crucial component of the training programme – demolitions:

> The type of training you had to do made it so you were always tired, you were always at the full gallop and then suddenly they would say 'Right, into the Nissen hut for a lecture'. Well, of course it was very difficult to keep awake. What he had done was he had these little fuses which he put under some of the seats and around the wall. You couldn't see them and you'd be sitting there and of course they'd go off![62]

The 'he' in question was another young officer who had followed the customary pre-Lochailort route of 5th Scots Guards ski training and irregular service in Norway for MI(R), whence he too had returned without having an opportunity to achieve a great deal. This was Captain Michael Calvert, a Royal Engineer who later earned the rather suspect sobriquet 'Mad Mike' for his daring and effective exploits with 'Chindit' special forces operating behind enemy lines in Burma. In only six weeks at Lochailort acting as assistant to chief demolitions instructor Captain Jim Gavin, Calvert found his niche teaching the rudiments of explosives, fuses, timing devices and booby traps. One student retained a mental picture of these lessons:

> Daily we sat, like a conspiracy of Anarchists, at the feet of Sapper officers who instructed us in the use of incendiary bombs, time-pencils, pressure switches, mines and gelignite and ammonal.[63]

Following the principle that 'the object of the course is to teach you how to destroy things quickly', when they were familiar with the rudiments of explosives students progressed to thinking about where and how to use them.[64] This took them from the blocking of roads with craters to placing hidden charges for the sabotage of railways and bridges. A favourite exercise was 'The Wrecker', where the objective was to derail a theoretical enemy ammunition train passing through Lochailort on its way to 'the Naval Base at Mallaig'. Students had 45 minutes to leave the lecture room, stalk up to the railway, place and conceal pressure switch charges. Later courses took students further afield on trips into Lochaber to look at the Caledonian Canal lock-system at Banavie and the aluminium smelter at Fort William, and to consider, in theory, how they might best be put out of action.[65] There was even among the explosives experts a former convict who passed on his ill-gotten expertise in setting small charges to break locks and get into safes.[66] This is believed to have been Johnny Ramensky, a frequenter of Barlinnie and Peterhead prisons who had been released from the former by special arrangement in return for offering his services to the war effort. He is known to have been teaching at the Commando training depot at Achnacarry in early 1942, and later passed on his undoubted skills for the benefit of one of Special Operations Executive's training schools at Beaulieu in Hampshire.[67]

For Michael Calvert, time spent at Lochailort was appreciated as useful experience gained among a group of fellows sharing and developing a philosophy of irregular warfare that chimed with his own:

> It was good to be in the company of men who were pioneering the type of fighting that had begun to intrigue me; the small force, which acted on its own, harried the enemy and upset their balance. Such forces could not win wars alone, of course, and none of us ever pretended that they could. But they had tremendous value as the spearhead of a big attack, or the annoying jolt which distracted the enemy from the central front, or the means of destroying a vital strategic point which for some reason or other the main force could not reach. They could dart in quickly and silently from the air, from the sea or on land and do their deadly work before the other side really knew what was going on.[68]

This was a philosophy that Calvert would take to guerilla warfare students in the Far East and to his subsequent career with the Chindits and the Special Air Service.

* * *

The first objective of the Lochailort training was guerrilla warfare as defined by Gubbins in his pamphlets. Fieldcraft and adjuncts such as rock-climbing could put guerrilla operatives in place to engage targets in enemy or neutral territory and, ideally, get them out again. Skill in demolitions enabled those targets to be destroyed, be they supply depots, munitions, communications or industrial installations. It was expected that these targets would usually be guarded, and one express purpose of attacks of this kind was to compel the enemy to dissipate his forces in guarding against 'hit and run' attacks throughout the territory he controlled. Although prolonged fighting with enemy forces was unlikely to be the hallmark of a successful sabotage operation or raid, violent encounters, often at close quarters, were necessarily part of the guerrilla role. Consequently much time at Lochailort was devoted to developing proficiency with rifle, sub-machine gun, revolvers and self-loading pistols, together with hand grenades and heavier weapons such as the aforementioned Boyes anti-tank rifle. Some of the Army's finest shots were recruited as weapons instructors, premier among them Warrant Officer First Class (soon to be Captain) P. A. Walbridge, a member of the British Army's competition shooting team who had transferred from the British Expeditionary Force sniping school in France. For rifle shooting Walbridge's creed was that he could teach his students to increase the number of well-aimed shots they could fire from the 15 per minute considered a good standard from a trained infantry soldier, to 20 or even 25 rounds per minute.[69] This was achieved with the standard issue Short Magazine Lee Enfield rifle, a superbly efficient and reliable weapon in the right hands. Walbridge was also adept with the Bren light machine gun, and supervised the introduction of a famous United States import, the Thompson sub-machine gun or 'Tommy gun'. A compact, short-range weapon with a high rate of fire, the Tommy gun was well suited to guerrilla operations. The model demonstrated at Lochailort was an updated version of the weapon that was a well-known favourite of American gangsters of the 1920s. Its Hollywood-fuelled reputation sat well with the unorthodox approach to warfare it was now to be used for.

With deerstalkers on the staff, Walbridge did not have a monopoly on shooting skills. The fieldcraft instructors drawn from the Lovat Scouts had trained at the small arms school at Hythe in Kent, and Walbridge had brought one colleague with him from the sniping school in France.[70] There were others too who could perform feats with the rifle. Lieutenant R. T. S. (Tommy) Macpherson, a Commando officer training at Lochailort in the summer of 1940, a man who knew a good deal of stalking and shooting, was impressed by the skills of one particular individual:

> There was a remarkable collection of instructors there. There was a fellow called Mackworth-Praed, an ex-guardsman, who was a weaponry instructor, and he had to be the finest shot I have ever seen. With a .303 standard bolt-action he could get three magazines off in a minute and they would all be on or just beside the bull's eye at 300 yards. He was a remarkable chap. He used his third finger on the trigger and flicked the bolt, which had a very easy action, with his second finger after each shot, and the speed of it was astonishing.[71]

Cyril Mackworth-Praed was another former Scots Guards regular officer, and was a 1924 Olympic gold medallist in shooting with his record-holding forte in the Running Deer discipline. He later established a new Olympic record in this event in the 1952 Helsinki games.

A different kind of shooting was taught by perhaps the most remarkable among the array of specialist fighting talents employed at Lochailort: two former policemen recently arrived from the Far East. William Fairbairn and Eric Sykes (known as 'Bill') brought the specialised brand of pistol shooting and methods of unarmed combat they had studied, used and refined during long service in China with the Shanghai Municipal Police in the 1930s. A centre of opium trafficking and prostitution, the international city of Shanghai was blighted by criminal gangs perpetrating a nightly catalogue of violent robbery, kidnap and murder. Distressed by the death toll among his police colleagues, Fairbairn had conceived a new approach to shooting that corresponded far more closely to the dangers they faced than the straightforward target shooting previously practised.

In pursuit of what he later called 'shooting to live', Fairbairn created a pistol range in a Shanghai warehouse which replicated the typical lodging house into which he and his police colleagues took their dangerous duty. In near darkness the policemen reacted to a series of surprises from pop-up targets, firecrackers and other hazards; this was the original 'Mystery House', the direct forerunner of the range created beside Inverailort. The intention was to inculcate split-second decision-making and reflexes, where the pistol was drawn with great speed and fired at a target by instinct, without a deliberate aiming action or use of sights, much as one would point a finger at someone or something without thinking about it. Two shots were to be delivered to the target, to ensure that in the real event none were returned. Fairbairn reckoned that in most shooting affrays in Shanghai the distance at which firing took place was not more than four yards. In these deadly, close-quarter exchanges, the instinct method was both life-saver and effective life-taker.

Fairbairn and Sykes retired from police work in China early in 1940 and returned to the United Kingdom where their work was already known. Fairbairn had published a manual of *Scientific Self Defence* in 1931, and it appears the pair had already been in contact with the British Secret Intelligence Service when they offered their services to the War Office.[72] Perceiving a theoretical connection between the underworld violence of the Shanghai waterfront and the likely undertakings of guerrilla warfare, they had been recommended to MI(R) and were both sent to Lochailort with the rank of Captain. There they collaborated with Walbridge and the other shooting instructors, while Fairbairn worked also closely with the physical training wing. Physical Training (PT) at Lochailort therefore encompassed exercises rather more choice than the assault courses behind Inverailort and the regular slogs up An Stac. The second Fairbairn and Sykes speciality imported from Shanghai was a vicious collection of unarmed combat and knife-fighting techniques. Fairbairn was a martial arts expert, but the methods he taught were somewhat removed from the refinements of ju-jitsu at which he excelled in its purest form.

By all accounts the most surprising thing about Fairbairn and Sykes was their outwardly gentle demeanour and unthreatening appearance. Given their age (both were in their late fifties) this was perhaps merely the preconception of their relatively youthful students, but they evidently took delight in overturning first impressions:

On the first morning we met 'Dan' Fairbairn and 'Bill' Sykes. We were taken into the hall of the Big House and suddenly at the top of the stairs appeared a couple of dear old gentlemen (we later discovered one was 56 and the other 58). Both wearing spectacles, both dressed in battle dress with just a plain webbing belt. They walked to the top of the stairs, fell tumbling, tumbling down the stairs and

ended up at the bottom, in the battle crouch position, with a handgun in one hand and a fighting knife in the other – a shattering
experience for all of us.

Having made this initial impact on 2nd Lieutenant Ronald Hall and
his fellows, in the following weeks Fairbairn and Sykes took them through
a prospectus of lethal disciplines:

They said, 'If you think our methods are not cricket, remember that
Hitler does not play this game'. They taught first of all how to fall, a
continuation of their falling down the stairs. They taught handgun
and knife work and neck breaking …. We were taught releases – if
you are grabbed by somebody from the back, front, side or whatever,
how to get out of their grip. We were taught 'come along' grips –
how to take a prisoner along without him being able to escape. We
were taught the use of sticks, anything from four inches to six foot.
A four inch stick is just held in the hand and you can strike with the
end of the stick, and give a chap a nasty knock with it …. They taught
the use of coshes (they preferred the spring type best), longbows,
crossbows, catapults, garrotting with anything that happened to be
handy … the use of shovels – any good soldier always carries either a
pick or a shovel and they simply use it to chop off a chap's head, or
whack him on the shoulder or just use it like a battle axe. You can do
the same with a tin hat …. We were taught mouth slitting. If you are
being gripped by somebody you can stick your thumb in the corner
of his mouth and split his cheek up to his ear; ear smacking – cup-
ping both your hands and hitting both his ears at the same time,
which of course breaks his ear drums; ear tearing – the easiest way to
tear a chap's ear off; eye gouging; the gralloch. A nice little tip Dan
Fairbairn told us, if you gralloch anybody, keep the point of your
knife down because otherwise when it comes up you might hurt the
sharpening of the blade where it might catch on his belt or buckle;
rib lifting – grabbing a fellow under the ribs and lifting him hard;
nose chopping – chopping downwards or upwards with your hand
or anything else; shin scraping – giving a fellow a good kick if, say,
he is holding you from behind, a good kick on the knee with your
boot, scraping it down his shin and ending up with a good stamp on
the instep; shoulder jerking – a sharp jab downwards of the arm

which will dislocate the shoulder; the bronco kick – if you get somebody on the ground you jump on him hitting him hard with both heels at the same time which will break the particular part that you hit; the bone crusher – a blow used on the sternum they recommended, where you put the tips of your fingers against the sternum and then with the full force of your body hit him with the ball of your hand, and it will smash his ribs or it can be used on any other part of the body, particularly under the chin; and how to tie up a man – tying his wrists with a good old-fashioned sailor's handcuff knot, and they also taught a way of tying the fellow's wrists behind his back and pulling his ankles up as well with the same piece of cord, and then putting a loop round his neck so that if he struggled he strangled himself.[73]

Brutalities of this kind were another feature of the course that entailed a degree of risk to the trainees. Notes for Lochailort instructors teaching the Fairbairn-Sykes unarmed combat programme carried a warning:

To avoid accidents in practice, great care must be used with all holds, throws, blows and counters underlined. The 'Japanese Strangle', the edge of the hand blows and the 'arm throw' require extreme care. On NO ACCOUNT should the Chinese 'rock crusher' be practised over the heart.

The unarmed combat syllabus was held to be particularly sensitive, and the instructors' notes were headed with an embargo that none of the information therein was to be 'communicated directly or indirectly to the Press or to any person not holding an unofficial position in His Majesty's Service'.[74]

Nevertheless, in 1942 Fairbairn published a guide to unarmed combat in illustrated manual form under the title *All-In Fighting*. Its teachings were shockingly violent, even to a nation at war, but this he justified in relation to the type of war that was by then being fought, the character of the enemy and German successes to date:

Some readers may be appalled at the suggestion that it should be necessary for human beings of the twentieth century to revert to the grim brutality of the Stone Age in order to live. But it must be realised that, when dealing with an utterly ruthless enemy who has clearly expressed his intention of wiping this nation out of existence, there is no room for any scruples or compunction about the methods to be employed in preventing him.[75]

The book was prepared at Lochailort with the assistance of Walbridge, who contributed much of the shooting content. And this was only one of Fairbairn's offerings to a readership far wider than the students under his instruction. In the same year he and Sykes published a guide to their pistol method as 'Shooting to Live with the One-Hand Gun'. Fairbairn also brought forth a 1942 pamphlet 'Self Defence for Women and Girls' which outlined some rather less homicidal but nonetheless effective actions for threatened females, such as 'The "Cinema" Hold, a Defence against Wandering Hands'.[76]

Together the names of Fairbairn and Sykes are remembered principally in connection with another product of their time as instructors at the Special Training Centre. In November 1940 the two men visited the London premises of Wilkinson Sword Limited, a firm that had produced sword blades for the British Army for generations. They brought with them designs for a new kind of knife, one they had determined would better meet the fighting requirements of special service soldiers. Their concern was that existing sheath knives, and the knives with knuckleduster hilts that such soldiers had taken to carrying, were limited in the effectiveness with which they could be used in different situations. The knife they had in mind was to be realised as a dagger of the stiletto type, with a double-edged $7\frac{1}{2}$-inch blade and a brass hilt with a chequered grip. It was sheathed in a leather scabbard that could be worn from the belt or strapped to the calf of the leg by means of cross tapes. The knife could be used as a survival knife and as a slashing weapon, but its principal application was in the practise of 'silent killing', above all to their recommended method of despatching sentries and other unwary targets by a thrust to the carotid artery in the neck.

Leaving a sketch with John Wilkinson-Latham and returning to Lochailort, Fairbairn and Sykes soon received a trial model that met with their approval. Wilkinson Sword hand-produced the first 50 of the 'F-S Fighting Knife', with the designers' initials etched on the ricasso of the blade, in January 1941. Another 1250 followed and, after a simplification of design, a Second Pattern went into mass production. Its materials would soon be simplified further into a Third Pattern which was produced in tens of thousands.[77] This knife, conceived and tested at the Special Training Centre Lochailort, became the weapon *par excellence* of the Commando, or special service, soldier. Its utility was practical, but it came to stand for something more. An efficient, cold-blooded killing weapon, it symbolised the whole ethos of irregular warfare with its uncompromising and lethal intent. As such, the knife was adopted as an emblem into the insignia and lore of the special service units that were being formed and trained for action.

Coping with hard country, fitness, the ability to destroy and de-rail, killing with rifle, machine gun, pistol, knife and bare hands, these were the main features of the Lochailort training syllabus and of the type of guerrilla warfare that MI(R) sought to disseminate. But from the first, Colin Gubbins had drawn attention to the importance of intercommunication as part of his 'Guerilla's Creed' and stressed the care and skill with which it needed to be employed in order to avoid detection by the enemy.[78] Signals training at Lochailort might begin with simple instruction in basic semaphore, but it extended into sophisticated instruction in wireless transmission, coding and maintenance that covered different types of possible operation. The staff of the signals wing came from a three-man team that had been despatched to Norway by MI(R) shortly before the ill-fated Operation *Knife* venture. Captain Peter Fleming and Royal Corps of Signals Sergeants Bryant and Beriff were flown to Namsos by flying boat to erect and operate a transmitter whereby they could put Norwegian forces directly in touch with the British expedition that was to follow. Although, unlike *Knife*, the team at least managed to reach Norway, there was little that they were able to achieve before the general evacuation. They brought their wireless equipment back with them, and it was with this equipment, and a stock of prototype portable radios, that a wireless station site on the hill above the Lochailort Inn was begun, placed at a sufficient remove from the bulk of An Stac to allow reception.

A full account of life on the signals staff at Lochailort was written in later life by Lieutenant-Colonel A. F. Austen, in 1940 a Royal Signals sergeant who was brought in to assist Bryant and Beriff. Austen notes the rapid defection of the mercurial Peter Fleming, a journalist, writer and something of an adventurer (brother of novelist Ian, creator of the 'James Bond' character), who quickly moved over to work with Lord Lovat's fieldcraft wing. Austen stuck with signals and his first day at work saw him aboard a herring drifter in the Sound of Sleat off the Isle of Skye, testing ship to shore communications:

This involved one of our party on an isolated beach with a radio and a time schedule of transmissions at increasing distance from the shore. All very interesting and a feeling of doing something of use in the war effort – the people organising the early small scale raids had realised the need for a small, hand held radio to cover the vital link between small boat and landing party.[79]

Austen spent some months at Lochailort passing on the basics of radio communication:

We did quite a lot of individual tuition, mainly with Special Mission people, some of quite advanced years, who had either forgotten or never bothered to learn the Morse Code. In time we devised a crash course which enabled them to master the code and a moderate speed in a few days, depending on their keenness .... Corporal Smith our Instrument Mechanic, was able to pass on the rudiments of wireless theory knowledge which would enable an operator to do emergency repairs and improvise tools and spares.[80]

Finally, the Lochailort training embraced the expertise of the Royal Navy. When, in July 1940, Commander Sir Geoffrey Congreve sent a telegram from Lochailort to Mrs Cameron-Head informing her that he had requisitioned four of her dinghies for the use of the Special Training Centre, this may be taken as one of the original sources of British 'Combined Operations' training during the Second World War.[81] Preparations to co-ordinate the efforts of the Royal Navy, the Army and the Royal Air Force towards the execution of sea-borne assault landings were to become a vital element of the British war effort in the following months and years, and much of it would be rehearsed on Scottish sea-lochs. But the initial efforts at Lochailort were necessarily of a more modest order, geared towards the preparation of small raiding parties to be landed upon, and picked up from, enemy-controlled shores. Between the boat-house at Inverailort itself and the (now demolished) Dorlin House on the South Channel of Loch Moidart, the naval element of the Special Training

Centre taught the rudiments of boat handling in all sea conditions, by day
and by night, and with an emphasis on silence.

The small-boat work was initially under the hand of Congreve, who
arrived at Lochailort directly from service in the Norway campaign
commanding a group of four anti-submarine trawlers that was attacked
off Namsos with the loss of two of the four vessels. Congreve received the
Distinguished Service Order for his contribution in Norway, living up to a
tough family standard; both his father and brother were holders of the
Victoria Cross. He himself had served as a young Midshipman at the
Battle of Jutland in 1916. Congreve left Lochailort after only a matter of
weeks, but his influence in special operations grew as he became a fixture
in early Commando raids.[82] His contribution came to a much-lamented
end when, in July 1941, he became the first from the Lochailort instructing
staff to lose his life on active service. Waiting aboard a landing craft for the
return of a small raiding party on a reconnaissance mission along the
beaches at the mouth of the River Slack in the Pas de Calais, he was killed
by machine gun fire from the shore. Congreve's place at Inverailort and
Dorlin had earlier been taken over by another experienced Royal Navy
officer, Commander C. G. Vyner. In the following years Vyner's west
highland boat stations served not only Lochailort students, but also
special service units developing canoe and other small-boat raiding
techniques, and parties from the major Combined Operations training
centres in Argyll. In March 1942 the Dorlin establishment was detached
from its administration by STC Lochailort and taken over entirely by the
Royal Navy. As HMS *Dorlin* it operated as one of the numerous specialist
Combined Operations training establishments along the Scottish west
coast. It was supported by accommodation and stores at Shielbridge,
Salen, Glenborrodale, Glencripesdale and Roshven.

* * *

Together with occasional visiting lecturers, like First World War escape
specialist Flight Lieutenant A. J. Evans and espionage theorist Bernard
Newman, these then were some of the original Lochailort teaching staff
who put together the first special training courses. They were a curious
collection of talents and personalities. Several were to demonstrate the
worth of the methods they taught by distinguishing themselves on operational service later in the war. But the students they tutored at Lochailort

were also an eclectic group, directed there for a variety of purposes, most of them special service volunteers, others unsure, indeed quite unaware of precisely why they had been sent there at all. The very first group of students were remembered by Peter Kemp as 'twenty-five puzzled sub-alterns, some of them volunteers, others arbitrarily despatched by their commanding officers. They were supplemented by an equal number of NCOs'.[83] Among this first intake was one volunteer from civilian life, the traveller and writer Fitzroy Maclean, then in the employ of the Russian desk at the Northern Department of the Foreign Office and recently returned from diplomatic service in Moscow. Maclean was unable to enlist in the Army as he wished, bound by the wish of the Foreign Office to retain his expertise, but able to pull sufficient strings to obtain a taster of irregular warfare and the military life at Lochailort. Maclean was later to prove a highly proficient exponent of irregular warfare, first with the Special Air Service in North Africa, then operating with partisans against German forces in Yugoslavia.[84]

The initial course was presumably a learning experience for all concerned, including the instructors, but there was to be little time for experimentation and fine tuning. While Inverailort was undergoing transformation into the Special Training Centre, events were unfolding on a greater stage that suddenly gave added urgency to this obscure initiative in its quiet highland location. On 10 May 1940, while the Operation *Knife* team were still awaiting instructions at Keir, the 'Phoney War' of stand-off in western Europe had come to an abrupt end. German forces poured into France and the Low Countries and their *Blitzkrieg* advance pushed back the home and British forces with stunning speed. While Mayfield, Stirling and Lord Lovat were summoning instructing staff to their chosen location in the Scottish highlands, far removed from the battle front, the military situation in France was deteriorating rapidly. As the first students arrived off the train at Lochailort in the first week of June, the campaign in Flanders was coming to its calamitous end. The bulk of the British Expeditionary Force was evacuating the Continent, embarking in small vessels from the beaches of Dunkirk. Less than three weeks later, on 21 June, the French government capitulated and the Battle of France was over, leaving western Europe under German domination. MI(R) originally envisaged irregular warfare as a potential weapon in eastern Europe where enemy forces were thought likely to prevail. With British regular forces thrown into disarray and defeat in the west, and with the enemy just across the English Channel, it suddenly looked a very serious proposition much closer to home.

In Norway the situation was little better. MI(R)'s modest efforts operated on the fringes of an Anglo-French expedition that landed some 10,000 troops at Namsos, Andalsnes and Narvik in mid-April. Their objective was to prevent German invasion forces from advancing north-ward up the coast from the foothold they had already established in the south of the country. This proved impossible, as German air attacks launched from captured air bases in the south took a heavy toll. Although there were successes in Norway, including the capture of the important northern port of Narvik and the serious harm inflicted on the German surface fleet, the campaign could not be sustained. With the position in France descending meantime into deep crisis, Norway was evacuated by Allied troops on 8 and 9 June.

Among the British troops that returned from Norway were a new kind of unit, the experiment that was MI(R)'s main contribution to the campaign. These were the 'Independent Companies', conceived by MI(R) in response to the German invasion of Norway in early April, and put into being by the end of that month. The plan was to land self-supporting guerrilla warfare units along the coast of northern Norway, with the task of hampering German exploitation of the long coastline between the separate Allied landing zones at Namsos and Narvik further north. The first idea had been to form a single Special Infantry Battalion made up of guerrilla companies, whether by transforming the Lovat Scouts or by recruiting a unit of volunteers from Regular Army regiments. Officers and men with experience of mountaineering would be considered an asset, although such skills would not be mandatory, and the intention was to locate the new unit in mountainous country as soon as possible for tactical training and 'physical hardening'.[85] The companies would be ship-borne, otherwise without transport, lightly armed with rifles and Bren light machine guns, and expected to operate without support for periods of up to one month. An important element of their equipment would be hard cash, £4000 in Norwegian and British currency, to aid their survival and operation amidst what was hoped would be a friendly local population.[86]

The MI(R) officer who created and commanded this force was Colin Gubbins, promoted to the rank of Brigadier. Rebuffed by the Lovat Scouts and with concerns about recruiting from the heavily committed Regular Army, the call for volunteers went out instead to Territorial Army formations stationed in the United Kingdom. The Territorials were asked to provide ten Independent Companies altogether, made up of 20 officers and 270 other ranks apiece. The response was enthusiastic, as demonstrated among the volunteers from 66th Division:

> The idea, we were told, was a small unit of two or three hundred men, self-sufficient in weapons and explosives and furnished with a bag of gold sovereigns, committed to guerrilla operations behind the enemy lines. The target, as was later intimated, would be German communications in the Norwegian mountains, to be attacked from a landing in some dark fjord.
>
> Without heroic delusions, by no means anxious for bloodshed or death but craving excitement, eager to get on with the War and impatient of my current administrative role, like lots of Galahads of that time, I joined the 10th Independent Company at once.[87]

The desire to get on with the real business of war expressed here by 2nd Lieutenant A. R. H. (Arthur) Kellas left the Independent Companies greatly oversubscribed in certain formations. This required a selection process, as occurred among the Territorial soldiers of the 1st Battalion London Scottish, Private Dallas Allardice among them:

> I was beginning to compare my early days in the army to days in a holiday camp when a notice came round asking for volunteers to go on a special assignment.
>
> The notice aroused tremendous interest and most of the Battalion volunteered. This led to interviews and eventually four officers and thirty-four other ranks were selected. The main qualifications for selection seemed to be knowledge of mountaineering and the ability to ski. I was one of the thirty-four to be selected .... [88]

Such was the urgency of the situation in Norway, there was almost no time to augment such qualifications with special training of any kind. The Independent Companies were formed and rapidly despatched to Gourock on the Firth of Clyde, from whence five of the ten Companies sailed for Norway under the codename *Scissorsforce*. Much as with MI(R)'s other Norwegian adventures, they found little time to prepare or carry out their allotted tasks, and on landing from the Norwegian fjords they found themselves almost immediately engaged by the enemy. Gubbins arrived at Mosjöen with two of his Independent Companies to find that the French ski troops who were supposed to be covering their flanks were instead preparing for evacuation. German forward troops appeared soon after, and although these were successfully ambushed there was no prospect of taking on the main body of highly trained Austrian ski units that was approaching behind them. The two Independent Companies re-embarked within a matter of hours and joined their brethren further up the coast around Bodö.

A similar if more drawn-out story unfolded in the area of Bodö. The Independent Companies could do little in the face of a German advance that was reaching into the northernmost quarters of Norway far quicker than anticipated. With the enemy upon them, and Bodö under air attack, there was no opportunity to develop the guerrilla strategy. *Scissorsforce* was not a success. In the general crisis Gubbins was transferred to command a regular formation in the main body of the Allied expedition, and the Independent Companies were restricted to fighting as conventional infantry in the defensive role. Their only guerrilla contribution came on the point of precipitate departure, sabotaging installations and fuel supplies to deprive the enemy of their use. Such acts were little more than gestures of defiance. As Norway was left to its fate *Scissorsforce* returned to Scotland. There the remaining five of the ten Independent Companies had been waiting in vain for their chance to sail for Norway, some of them actually embarked and ready to leave. They were now stood down.

One of the Companies that did not set sail was No.6, formed from 9th (Highland) Division, a 'second-line' or reserve formation of the Territorial Army. The original volunteers were whittled down by drawing lots and in late April the winners assembled at Buddon Camp in Angus on the links of the Scottish east coast. Second Lieutenant R. A. C. (Ralph) Cameron was one of them:

> Organisation was followed by a fortnight's training, chiefly in small arms and night work. The Company then moved to the Trossachs for training in steep country. Each man was expected to carry a rucksack (as opposed to a pack) which was said to weigh 108 lbs. I do not think it was an exaggeration. To get to one's feet after being loaded up, the best method was to imitate a camel's approach to the problem,

substituting 'Christ' for the customary moan. At the end of May the Company embarked at Glasgow on the *Monarch of Bermuda*.[89]

After some days aboard ship, the Company was ordered to disembark and found itself waiting with little purpose at Wishaw in Lanarkshire alongside No.7 Independent Company. In July it moved to Cornwall to take up defensive duties, quite the opposite of the tasks for which the men had volunteered and an indication of the crisis that the threat of invasion suddenly posed. Nevertheless, unlike 5th Scots Guards a month earlier, the Independent Companies were not to be entirely dispersed. Those that avoided diversion into emergency defensive duties on the English south coast remained in the area around Glasgow. After a brief period of leave, the men were ordered a period of proper training, an opportunity that had been all too clearly lacking for those rushed out to northern Norway and asked to operate there in severe winter conditions. The training was to take place in the west highlands of Scotland.

* * *

The Special Training Centre Lochailort began its work in earnest by taking in and training the Independent Companies in rotation. While waiting their turn to go to Inverailort, the troops were housed in the other properties that had been requisitioned in the vicinity. From these, each Company conducted training of its own. No.4 Independent Company went to Traigh House, one of Miss Astley-Nicolson's numerous properties in Morar, while Private Allardice's No.5 Independent Company had the run of her larger house at Arisaig:

> It was a most beautiful building situated in spacious grounds, over-looking a small beach with the magnificent scenery in the distance of Eigg, Muck and Rhum: the land of Bonnie Prince Charlie. The house, built with Aberdeen granite, and owned by a Miss Nicholson, was full of antique furniture with pine wood walls supporting stag heads and family portraits ....
>
> On the morning of our first day together, Major Peddie gave an introductory pep talk. He informed us that we would be undergoing a rigorous training programme in the mountains and that special instructors including Lord Lovat and his Lovat Scouts would train us.

There would be deer stalking, forced marches, living and surviving in the hills and operating with the Navy landing on Islands on the West Coast. All this to me was unbelievable, as it would have been my choice of an ideal holiday and resembled some of the activities that my friends and I had been doing in pre-war summers.[90]

The appeal was less immediate for one of Allardice's officers, 2nd Lieutenant A. D. C. Smith, who in letters to his mother held the weather unreliable and the locals thin on the ground:

I arrived here this morning – it is a really magnificent bit of country and would be even better if one could see it ….

Another thing that surprises me – and disappoints me – is the lack of hospitality of the Scots. You write of having had the local military to dinner and so forth, but not a soul has called on our mess and not one of the local worthies has asked any of us to dinner – or even in for a drink! It would make such a difference.[91]

Diffidence from the civilian population would not be the typical experience as they grew accustomed to the military presence suddenly imposed upon them, but given some of the activities of No. 5 Independent Company described by Private Allardice, the new arrivals were perhaps fortunate relations did not deteriorate into downright hostility:

At the beginning of our training we were encouraged, at the end of the day, to go out deer stalking. This was both exciting and enjoyable but eventually it became uncontrollable and the mountainside was reminiscent of a battlefield with some firing at deer from long range resulting in many of the deer being wounded. This, of course, did not please the locals and an order came out that there would be no more unofficial stalking. Instead we managed to do a little poaching in the rivers with the help of a primer and detonator.[92]

Friendly and discrete relations between soldiers and residents would nevertheless prove to be a positive memory overall for those on both sides of the equation, despite occasional lapses. Meanwhile, No. 5 Independent Company went through seven weeks of concentrated training at Arisaig and Lochailort, leaving it 'fit, hard and remarkably proficient with its weapons'. It then moved south to the Isle of Wight to prepare for a raid on the coast of France, an operation that was cancelled.[93]

Second Lieutenant Kellas and No. 10 Independent Company spent much longer in the highlands. Over the best part of six months they moved between the Special Training Centre at Lochailort, Achdalieu Lodge on Loch Eil, Glenfinnan Lodge at the head of Loch Shiel and, further east into Lochaber, accommodation at Achnacarry and Torcastle Lodge. Within that period Kellas' notebooks record a timetable for three weeks of intensive Lochailort training. The syllabus covers instruction in unarmed combat, semaphore, use of the sub-machine gun, stalking, close combat, compass work, running, fieldcraft ('movement through woods'), patrolling, map reading, route marches, physical training, sport (running, boxing, football), demolitions, grenade throwing, two full days ominously marked 'hills', messages, a semaphore competition, a night scheme, lectures on fieldcraft, patrolling and compass work, and two examinations.[94]

No. 10 Independent Company was formed from a Territorial Army formation recruited largely from the industrial towns of Lancashire and the English Midlands. Kellas' published memoir records that it took his men some time to become accustomed to the alien scenery and associated physical discomforts of the west highlands:

Uprooted out of Liverpool slums and Midland mills and offices, the men were sometimes worn out as we climbed about in those hills, and cursed and swore and laughed and blasphemed .... As the weeks passed, however, the best of them began to respond to the challenge and even enjoy it, and there were times of exhilaration for all of us. Indeed when the weather broke it seemed to me that the worse the conditions the more robust the mood.[95]

When the nights shortened, and the weather conditions grew characteristically challenging, the work went on:

We ran for miles across country; we hung a rope bridge over the narrows of the Lochy torrent under the castle rock and swarmed across and tumbled into the water; we felled trees, sawed logs and built a raft; we shot pheasant and hunted rabbits and rats with our pistols; we route-marched in the rain; we scrambled up to the snow and splashed through the bog and waded the burns. We played war-games in the woods on stormy nights, wiring our defences with explosive devices.[96]

In the midst of these exertions, Kellas experienced another feeling beneath the exhilaration, a nagging doubt that underlay his men's ritual moans against the toughness of the military life in the Rough Bounds and grudging appreciation of its compensations. These after all were men who had volunteered for special service, enticed by the promise of activity and a chance to get into action. Processing across the hills to Loch Morar, or forcing a route march through a sleet-driven Glendessary, the Independent Companies were still a long way from the real war. Their own disquiet at the brevity of the Norwegian campaign was compounded by the depressing, humiliating news from France and their current impotence against what looked like an all-conquering German foe. Kellas found himself wondering if Britain, never mind his platoon, had the stomach for the fight. He at least derived some comfort from the attitude espoused at the Special Training Centre, as he observed following a night exercise:

> … on the weary way along Loch Ailort that morning the Company Commander was exhausted and lay very still in the ditch when we halted at the roadside in the dripping birch-wood. Colonel Stirling, chief instructor, unmercifully rebuked him for having abandoned the assault on the town of Mallaig, the object of the operation, after that ghastly night in the hills. The rest of us gave thanks to God that the wretched major had called off that lark; but I agreed with Stirling. For, as I sternly recorded in the diary, 'I keep comparing ourselves with German troops, who cover thirty miles a day with a kind of crusading zeal in the name of the Third Reich'.[97]

Kellas may easily be forgiven his doubts. There can have been no hiding that this extended period of training in and around the Rough Bounds was nothing if not an exercise in improvisation. Officers and men must have been conscious that the test awaiting them was an enemy that had already demonstrated his efficiency and ruthlessness with stunning success. For those determined to fight fire with fire, as those driving the special operations idea certainly were, the comparisons at this early stage must have been troubling.

Towards the end of its time in the highlands, No.10 Independent Company had to endure the frustrating experience of embarking on a long voyage for a raid that never happened. This was Operation *Menace*, a scheme to enter Dakar in Senegal, French West Africa, in support of a French force that would seize the colony for the Allies. When the mission was called off, the Independent Company found itself back in Lochaber in late October. The feeling of anti-climax with which they returned was something British special service forces would have to learn to live with over the next 18 months, as their efforts at raiding proceeded tentatively and on a trial and error basis. Independent Company guerrilla operations had begun as early as the end of June 1940 when raiding parties from No.11 Independent Company approached the French coast around Boulogne. Those two parties that actually managed to land achieved little more than brief exchanges of fire and retired without casualties. For the majority of Independent Company volunteers, any awareness they had of small raiding activity, even on a scale as limited as this, was a source of frustration in itself. No.11 Independent Company had been added to the complement specifically for special operations, while the majority of their counterparts in the original ten companies were stuck in defensive duties on the British mainland.

* * *

From the Independent Companies also came the second Commanding Officer at STC Lochailort. Lieutenant-Colonel Hugh Stockwell, later of Burma, Malaya Emergency and Suez Crisis repute, took over from Bryan Mayfield in September 1940. During the Norway campaign, Stockwell commanded No.2 Independent Company and he returned from that dismal experience convinced of the urgent need for change in how the British Army approached training across the board. In a memorandum drafted for the attention of his superiors, he stressed that soldiers needed suitable ground to train over and better approximation of real battle conditions:

> ... it is necessary to be absolutely ruthless in obtaining the grounds we require, & in relaxing at reasonable risk the safety precautions which have so handicapped field firing and artillery practice camps in the past; every day in peacetime the Navy and Air Force take

justifiable training risks which have never been accepted for Army training.

Further, he wanted to see all soldiers fitter, individually motivated and accustomed to using their initiative:

> ... it is necessary in our training to pay the utmost attention to the development of every man we have in the fighting line – this, I understand has already been commenced. Undoubtedly, drill gives steadiness and encourages discipline, but only the minimum necessary time should be spent on this – what is most necessary is training in the use of ground, the stalker's instinct, absolute confidence in the weapon, & complete reliance on the determination of one's comrades to stand and fight.[98]

Command at Lochailort gave Stockwell the opportunity to put these recommendations into practice. He did not change the essential features of the course; fieldcraft, fitness, unarmed combat, weapons, demolitions, communications remained the standard. But administration was tightened up, facilities were improved and extended, and the throughput of students increased. The teaching was still unorthodox, but the character of the Centre departed somewhat from its experimental origins with MI(R) as it came under more conventional structures of military organisation. Training special service troops would remain the fundamental function, but STC Lochailort would also be concerned with teaching guerrilla methods for the benefit of normal infantry soldiers.[99]

As preparations to combat any German invasion of the British mainland intensified in the summer of 1940, officers and NCOs from defensive formations in the south of England were selected for training in irregular warfare. These were drawn from the XII Corps Army formation under the command of Lieutenant-General Andrew Thorne, tasked with defending the vulnerable coasts of Kent, Sussex and parts of Hampshire and Surrey, and having to do it with resources far from adequate for the job. Thorne's plan was based on mobile columns of troops operating behind a defensive 'crust' of forces in coastal areas. The mobile columns would intercept and harry any enemy forces penetrating the crust before they reached a second defensive line towards London. Thorne badly lacked trained troops and sending a small number to Lochailort, in order to have them return and pass their new knowledge on, was part of the effort to increase their overall capability.

Young officers and non-commissioned officers who had not been in the peace-time Army had little practical experience of the minor tactics of battle and fieldcraft, and yet they were expected to train their troops in these very disciplines. XII Corps, under a new commander General Bernard Montgomery, would become one of the most innovative formations of the field army in developing its own training schools in minor tactics, but initially it had to make the best of anything that was available.[100] Second Lieutenant Ronald Hall was one of those despatched to Lochailort from his infantry unit, the 4th Battalion Dorsetshire Regiment then in Kent, to learn what he could of irregular methods and return to impart whatever was relevant to his own troops:

> Sergeant Davidson and I were chosen by Harold Matthews our Commanding Officer to go to the irregular warfare training centre for what they called an advanced assault course and to come back and form our own battle patrol.[101]

Lochailort's utility in teaching irregular methods to conventional infantry soldiers proved to be one of the attributes that kept it functioning for two years, latterly after the focus of special operations training had moved elsewhere. Its students came from units of British Home Forces, and also included representatives of Canadian and Polish Army units stationed in the United Kingdom. STC Lochailort staff expressed the opinion that it might be more effective to form and train dedicated Assault Companies as specialist units within larger infantry formations. However, the training of assault troops proceeded on the basis of selecting 180 non-commissioned officers and officers at and below the rank of Captain from across an infantry division, or equivalent numbers from smaller formations. The selected trainees received a 30-day long programme of instruction with five days allocated to each subject (close combat, assault, demolitions and fieldcraft), a full week of tactical exercises and three free days.[102] In autumn 1941, 2nd Lieutenant Norman Craig of the Welch Regiment passed through the assault troops course as part of his training as a junior officer newly-commissioned from the ranks, and identified it as 'the prototype of the battle schools, which later had such a vogue in England'. The syllabus still followed the format pioneered in the summer of the previous year:

The programme was full, varied and exacting. We did practical map-reading in the hills, although there were few convenient landmarks to help us. We carried out opposed landings from the loch and were sniped at with live ammunition. We practised street fighting, mess-tin cooking and unarmed combat. Those who were not completely exhausted by the day's work spent their leisure hours doing yet more mountain climbing or shooting deer.[103]

Scottish infantry units also found themselves at Lochailort. In October 1941 the 51st (Highland) Division was an untried formation that assumed a famous identity borrowed from Scotland's most celebrated military formation. The original 51st, inheritors of a prestigious reputation won during the First World War, had not returned from France in 1940. Its surrender at St Valéry-en-Caux was something of a Scottish national trauma amidst the general calamity of the German victory in France. The new division, formerly the 9th, trained hard for more than a year to prepare for what would be expected of it in its new guise as the 51st. As part of the process the divisional commander Major-General Wimberley sent one platoon from each of the nine infantry battalions under his command to learn the techniques of assault landing and all the other features of the course. For accommodation they were imposed upon another collection of unfortunate property owners in houses as far south of Lochailort as the shores of Loch Sunart.[104] Recruits for other Scottish infantry battalions also encountered the Lochailort regime, sent there from the other side of the country by No.9 Infantry Training Centre at Aberdeen.

Other recipients of special training were Local Defence Volunteers (LDV) across the highlands, from July 1940 renamed as the Home Guard. Something of a training roadshow went out from STC Lochailort to LDV units in the Inverness area. Three instructors stopped off at Newtonmore, Aviemore, Grantown-on-Spey and Inverness, imparting a condensed version of the course to these highly enthusiastic volunteers all anxious to know what methods might be at their disposal should a German invasion somehow reach as far as the deer forests of Badenoch. At this early stage, where local efforts tended to run ahead of national organisation, there was much enthusiasm among LDV/Home Guard units across the United Kingdom as a whole for this kind of training. The guerrilla army approach was being heavily promoted by the journalist and Spanish Civil War veteran Tom Wintringham, who in July 1940 opened his own irregular warfare weekend school for Home Guard members at Osterley Park near London. Wintringham's communist sympathies tended to reinforce reluctance in the War Office to see the Home Guard develop in this direction and, in Scottish Command as elsewhere, the units were quietly eased into more conventional modes of defence training.[105] Nevertheless, in the ensuing years Scottish Home Guard units continued to take advantage of the highland special training centres within their reach. To accommodate the fact that the Home Guard were part-timers with jobs to hold down, STC Lochailort offered a weekend version of their course with exercises in the core subjects morning, noon and night over the two days.[106]

Back in the south-east of England, General Thorne's front-line defence planning embraced guerrilla methods with rather greater urgency. Thorne applied to the War Office for an officer to help him train selected local civilians in the rudiments of guerrilla warfare and organise them into 'stay-behind parties'. In the event of a German invasion force penetrating his coastal defences, these could operate from hide-outs and attack enemy communications and supply, disrupting any preparations for an assault on London. The idea was one that had already been floated by MI(R), and the officer identified for the job was Captain Peter Fleming. Fleming took what he could from a brief stay at Lochailort, and what he knew from his private adventures in South America and China, to confer irregular warfare wisdom upon the yeomen of Kent.

The civilian stay-behind parties that were nurtured in the XII Corps area were quickly subsumed into a larger clandestine organisation, operating on the same principles, that made such preparations as it could in all vulnerable points in the country, using the Home Guard as a cover for its activity. These 'General Headquarters Auxiliary Units' were recruited, trained and equipped under the aegis of MI(R) and placed under the direct command of Colin Gubbins. They attained a quite sophisticated level of organisation and preparedness, extending the length of the country, if patchily, including parts of Scotland. Their training was partly based on MI(R) guerrilla methodology taught at Lochailort, including the full range of unarmed combat skills introduced by Fairbairn and Sykes. The Lochailort influence was passed on directly by Fleming's assistant in this work, Captain Michael Calvert, who was posted to advise the Auxiliaries directly from his role as demolitions instructor at the Special Training Centre, and also by polar explorer Andrew Croft who had briefly taught fieldcraft there. Fleming and Calvert first surveyed the area in which the units would operate, selected the men and began their training. There is evidence too that the Auxiliary Units received instruction from regular soldiers who had passed through the Lochailort course, including 2nd Lieutenant Ronald Hall from whom the local 'resistance' in Kent absorbed some of the unarmed combat syllabus.[107]

Never tested, the extent to which the Auxiliary Units would have proved operationally effective following a German invasion is necessarily a matter of conjecture, but Calvert was in no doubt. When the initial invasion scare passed, thanks to the defeat of the German Air Force in the Battle of Britain, Fleming and Calvert's work was over:

> Peter and I were recalled and I remember thinking as we returned to London that, if it had been called to action, the Resistance Army of Kent and Sussex would have had at its core some of the toughest and most determined men I have ever met. Their farms and shops and their homes would have been highly dangerous places for any enemy soldier to enter. Although the Germans didn't know it, they should have thanked the R.A.F. boys for keeping them away from Britain.[108]

*   *   *

If special service troops were far from being the sole customers of the Special Training Centre, from late summer 1940 its priority students were nevertheless a steady stream of officers and men who were not from infantry regiments or the Home Guard, nor from formed Independent Companies. A small number were foreign, or had particular language skills or local experience that suited them for covert operations and liaison work in enemy-occupied countries. These men were being specifically prepared for deployment by a new organisation that took on from MI(R) the role of co-ordinating and supporting overseas resistance networks under the title Special Operations Executive. But the majority of the new students had answered a general call for volunteers issued throughout the Army in July 1940. They were training to join, and to train in turn, a new kind of fighting unit, an aggressive raiding force that was designed to keep an offensive edge to the British war effort by conducting sea-borne assaults all along the coasts of continental Europe. The new force was called the Commandos. To further a broad training effort to support the development of Commando forces 5000-men strong, overall control of the Special Training Centre was detached from MI(R) and firmly placed within the formal command structure of the Army. The days of improvisation and experimentation at Lochailort were coming to an end.

Like the volunteers they taught, the original cadre of Lochailort instructors were men anxious to get into the war. Though a few stayed on, Mayfield, the Stirling brothers, Lord Lovat, Spencer Chapman, Gavin, Lindsay and Calvert remained at Lochailort only long enough to establish the Centre and see it working in the hands of staff made ready to succeed them. Bryan Mayfield was one of those who quickly returned to more conventional soldiering, taking command of the 2nd Battalion Scots Guards on active service in North Africa. Others established individual reputations fighting in the field of special operations that they had helped to bring into being. Chief Instructor Major Bill Stirling and Spanish Civil War veteran Captain Peter Kemp passed into the service of Special Operations Executive (SOE). Stirling left Lochailort at the end of 1940 with an SOE team under the name 'Yak Mission'. This was an ultimately unsuccessful effort to recruit and train guerrilla fighters from among Italian prisoners of war in the Middle East. The team, led by Peter Fleming, went through the Lochailort course before departing for Cairo.[109]

In the Commandos Lord Lovat became an elemental influence and something of a public figure following the widely publicised exploits of his No.4 Commando during the Dieppe raid of August 1942, a propaganda iron pulled from the fire of an otherwise disastrous operation. Lovat's Lochailort colleague Martin Lindsay also volunteered for the new Commando force. This brought him to the fore in pioneering parachute training with No.2 Commando at Ringway airfield near Manchester, from which first British experiments in airborne warfare grew the Parachute Regiment. From there Lindsay moved on to regular infantry operations with 1st Battalion Gordon Highlanders in the north-west Europe campaign.[110] Fieldcraft instructor David Stirling was another Commando volunteer. After serving as a Commando officer in the Middle East, he came up with a scheme to attack desert airfields deep behind enemy lines in North Africa. This he achieved by creating a small raiding force named (misleadingly) the Special Air Service (SAS), which operated with such success that it survived Stirling's capture in 1942 and developed into the force that still operates today. In the closing years of the war the SAS embraced the talents of the elder Stirling and of Michael Calvert in senior command positions.

Fieldcraft instructor Freddy Spencer Chapman was one of those who directly exported the Lochailort syllabus for the instruction of others farther afield. In early autumn 1940 he and Calvert were sent to Australia to set up a training school amidst the mountains, eucalyptus forest, swamps and beaches of Wilson's Promontory, the southernmost point of Victoria. Their students were the Australia and New Zealand Independent Companies, guerrilla forces newly created on the British model with a view to combating the Japanese in the islands of the Pacific should, as soon transpired, Japanese aggression come to pass:

> The training was the natural development of the Lochailort course and was as practical as we could make it. Calvert, with his infectious enthusiasm, taught them how to blow up everything from battleships to brigadiers, and I can see now the gleam that used to come into his eye as he looked at a bridge and worked out exactly how much explosive to use and where to place it. I taught them how to get any party from A to B and back by day or night in any sort of country and to arrive in a fit state to carry out their task. This included all sorts of sidelines, a new conception of fitness, knowledge of the night sky, what to wear, what to take and how to carry it, what to eat and how to cook it, how to live off the country, tracking, memorising routes, and how to escape if caught by the enemy. The course culminated in a three-day-and-night scheme in which the Australians 'fought' the New Zealanders all over the Promontory; and this was followed by a heated post-mortem on a twelve-foot-square sand table model of the area.

The similarity between the Australia courses and their Scottish originator was close; Spencer Chapman could easily be describing Lochailort itself, right down to the sand table models that were a feature of exercise planning and de-briefing at the original Special Training Centre.[111]

Again, once Spencer Chapman and Calvert had trained a cadre of instructors to pass the methods on, they were free for similar employment elsewhere. Calvert went to Burma and a job training British and Australian officers and NCOs in guerrilla methods for covert operations against the Japanese in China. Spencer Chapman teamed up once again with

Lochailort colleague, Jim Gavin, at another special training school, this one run under the aegis of Special Operations Executive at Tanjong Balai in Singapore. Here the threat from the Japanese was much closer than it had been in Australia, though general faith in the conventional defences of Singapore and Malaya meant that no great sense of urgency characterised the work of Gavin's No.101 Special Training School. It was nevertheless with the conception of potential Japanese victories that Gavin, Spencer Chapman and other specialists began to train military and civilian personnel in irregular warfare methods that could be employed should 'the unthinkable' happen. Efforts to create intelligence networks and 'stay-behind parties' throughout south-east Asia had barely got going when the Japanese advance into Malaya began. When British defences were quickly overwhelmed, Spencer Chapman was one of those who did stay behind, leading anti-Japanese guerrilla operations in the Malayan jungle for some three years.

For such individuals as Lord Lovat, David Stirling, Michael Calvert and the others, the weeks and months spent amidst the Rough Bounds of the west highlands constitute only a brief prelude to spectacular war careers that earned high accolades and awards. Others, like Fairbairn and Sykes, Wedderburn and Murray Levick, we shall meet again by dint of their influence in developing the training regimes of the Commandos and Special Operations Executive. In time these new organisations developed their own training establishments, including others situated in the Scottish highlands and one in particular whose reputation came to overshadow those initial steps taken in the hard country around Inverailort. The influence of the STC Lochailort training syllabus is plain in those that followed. With the foresight of Holland and Gubbins' MI(R) think-tank behind them, and through a perspicacious opinion of what warfare against a power like Nazi Germany must entail, the original Lochailort team saw to it that the training and development of British special service forces had somewhere to start from. At a time of national crisis and great danger, this was no small contribution.

NOTES TO PART ONE

1. R. Henriques: *The Commander. An Autobiographical Novel of 1940-41,* (London: Secker & Warburg, 1967), p. 69.

2. All quotes and figures from correspondence in the Cameron-Head Papers, Highland Council Archive, D271/B/III/1.

3. Guest books of the Lochailort Inn. Courtesy of Ms A. M. Keenan and Mr R. Mungin, Roshven.

4. P. Wilkinson and J. Bright Astley: *Gubbins and SOE* (London: Leo Cooper, 1993), pp. 33-37; and MI(R) papers in records of Special Operations Executive, National Archives, Kew, HS8/256 and HS8/260.

5. The branch was originally designated General Staff (Research), GS(R).

6. D. Fitzpatrick: 'Militarism in Ireland, 1900-1922', in T. Bartlett, *et al.*: *A Military History of Ireland* (Cambridge: Cambridge University Press, 1996).

7. Quoted in Wilkinson and Astley: op. cit., pp. 8-9.

8. MI(R) papers in Special Operations Executive records, National Archives, Kew, HS8/256. A full transcription of 'The Partisan Leader's Handbook' is given as Appendix 2 to M. R. D. Foot: *SOE in the Low Countries* (London: St Ermin's Press, 2001), pp. 447-72.

9. War Office records, National Archives, Kew, WO208/340.

10. W. Mackenzie: *The Secret History of SOE* (London: St Ermin's Press, 2002), pp. 52-54 and MI(R) papers in the records of Special Operations Executive, National Archives, Kew, HS8/263.

11. J. Warwicker (ed.): *With Britain in Mortal Danger, Britain's Most Secret Army in WWII* (Bristol: Cerberus Publishing Ltd., 2002), pp. 9-21.

12. Lindsay's own account was published soon after: M. Lindsay: *Sledge. The British Trans-Greenland Expedition 1934* (London: Cassell & Co., 1935).

13. F. Spencer Chapman: *Helvellyn to Himalaya* (London: Chatto & Windus, 1940).

14. F. Spencer Chapman: *The Jungle is Neutral* (London: Chatto & Windus, 1950), p. 3.

15. C. Steven: *Eye to the Hills. A Scotsman's Memories of an Outdoor Life* (Derby: Breedon Books, 2001), pp. 72-73.

16. Steven need not have worried. Following the early demise of 5th Scots Guards, his abilities took him through service with the Intelligence Corps in Iceland, the course at the Special Training Centre Lochailort, and into the Commandos as a commissioned officer. He ended the war as an instructor at the Commando Mountain Warfare Training Centre at St Ives in Cornwall.

17. 'Notes on the Preparation of a British Ski Force', 18.3.1940. War Office records, National Archives, Kew, WO193/21.

18. D. Erskine (ed.): *The Scots Guards, 1919-1955* (London: William Clowes and Sons Ltd., 1956), p. 26.

19. War Office memo (12 December 1939) from the Director of Military Operations to the Director of Military Intelligence had noted: 'This unit is not required ... we cannot justify the raising, equipping and maintenance of such a unit. Regretfully we must check their ardour – whether you command enough adjectives to do so in appropriate language, I doubt.' National Archives, Kew, WO193/21

20. P. Kemp: *No Colours or Crest* (London: Cassell, 1958), pp. 13-14.

21. Keir Visitors Book for 1937, in the collection of the Stirlings of Keir.

22. Kemp: op. cit., pp. 18-19.

23. F. Mackay: *Overture to Overlord. Special Operations in Preparation for D-Day* (Barnsley: Pen & Sword, 2005), pp. 53-56.

24. F. H. Hinsley and C. A. G. Simkins: *British Intelligence in the Second World War, Volume 4, Security and Counter Intelligence* (London: HMSO, 1990), pp. 25-26.

25. MI(R) War Diary, 10 October 1939, and 12 April 1940, Special Operations Executive records, National Archives, Kew, HS8/263

26. Ibid., 18th April 1940.

27. Lord Lovat: *March Past* (London: Wiedenfield & Nicolson, 1976), p. 176.

28. P. Kemp: op. cit., p. 19

29. Lord Lovat's memoir seems to suggest this, although there are minor discrepancies between Lovat's quoting of Kemp and Kemp's published account. Lovat: op. cit., pp. 177-78.

30. Later Major General J. M. L. Gavin. Interview with James Merrick Lewis Gavin, Imperial War Museum Sound Archive, 12308, Reel 1, 1983. Source: BBC Radio 4 'Set Europe Ablaze'.

31. Major R. F. Hall MC: 'The Big House', unpublished transcript of a lecture to Moidart Local History Society, 13 August 2001.

32. N. Craig: *The Broken Plume. A platoon commander's story* (London: Imperial War Museum), 1982, pp. 29-30.

33. F. Spencer Chapman: *The Jungle is Neutral*: op. cit., p. 6.

34. Examples kindly donated to the National War Museum by Mr and Mrs H. Clyne of Lochailort.

35. Cameron-Head Papers, Highland Council Archive, D271/B/III/1.

36. Hall: op. cit.

37. Mackenzie: op. cit., p. 54.

38. A letter of Lieutenant-General R. C. Firebrace, Commander-in-Chief, Scottish Command, to the Under Secretary of State, MI5, refers to this arrangement at Inverlochy as late as 18 December 1940. Letter from the papers of Major A. A. Fyffe, then with 49 Field Security Section Intelligence Corps, later an officer of Special Operations Executive. Information on requisitioning of these properties is confirmed in Valuation Rolls of the parishes concerned held in public records at the National Archives of Scotland.

39. War Office records, National Archives, Kew, WO260/8.

40. Hall: op. cit. Bangalore torpedoes were simple explosive devices with charges placed within a long, extendable tube. They were developed in 1912 by Indian Army engineer officers serving at Bangalore. In the First World War they had been used on the Western Front to clear barbed wire defending enemy positions before an attack.

41. D. Niven: *The Moon's a Balloon* (London: Hamish Hamilton, 1971). Niven went on to serve with the special battlefield intelligence unit 'Phantom', the General Headquarters Liaison Regiment. Reproduced by permission of Penguin Books Ltd.

42. Later Colonel David Sutherland of the Special Air Service and Special Boat Service. D. Sutherland: *He Who Dares. Recollections of service in the SAS, SBS and MI5* (Barnsley: Leo Cooper, 1998), pp. 29-30.

43. Kemp: op. cit., p. 19.

44. D. Sutherland: op. cit., p. 28.

45. 'Special Training Centre Lochailort. Suggested fieldcraft games and competitive exercises for troops', Stockwell Papers 3/10, Trustees of the Liddell Hart Centre for Military Archives, King's College London.

46. Oral testimony of Major William McHardy, Gordon Highlanders, in D. Atherton (ed.): *We're Far Fae Home Now! Aberdeen and the North East's experience of military service abroad, the Great War to the Gulf* (Aberdeen City Council, 1999), p. 27.

47. Unpublished memoir by Lieutenant-Colonel E. H. Van Maurik OBE, supplied by him to the National War Museum.

48. Mr Angus Mackinnon: transcript of National War Museum recorded interview, April 2002.

49. Ibid.

50. Lieutenant-Colonel A. F. Austen MBE, BEM: 'The Special Training Centre Lochailort, Inverness-shire, A Personal Memoir', Royal Signals Museum Archive, Ref. 936.4, pp. 41-42.

51. Imperial War Museum: Gavin: op. cit.

52. F. Spencer Chapman: op. cit., 1950, pp. 6-7.

53. G. Murray Levick: *Antarctic Penguins, a Study of their Social Habits* (London: William Heinemann, 1914).

54. Combined Operations Pamphlet no. 27, 'Hardening of Commando troops for Warfare' (1944), National Army Museum, Department of Printed Books, 356.168.

55. Austen: op. cit., p. 8.

56. 'Three Days Venture', Stockwell Papers 3/24, Trustees of the Liddell Hart Centre for Military Archives, King's College London.

57. Posting order in Regimental Archives Scots Guards, 'P' file no. S3.

58. Scottish Mountaineering Club Papers, National Library of Scotland ACC 11538/17, p. 101.

59. Ernest Alexander MacLagan Wedderburn 1912-44, 'In Memoriam', obituary by N. E. Odell, *Scottish Mountaineering Club Journal 1945* (Edinburgh).

60. 'Crag and Sea-Cliff Climbing Course, STC Lochailort. Suggested Extension of Training', 10 July 1941, War Office records, National Archives, Kew, WO193/21.

61. Austen: op. cit., pp. 7-8.

62. McHardy and D. Atherton (ed.): op. cit.

63. A. Kellas: *Down to Earth [or Another Bloody Cock-Up]. A parachute subaltern's story* (Edinburgh: Pentland Press, 1990), p. 27.

64. 'Lochailort fieldcraft course. Offensive Demolitions December 1940', Stockwell Papers 3/1, Trustees of the Liddell Hart Centre for Military Archives, King's College London.

65. 'Special Training Centre, Lochailort. Demolitions Course Programme: 17-31 May 1941', Stockwell Papers 3/6, Trustees of the Liddell Hart Centre for Military Archives, King's College London.

66. Interview with Tommy Macpherson, Imperial War Museum Sound Archive, 17912, Reel 1. 1998.
67. C. Cunningham: *Beaulieu. The Finishing School for Secret Agents* (Barnsley: Leo Cooper, 1998), pp. 72-73.
68. M. Calvert: *Fighting Mad* (London: Jarrolds), 1964, p. 49.
69. J. Dunning: *It Had To Be Tough. The fascinating story of the origins of the Commandos and their special training in World War II* (Durham: Pentland Press, 2000), p. 71.
70. Mackay: op. cit., p. 57.
71. Later Sir Thomas Macpherson of Biallid, 11 Commando and Special Operations Executive and President of the Commando Association. Interview with Tommy Macpherson Imperial War Museum Sound Archive, 17912, Reel 1, 1998.
72. M. Binney: *Secret War Heroes* (London: Hodder & Stoughton, 1985), p. 17. No documentary evidence has emerged to substantiate accounts that Fairbairn and Sykes first ran a cadre course for close combat instructors at Auchinraith House, Lanarkshire, on behalf of the Secret Intelligence Service.
73. Hall: op. cit.
74. 'Syllabus. Specialist Close Combat, Special Training Centre Lochailort. Appendix C: Unarmed Combat', Stockwell Papers 3/10, Trustees of the Liddell Hart Centre for Military Archives, King's College London. This unarmed combat syllabus from 1941 is based on 'Notes by W. E. Fairbairn and E. A. Sykes, Inverailort, July 1940. Revised November 1942.'
75. W. Fairbairn: *All-In Fighting* (London: Faber & Faber, 1943), pp. 7-8.
76. W. Fairbairn and E. Sykes: 'Shooting to Live with the One-Hand Gun' (Edinburgh: Oliver & Boyd, 1942); W. Fairbairn: 'Self Defence for Women and Girls' (London: Faber & Faber, 1942).
77. F. Stephens: *Fighting Knives. An Illustrated Guide to Fighting Knives and Military Survival Weapons of the World* (London: Arms and Armour Press, 1980), pp. 90-95.
78. 'The Art of Guerilla Warfare' (pamphlet), MI(R) papers in Special Operations Executive records, National Archives, Kew, HS8/256.
79. Austen: op. cit., p. 20.
80. Ibid., p. 57.
81. Cameron-Head papers.
82. Diary of Commander Sir Geoffrey Congreve Bt., Imperial War Museum, Department of Documents, P280 and PP/MCR/149.
83. Kemp: op. cit., p. 20.
84. F. McLynn: *Fitzroy Maclean* (London: John Murray, 1992), p. 84. In 1941 Maclean escaped into uniform on a technicality by proposing to stand as a Member of Parliament, a situation incompatible with Foreign Office service.
85. War Office records, National Archives, Kew, WO260/32.
86. J. Ladd: *Commandos and Rangers of World War II* (Book Club Associates, 1978), p. 236.
87. Kellas: op. cit., p. 21.

88. D. Allardice: 'Friendship in a time of War (1939-45)', unpublished memoir, National Museums Scotland Library 220919, p. 29.

89. Major R. A. C. Cameron MC, DCM (Greece) MA: letter to the National War Museum, 17 March 2002.

90. Allardice: op. cit., pp. 48-49.

91. Papers of Major A. D. C. Smith, National Army Museum, Department of Archives, Photographs, Film and Sound, 8512-32/038-044.

92. Allardice, op. cit, pp. 49-50.

93. C. Barclay: *The London Scottish in the Second World War, 1939-1945* (London: William Clowes & Sons, 1952), p. 896.

94. Notebooks of 2nd Lieutenant A. R. H. Kellas, 1940, National Museums Scotland M.2003.3.1-2.

95. Kellas: op. cit., p. 30.

96. Ibid., p. 47.

97. Ibid., p. 31.

98. This and previous quote, 'Observations on the organisation, equipment, training & discipline of the British Army, based on the recent fighting in Norway', Stockwell Papers 2/8, Trustees of the Liddell Hart Centre for Military Archives, King's College London.

99. 'Training of Assault Troops memorandum No. 2', Stockwell Papers 3/20, Trustees of the Liddell Hart Centre for Military Archives, King's College London.

100. T. Harrison Place: *Military Training in the British Army, 1940-1944. From Dunkirk to D-Day* (London: Frank Cass, 2000), pp. 43-48.

101. Hall: op. cit.

102. 'Training of Assault Troops Memorandum No. 2', Stockwell Papers 3/20, Trustees of the Liddell Hart Centre for Military Archives, King's College London.

103. Craig: op. cit., p. 30.

104. J. McGregor: *The Spirit of Angus. The War History of the County's Battalion of the Black Watch* (Chichester: Phillimore, n.d.), pp. 13-14.

105. S. P. Mackenzie: *The Home Guard. A Military and Political History* (Oxford: Oxford University Press, 1995), pp. 68-77.

106. 'Home Guard Weekend Course III, 19/20 April 1941', Stockwell Papers 3/3, Trustees of the Liddell Hart Centre for Military Archives, King's College London.

107. Warwicker: op. cit., pp. 78-84.

108. Calvert: op. cit., p. 56.

109. Mackenzie: op. cit., p. 170.

110. His book *So Few Got Through* (London: Collins, 1946) was a widely read account of his later service.

111. Spencer Chapman: op. cit. (1950), pp. 8-9. Austen: op. cit., p. 13, attributes the prevalent use of sand table models at Lochailort to the skilled work of Trooper Craig, Royal Armoured Corps.

PART TWO

The March of the Cameron Men

COMMANDO TRAINING

... An almost solid stream of German machine-gun tracer bullets was whizzing past at about head height. We were forced to run like half-shut knives, our bodies bent forward, as if we were forcing our way against a strong wind.

The private took a couple of glances – one up at the arc of enemy fire, the other across at me. Then out of the side of his mouth he panted: 'Jesus Christ, sir, this is nearly as bad as Achnacarry!'

THE SETTING OF this story from Donald Gilchrist's *Castle Commando* is one of the pebbled beaches at Dieppe on the coast of occupied France during the disastrous Allied amphibious landings of 19th August 1942.[1] Captain Gilchrist and the man beside him were members of No.4 Commando, a special service unit whose efficient destruction of a coastal gun battery on the flank of the main assault would prove to be one of the few successes of the day. The private soldier's allusion to Achnacarry was a reference to the Scottish highland estate between Loch Arkaig and Loch Lochy, seat of Clan Cameron, where since February that year Commando training had been centralised. Both men under fire on the Dieppe beach enjoyed the joke, and understood it as an impromptu tribute to the challenge they had recently been put through in the wild country of Lochaber. The toughness of Commando training at Achnacarry became legendary, a fixture in the memory of thousands of men who trained there, and celebrated thereafter thanks in some part to Gilchrist's classic book published nearly 20 years later. But the story of the Commandos and their training does not begin and end there.

At the beginning of June 1940, Winston Churchill was a new Prime Minister, in office for only three weeks. Replacing the discredited government of Neville Chamberlain, he had offered Parliament and the British public not optimism and empty reassurance, but rather his determination and defiance of the enemy: 'blood, toil, tears and sweat.'[2] Almost immediately Churchill's new government had to absorb defeat in the campaign in Norway, and abject disaster in France. As French defences broke before the German *Blitzkrieg*, the British Expeditionary Force proved impotent. The 338,000 British troops evacuated from Dunkirk were thankful to avoid capture, but were compelled to leave much of their equipment and many of their fellows behind them. With the fall of France two weeks later, German forces were just across the Channel; suddenly defence of the British mainland was the urgent priority. But in facing these dire reverses, Churchill was at pains to stress that the British empire remained a fighting power to be reckoned with, and that British forces would attack as well as defend. On 5 June he wrote an instruction to the Chiefs of Staff of the British armed forces, to provide a swift means of return to the coasts of France in 'hit and run' guerrilla raids against the enemy:

> Enterprises must be prepared with specially trained troops of the hunter class who can develop a reign of terror first of all on the 'butcher and bolt' policy. I look to the Chiefs of Staff to propose me measures for a vigorous enterprising and ceaseless offensive against the whole German occupied coastline.[3]

The response to this instruction in the War Office was a hastily prepared scheme to form a raiding force of 5000 men that could strike in small and frequent raids all along those German-held coasts. The practical purpose was to oblige the German Army to commit substantial manpower and resources to garrison the fringes of its conquered territories, and to impede the build-up of invasion forces by impelling the enemy to spread his garrisons thinly. But at least of equal weight was the psychological message. Churchill was convinced that the 'completely defensive habit of mind' had been the ruin of the French.[4] For the sake of British forces, and for the attitude of the British people at large, whose confidence had been shaken by the calamities in France, he thought it critical that an aggressive spirit be fostered and fed by active operations. To await invasion without an offensive strategy would be to court disaster.

But the War Office had to allow that, in the short term at least, every organised fighting force available on the British mainland was required for the defence of home soil. Rather than commit any existing infantry division to special operations and so deny its immediate deployment on defensive duties, the decision was taken to call for volunteers for an entirely new force. The original scheme for establishing these special service troops was drawn up by Lieutenant-Colonel Dudley Clarke, a senior staff officer working for the Chief of the Imperial General Staff. Clarke had served before the war in the British mandate territory of Palestine and knew what trouble Arab guerrilla fighters had given the British garrison there. But his inspiration came from further back in time, from the Boer farmers who successfully harried and eluded numerically superior British forces in the South African War at the turn of the century. It was Clark who came up with the name 'Commandos', borrowed from those same Boer forces.

By Clark's own account the suggestion was brought to mind by the books of former Boer commando soldier Denys Reitz, the first entitled *Commando*, which enjoyed considerable popularity in British and American markets during the 1930s.[5] The 'Commando' title struck a chord with Churchill, whose personal experience of the war in South Africa included capture by Boer forces in November 1899 and escape a month later. The example that Churchill himself had in mind, however, was borrowed from the enemy of less distant days. He had noted the use of German 'storm troops' in the defeat of France, where fast-moving mobile infantry followed up armoured 'spearheads' thrusting deep behind Allied defensive lines. The storm trooper doctrine was a German idea of the latter years of the First World War. It used heavily armed and highly trained infantrymen to take enemy positions and advance onward, leaving it to slower-moving formations to reduce the most heavily defended positions that the storm troopers had simply bypassed and isolated. This concept had been tested to good effect on the Eastern and Italian Fronts in 1917, and applied in the highly successful, if ultimately unsustainable, German offensive in the west in the spring of 1918. Its revival and refinement in 1939-40 as an element of the *Blitzkreig* doctrine of lightning warfare had thoroughly overwhelmed the armies of Poland, the Low Countries, the French and the British. Taking the all-conquering German model, Churchill wanted his British Commandos to be storm troopers as well as guerrilla fighters.

Perhaps most striking about Churchill's language in his early pro-nouncements on the subject of raiding forces is his unequivocal use of terms of intimidation. The phrases 'butcher and bolt' and 'reign of terror' are not the stuff of which the conventional British self-imagery of the Second

World War is made. Quite the contrary, for these are concepts that have been readily attached to the enemy, the dark panoply of Nazi ideology, to the Schutzstaffel (SS) and other organisations that imposed it, and the war crimes that were perpetrated in its name. But with British fortunes at their lowest ebb, and even before the full horror of the Nazi way of war unfolded in eastern Europe, Churchill did not demure from directing his Commandos to instil fear into the enemy. This aim was as much part of the moral purpose of their existence as the fostering of an aggressive spirit among the Army and the public at home.

The Germans would react to this. Resistance and guerrilla warfare were one thing. Occupying forces might expect to encounter, and counter, defiance and danger from elements among the peoples they had conquered. The prospect of British soldiers crossing the Channel with the express purpose of slitting German throats was something else again. Almost as unhappy with the idea were individuals within the command structure of the British field army, where a sense of unease over the unorthodox and popular image of the Commandos became an underlying tension in the planning of operations and allocation of resources for which competition was intense.

It is unclear how much Churchill knew at this point about the activities to date of Military Intelligence (Research). MI(R) was not, at any rate, given the principal part in the creation of the Commandos. The Independent Companies were brought into the equation from the first, but, being derived from Territorial Army-generated units whose core were pre-war part-timers, they were not thought necessarily to be the best source of recruits. It was felt that the leadership qualities thought necessary might readily be found among Regular Army officers and 'Emergency Commission' (war service only) officers in particular. A call for volunteers went out from the War Office directly through the Army command structure and covered all serving soldiers in Home Forces: regulars, territorials, conscripts; infantry, cavalry, artillery and other corps. MI(R) would continue its activity in clandestine warfare meantime, but under the oversight of a new department of Military Operations that would be concentrating on larger-scale raids along the coasts of France, the Low Countries and Norway. Using its new Commando units, and with the Royal Marines Brigade brought under its sway, the Army would be in control. These initial command and administrative arrangements did not last long however. From the first, perpetual restructuring was a feature of Commando organisation, variously an invigorating influence or blight upon their efforts.

In July 1940, MI(R) was amalgamated with a branch of the Secret Intelligence Service to concentrate on nurturing resistance networks overseas. Although there was little practical change to what went on there, MI(R)'s irregular warfare school at Lochailort thenceforth came under the control of the Directorate of Military Operations. The Special Training Centre was placed under the overall command of a new appointment, a Director of Combined Operations, whose job it was to co-ordinate the naval, military and air support arms of amphibious warfare. The Combined Operations Directorate also inherited a small research and development establishment at Fort Cumberland near Portsmouth where experiments in amphibious landings and craft design had been pursued intermittently since 1937. From these two establishments would sprout the two main strands of specialist Commando training, on land and at sea.

The first Director of Combined Operations, appointed by Churchill on 17 July 1940, was Admiral Sir Roger Keyes. More than anyone Sir Roger Keyes could claim knowledge of how to launch a successful sea-borne raid. In the spring of 1918 Keyes organised an attack on the German U-Boat submarine bases at the Belgian ports of Zeebrugge and Ostend. The raid at Zeebrugge was one of the outstanding British successes of the First World War and, at a time when British forces on the Western Front were under great pressure from German attack, Keyes was hailed a much-needed British hero. Under Keyes' plan an explosives-packed submarine blew open the dock gates, and the light cruiser HMS *Vindictive* entered the dock and disgorged landing parties to wreak substantial damage on the installations before withdrawing. Zeebrugge had been a major operation, far greater in scale than anything Sir Roger's new Combined Operations Directorate could possibly expect to muster for many months; but it was very much the kind of attack that the Commandos would be working towards.

* * *

The mechanics of the Commando volunteering and selection process were simple and deliberately reflected the self-sufficiency with which the units would be expected to operate in action. In each of the Army's regional Home Commands, volunteers for special service were placed at the disposal of a selected commanding officer. The Commando leader would choose his own Troop leaders, each Commando being divided into fighting Troops of some 50 men. Troop leaders would in turn choose their own junior officers, non-commissioned officers and men, initially by interview. So a Commando would form around 500 strong, each chosen man temporarily seconded from his original unit.[6] Ten of these Commando units would be created, including, it was planned, one formed from the existing Independent Companies. Those Independent Companies that had seen active service in Norway were also a source of experienced officers who could be dispersed through the new units. Three commanders of the original Independent Companies went on to become commanding officers of Commandos. These included Lieutenant-Colonel Charles Newman who later won the Victoria Cross leading No.2 Commando on the St Nazaire Raid of March 1941.

Of the original ten Commando units drawn up on paper, two of them, Nos 9 and 11, were to be formed by volunteers from Army units of Scottish Command. As elsewhere, the special service volunteers had little idea of what exactly it was they were volunteering for. Personal motivation varied according to individual inclination, but tended to have one feature in common, that of boredom with their current lot. Commando volunteer Lieutenant Tommy Macpherson, serving with 5th Battalion Cameron Highlanders on garrison duties in Caithness, recalled what little he knew of what he was putting himself in for:

> Absolutely nothing because the Commandos were a new concept. The Scottish Commando was one of the first three formed, I think. And there was no precedent, but we were told in Churchill's speeches and by the chain of command that this was going to be, for some time, the only aggressive part of the Army in Europe .... I thought it would be fun. I suppose I was slightly bored in the Battalion and I was a pretty fit young man and I thought this would work out well.[7]

Private John S. MacKay was tiring of guarding docks and aerodromes with the 2nd Battalion London Scottish ....

> So I joined the Commando, or I went for an interview. There were two officers and we were called into a room and we were questioned ....

'Could you swim a mile?'

'Oh yes, I could do that.'

'Could you run a hundred yards in $11\frac{1}{2}$ seconds?'

'Oh yes, often did that,' and all this kind of thing. Really it was all on fitness and whether you were the type of person who would fit into a unit that would be doing, hopefully, special operations, secret operations, and hopefully get me off these dreadful guard duties.[8]

As to what a new Commando unit should be and do exactly, this was set out in the same War Office memorandum that established the selection process. After formation, each new Commando unit was to be allocated a home area for accommodation and training. It was determined that this would be a seaside town, so that boat work and landing operations could be practised offshore. Promoting the idea of a Commando unit as a self-supporting fighting force of resourceful individuals, the men would not be accommodated together in barracks or other formal quarters as was the norm for infantry soldiers, nor would they be in receipt of rations. Much as the Independent Companies had been sent on operations in Norway with hard cash for their keep, each Commando soldier was simply to be given a regular allowance from which it would be up to him as an individual to arrange his own lodging and feeding. This would prove to be manna for landladies of boarding houses and, with a little tolerance, for families in private homes in the towns where Commando units were placed. It would lead to a great many friendships, romances and no few marriages.

The thinking behind the practice was expounded by one senior Commando officer at the war's end, stressing how it was seen to foster the individual initiative which led Commandos to improvise when operations did not go according to plan:

We spent a good deal of time and trouble in the Commandos trying to instil initiative into the private soldier, and very often we found that the Regular soldier was the most difficult to teach. One of our methods made some of the more stereotyped officers hold up their hands in horror, but it worked: we refused to allow the men to live in barracks, but gave each an allowance of 6s. 8d. a day to feed and house himself, and to find transport to and from the places of parade but of course he could walk or bicycle if he liked. All we used to say was: 'Parade tomorrow is at such and such a cross-roads, or in the

Market Square at so-and-so, and the time is 0730 hours.' If any man turned up at 0731 and said he thought a bus ran that way but was mistaken, or said that his landlady hadn't got his breakfast in time or made one of a thousand other excuses, we told him he was the sort of chap who wanted at least an Orderly Corporal, a C.Q.M.S. and a Drill Sergeant to get him up, give him his breakfast and get him on parade and we sent him packing back to his old unit.[9]

The Commando unit would be training together around its home-town area, but it was not envisaged that it would necessarily fight together as a unit. Operational teams of various sizes would be picked and put together from the pool of trained soldiers created. On operations, a Commando force, however formed, was expected to be capable of operating without support for up to 24 hours. It would be composed of soldiers capable of splitting into smaller parties thinly spread, or proceeding as individuals if necessary. The definition of a raid was that, whatever the scale of operation or nature of the target, action would end with a withdrawal. There was no expectation that Commando units should engage enemy forces in any substantial number, or should have to overcome enemy defences and hold a position taken in the manner of conventional infantry. Their specialisation would be 'tip and run tactics dependent for their success upon speed, ingenuity and dispersion'.[10]

Commando capability was directed towards raids of four broad classes. Straightforward harassment raids would discomfit the enemy and hopefully compel him to devote precious resources towards maintaining a defensive and alert posture over wide expanses of occupied territory. Reconnaissance raids would obtain intelligence through observation, photography and capturing prisoners, often as an assessment of landing locations and enemy defences in advance of larger operations. Sabotage raids would attack industrial or strategic installations that could not be approached by Royal Air Force bombers. Finally, supporting raids formed part of a larger operation, either for the purpose of diversion or with the objective of destroying isolated targets that would allow a main attack to proceed with a greater chance of success.[11]

Essentially, that which would make a soldier a Commando soldier, that which would set him apart from the conventional soldiering from which he had been taken, would be his training. With the Special Training Centre Lochailort already in existence, it was briefly proposed that the training of all Commando cadres would be focussed there, but this was considered impractical and out of step with the idea of home-town bases, and the self-sufficiency of each Commando unit.[12] Instead, each officer leading a Commando unit was to be responsible for its own training programme centred on its allotted seaside location. Within the confines of broad requirements set out in formal training instructions for all Commandos, it was up to each Commando to make the best use of ground and expertise available. The STC Lochailort course would be available for specialised intensive training, but it was not foreseen that Commando units as a whole should necessarily pass through its test.

A War Office pamphlet issued in August 1940 was the first to codify the objectives of the training. Its spirit was summarised by an injunction appealing to individual self-reliance and resourcefulness as a complement to team spirit or *esprit de corps*: 'Training will differ from that normally given to the regular soldier in that the greatest stress must be laid on the ability of each man to decide his own course of action without being told what to do.'

Individually, each Commando soldier was to be physically fit, re-sourceful, motivated by 'the offensive spirit', and by a pride in his own ability. Collectively, Commandos would train for embarkation onto ships and assault craft, for assault landings therefrom, for movement from beaches to targets, in the tactics of raiding against all manner of targets from aerodromes to railway signal boxes, for withdrawal from close contact with the enemy, in street fighting, and in 'terror tactics among disorganised enemy troops and civilians'.[13] Individual training would entail numerous practices straight out of the Lochailort assemblage: speed marching, skill-at-arms, swimming and small-boat work, unarmed combat, map-reading and fieldcraft, demolitions and sabotage. By spring 1941 first aid was added to the requirement.[14] The requirements of collec-tive training naturally entailed a rather larger-scale approach.

The high state of readiness sought by commanding officers of Com-mando units was not, by its very nature, something that could be attained overnight. Private John S. MacKay recalled that on joining No.9 Commando at Whiting Bay on the Isle of Arran in the late summer of 1940, he did not find the training particularly advanced:

You must remember that No.9 Commando was a Commando in formation so all the people who were actually in that Commando had just joined it so therefore their training was very basic .... Everything we did was to make sure that you were one hundred and one per cent fit. And we were. We were young, I was nineteen, and we were very, very fit indeed .... Doing route marches, special route marches. Instead of resting every hour for ten minutes, as I think it was we used to on a route march, we would slope arms for ten minutes and carry on without a rest. All this kind of training ... and swimming in your clothes and things like that.[15]

To the present-day soldier this emphasis on fitness might not seem especially surprising. The physical fitness and endurance demanded of Commando soldiers in 1940 might not appear entirely outlandish to a regular infantry soldier in the British Army of today. But in 1940 it was revolutionary. Up to that point, drill, discipline and skill-at-arms were the principal features of infantry training at the individual level, with route marches characterising much of the attention to general service fitness. Formal physical training, under the guidance of the Army Physical Training School, emphasised gymnastics-based exercises and sport. The Commandos led the way in instilling physical fitness for battle conditions by replicating and exceeding the physical demands that would be part of actual operations. Thus physical training became less a matter of physical jerks and team games and more a programme of speed marches, endurance exercises over hard country, and assault courses.[16] With special operations held to be a matter of speed, reliant on the ability of special service troops to operate without support, a heightened state of fitness was essential to the whole philosophy. As at Lochailort, tests of fitness were built into almost every aspect of Commando training.

For training in this initial phase, and indeed later, Commandos were clothed and equipped much as the rest of the British Army, with 'battle dress' uniform or denim fatigues, webbing equipment, rifle or other individual weapon, and steel helmets. But for comfort and mobility the helmets were often dispensed with in favour of the multi-purpose 'cap, comforter', a sleeve-like tube of khaki-coloured wool closed at each end that could be worn around the neck but more usually was donned as a folded cap. Otherwise, individual Commando soldiers wore the soft headdress of their parent regiments or, in the case of certain Commando units, adopted as standard Scottish 'Tam O' Shanter' bonnets worn with regimental badges or unit insignia. Boots, all-important under training conditions that emphasised long marches in difficult terrain, were standard issue.

Over time, modifications and departures from standard equipment proceeded from experience of raiding operations, introducing features such as small inflatable life belts and the 'Bergen' rucksack. Inspired by innovative Norwegian design, a Bergen was a canvas pack on a metal frame allowing each soldier to carry considerable loads of field and demolition equipment and rations as befitted his self-supporting role. Standard boots remained, but Commandos also had recourse to rope and rubber-soled shoes for stealth and, from mid-1942, to composition rubber-soled boots. Each Commando soldier carried the Fairbairn-Sykes knife in models derived from the design drawn up at STC Lochailort; and also a 'toggle', a short length of rope with a loop attachment at one end and a wooden toggle at the other. These enabled the rapid assembly of lengths of rope for rock-climbing, river crossing and overcoming obstacles.

* * *

No.11 Commando was the first of the special service units raised from Scottish Command to be formed. In August 1940 the selected officers and men assembled at Galashiels in the Scottish borders under the command of Lieutenant-Colonel R. D. (Dick) Pedder, Highland Light Infantry (HLI). No.11 set about getting fit, marching and camping in the vicinity of Galashiels and swimming in the River Tweed. Captain Geoffrey Keyes joined No.11 Commando from his cavalry regiment the Royal Scots Greys, bringing with him a troop of cavalrymen for the Commando. He described the trials of the Galashiels-based training in a letter to his father who, being the Director of Combined Operations, had a particular professional interest in the proceedings:

> The first day's walk was rather a shocker, as we started off from
> scratch with eleven miles non stop in three hours, twenty minutes
> halt for lunch, then another four miles in one hour. No joke;
> I finished rather lame as did most of my cavalrymen, but we got a
> good chit from the C.O. for our spirit. We slept that night under the
> stars in a wood after a bathe in the Tweed – pretty cold, and, next
> day I was incredibly stiff. The C.O. sent me on next day to arrange

the night's bivouac, despite my efforts to be allowed to march (as it wasn't so far and I think I could have done it.) I felt pretty lousy leaving my chaps some of whom were nearly as bad as me .... [17]

In September, No.11 Commando moved from the borders to their allotted home area, the hamlet of Lamlash on the coast of the southern Hebridean Isle of Arran. Thanks to its proximity to the Clyde, Arran was a popular destination for holidaymakers from the Glasgow area and so had facilities that helped to accommodate the domestic requirements of the Commandos. More importantly it had mountains, rugged country surrounding them, and a long coastline along which assault landings and reconnaissance raiding could be practised. Arran was already well-known to Combined Operations command, having been the scene of a major Royal Marines exercise in 1935. [18] At Lamlash No.11 Commando was re-joined by Lieutenant Tommy Macpherson, fresh with what he had learned as a student, and temporary fieldcraft instructor at the Special Training Centre Lochailort where he had been sent within days of joining the Commando at Galashiels:

The Isle of Arran was particularly suitable because it had of course coastline where you did amphibious work. But it is a miniature of Scotland. It has its own highlands, lowlands and rolling border-type country. And it would correspond to most of the different types of country that we would be liable to be involved in. [19]

Indeed so suitable was Arran felt to be that it hosted no fewer than three Commando units in the late summer of 1940. No.11 Commando were in billets around Lamlash, No.9 were further down the island's east coast at Whiting Bay, and No.8 lived and trained in the north of the island at Lochranza. No.8 Commando included a concentration of recruits from the Guards regiments of the Household Division, and one of its officers was Lieutenant David Stirling of the Scots Guards, late of the instructing staff at Lochailort. The three units divided up between them the rugged country of the interior of the island, but were liable to meet in pursuit of a common goal, the 2867-foot summit of Goat Fell, the highest of its forbidding granite mountains.

Private John S. MacKay arrived on Arran with No.9 Commando and at first lived in billets at Knockenkelly, a little to the north of Whiting Bay:

It was a house away at the top of a hill and we had to go up there. It was obviously let as a holiday home in the summer time, or had been, and we were in an outbuilding and I can remember the bed was soaking wet, all the clothes we had in there were wet. But we didn't have much time because I think the best training I ever had was that we kept changing, going down to do some drills, running up to change and coming down again and doing a run. Then we would run up again and change again to do some square bashing. Then we would do route marches. And every time we had to run up to the house, which must have been a quarter of a mile up this hill, and I think we got very fit doing that.

MacKay's extra exertions at Knockenkelly were shortlived, however, as he transferred to the Signal Platoon of No.11 Commando a few miles to the north. In October 1940, in the first substantial reorganisation of raiding forces, various Commando units and Independent Companies were amalgamated together to form five larger Special Service Battalions. This change marked the end for the original Independent Companies, and some among their number chose to return to their former regular units rather than stick with the Commandos, their hopes of seeing early action by volunteering for special service having largely been frustrated.

The organisational change came in response to the first none-too-successful operational raids that had been carried out in the summer on the French coast about Boulogne and against the German-occupied Channel Island of Guernsey. These minor incursions were experimental in character and Churchill indicated that he was looking for something bigger and better as soon as possible. No.9 Commando and No.11 Commando joined together on paper to become companies of No.2 Special Service Battalion. The larger units were geared to be capable of more substantial attacks, but the overall change to the Commando establishment endured only a few months, and the concept of the 'Special Service Battalion' was dropped by February 1941. As Private MacKay remembered, the reorganisation had in any case made little difference in practice on the ground in Arran:

As far as I can recall there was absolutely no connection between the 9th and the 11th. Each really stuck to their own thing. I think the 11th always felt themselves a little superior to the 9th because the

9th were fairly new and the 11th were well trained and ready for action ....

One thing that No.11 Commando, which styled itself 11th (Scottish) Commando, had in abundance was unit identity:

> The first thing really was that we were given a black hackle so we really belonged to a unit, whereas before we always wore our own cap badges in the 9th – everybody had a different badge. We were now really a Commando and we had a recognisable badge which was the black hackle and we were all very proud to be able to wear the black hackle too, and we did. The training went up a gear. We started doing night route marches around the island .... At the end of the march you went off the end of the pier into the water and swam back. I can remember I think he was Major Pedder then but he became Lieutenant-Colonel Pedder, who was HLI, and he was a bit of a tartar, and he stood at the end of the pier waving his revolver for anybody who didn't want to go in. So everybody went in and made their way back to the shore and by the time they got back to the shore they were a pretty sorry sight I can tell you.[20]

The black hackle, or cap feather referred to here, was one means whereby Commando units attempted, at their officers' own initiative, to create the emblems of identity by which British Army units of all kinds had long defined themselves. This tendency rather flew in the face of the formal concept of special service troops as a general pool of trained soldiers from which teams for operations could be drawn up as required. Officially the Commando units were not to be thought of as regiments. Officers and men were merely seconded from their parent units, to which they could be returned if they failed to meet the standards required, or if they were deemed to be surplus to requirements. Competitive spirit was to be encouraged, but Commando units were not expected to be hidebound by fissiparous group mentalities and associated traditions that were such a strong feature of the British Army – an army which thus far in the war had not fared well.

And yet the urge to foster and display *esprit de corps* ran deep in most British soldiers. No.11 Commando's black hackle was worn on the khaki Tam-o-Shanter bonnet, giving officers and men a particularly Scottish

1. Commando landing exercise on Loch Fyne, 1941. Major Jack Churchill leads the way, sword in hand.

(IMPERIAL WAR MUSEUM)

2. Commandos on a three-day exercise from STC Lochailort, 1941.

(THE HONOURABLE IAN CHANT-SEMPILL)

3. Admiral Sir Walter Cowan, aged 69, on active service with No.11 Commando, 1941.

(NMS)

4. Lord Lovat at Newhaven, Sussex, on No.4 Commando's return from the Dieppe Raid, 19 August 1942.

(IMPERIAL WAR MUSEUM)

5. A soldier of No.1 Commando abseiling in Glencoe, November 1941.

(IMPERIAL WAR MUSEUM)

6. A canoeist of Captain G. C. S. Montanaro's 101 Troop of the Special Service Brigade training on a Scottish loch, 1941.

(TRUSTEES OF THE LIDDELL HART CENTRE FOR MILITARY ARCHIVES)

7. A wedding in Largs, 1942. The Best Man, seated right, is Corporal George Dixon of 40 RM Commando, later one of the unit's 'T' Company lost in the sinking of HMS *Fidelity*.

(MR PETER MILES)

8. French Commandos tackle an assault course at Achnacarry, July 1943.

(IMPERIAL WAR MUSEUM)

9. Richard Baxter, 45 RM Commando: 'We knew Achnacarry was the place where you became a Commando – or didn't.'

(NMS)

10. Wartime alterations to the interior of Achnacarry. The Officers' Mess featured murals by Corporal Brian Mullen, No.4 Commando, later killed in action on D-Day.

(CLAN CAMERON MUSEUM)

11. The Achnacarry flotilla of small boats on Loch Lochy, with a landing craft in the foreground.

(CLAN CAMERON MUSEUM)

12. Achnacarry commandant Lieutenant-Colonel Charles Vaughan inspects French Commandos on Bastille Day, 14 July 1943.

(IMPERIAL WAR MUSEUM)

13. Royal Naval Commandos advance under fire in an exercise at HMS *Armadillo*, Ardentinny.

(ROYAL NAVAL COMMANDO ASSOCIATION, LICENSED WITH PERMISSION OF GREENHILL BOOKS)

14. Sledge patrol from the Commando Mountain and Snow Warfare Training Centre, Braemar, winter 1942/43.

(FRANK SMYTHE ESTATE)

15. Frank Smythe (foreground) leads Commando ski training, Braemar, winter 1942/43.

(FRANK SMYTHE ESTATE)

military appearance that fitted the unit's self-image as the Scottish Commando. On joining with No.11 Commando in No.2 Special Service Battalion, No.9 Commando also adopted the black hackle. Others went further. No.4 Commando was stationed at Weymouth on the Dorset coast, going through training similar to that being carried out on Arran, when its commanding officer Lieutenant-Colonel C. P. D. Legard came up with a cap badge design which featured a death's head emblem. Early examples seem to have featured a crack to the skull as a particular embellishment. As a mark of unit identity, this was a choice laden with symbolism about how Commando officers saw themselves and their part in the war: an absolutely uncompromising response to the threat of Nazi Germany, expecting to be feared, entirely prepared to be ruthless. For a time, officers and men of No.2 Commando wore a lanyard from the shoulders of their battle dress blouses made up of entwined strands of black and white cord. This is thought to have been introduced at the behest of their commanding officer Lieutenant-Colonel Charles Newman and devised on the theoretical basis that, for the soldiers of No.2 Commando, the issues of the war were as black and white as the lanyard.[21]

While all this might have corresponded to the line of thought of Prime Minister Winston Churchill when he gave directions for a new special raiding force, it was too much for the War Office. Death's head cap badges and their sinister, piratical associations were disconcerting enough, but their equivalence to those worn by the German SS made them unacceptable, particularly when Combined Operations command made the administrative blunder of dubbing their raiding forces Special Service (or 'SS') Battalions. Commando soldiers were ordered to wear the cap badges of their original units. Only cap hackles, and one or two other aberrant practices of the kind, survived for long. No.11 Commando clung to its Scottish embellishments, aided by the presence in its ranks of Piper James Lawson, formerly of the Gordon Highlanders, who composed a march for his unit.[22]

*   *   *

The Commandos on Arran continued training, with their programme expanding to include Lochailort-style sessions in unarmed combat, climbing and fieldcraft. These extra elements were taught by specialist instructors brought in from outside the Commando units' own training regimes. Whether they were imported direct from STC Lochailort is unclear.[23] A certain urgency was added to larger exercises by the introduction of live firing, where Troop leaders fired live rounds over their soldiers' heads 'to impress upon them the horrors of war, and make them utilise the best cover'.[24] On the water the Commandos received some valuable help with their first steps towards proficiency in amphibious operations. Admiral Sir Walter Cowan was a highly decorated retired officer who had first joined the Royal Navy in 1894. Still fit at 69 years old, and anxious to be of use to his old friend Sir Roger Keyes, he obtained an appointment with Combined Operations in the relatively humble rank of Commander and proceeded to Arran to lend a hand. Cowan worked the Commandos hard along the beaches. He had a high regard for their attitude and approach, if not initially for the standard of their seamanship:

> ... the training of the two Scottish Commandos 9 and 11 in Arran during the autumn and winter of 1940 was the most vigorous and ruthless I have ever seen .... The pick of the Scottish regiments, and they laughed at hardship – wet through at least five days out of seven and often up to or over the waist ... they practised landing in merchant ship life boats, heavy and unhandy to a degree. Most of the men had no knowledge of boat work, and started learning to pull in these un-wieldy craft with heavy oars – it was a wonder it didn't break their hearts. Then someone had a brainwave. They took the paddles from Carley floats and went like the wind with them.
>
> The landings were mostly on shelving beaches and because of the tides the boats had to be hauled well up, which meant men up to their waists in water. To do it in the small landing craft of course was child's play but they were not often allowed them because of the wear and tear and shortage of these craft.[25]

Despite the inexperience of his land-lubbing charges, and the scarcity of equipment, Cowan stuck with it. And his involvement did not stop at training. When No.11 Commando finally departed for operational service in the Middle East at the end of January 1941, sailing from Arran as part of a composite Commando force, Cowan went with them. With No.7 Commando he took part in an unopposed landing at Bardia in Libya; and when the Commando force in the Middle East was later disbanded, Cowan obtained an attachment to an Indian Army armoured regiment and continued active operations. Remarkably, he was captured, repatriated by the Italians on grounds of his advanced years, and returned once more to service with the Commandos. In 1944 he was awarded a Bar to his Distinguished Service Order, a decoration he had first won for service in the Omdurman campaign in the Sudan in 1898.

Back on Arran, work with even smaller craft was also at hand. A Troop from No.6 Commando had begun working with German-style recreational 'folbots', one and two-man canoes made of rubberised canvas over a folding wooden frame. In conjunction with canoe expert (and African big game hunter) Lieutenant Roger Courtney of No.8 Commando, they had convinced Combined Operations Directorate that there was real potential for canoe sabotage attacks against enemy shipping. Courtney gave substance to his case by carrying out two mock sabotage attacks on vessels in Loch Fyne, Argyll, under the eyes of Admiral Sir Roger Keyes. His point made with sufficient impact, Courtney and his team were sent to Arran to develop the idea. Based at Sannox and Corrie, their experiments took them all around Arran and the coastal waters of the western isles.

From these beginnings their Commando Special Boat Sections concept developed into 101 Troop, a single canoe unit for the whole of 1st Special Service Brigade, commanded by Captain G. C. S. Montanaro. Efforts to develop this strand of Commando warfare continued on Arran through the winter of 1940/41. The exertions of 101 Troop were not, however, restricted to their chosen speciality. Canoeists and coastal reconnaissance specialists they might have been, but Commandos they remained, and their training diet took them out of the water and through weapons, demolitions, and fieldcraft exercises over the Arran terrain. The 101 Troop training programme for the first week of January 1941 lists day and night exercises over the hills immediately above their base: Maol Donn, Am Binnein and the Coire Nan Larach. These were divided by restful days at Corrie, practising with weapons and hearing such intriguingly titled lectures as 'The Guerrilla Warfare of Jenghiz Khan'.[26]

*   *   *

While Commandos under training in Scotland and elsewhere did what they could to rehearse assault landings with the craft available to them, Combined Operations Directorate was pressing ahead with provision of proper equipment. The principal requirement was for custom-designed landing craft to be used in beach assaults. Several designs had been prepared, but Combined Operations had to wait its turn amidst competing demands for scarce resources of manpower, production capacity and of finance. Nevertheless, by October in 1940 Combined Operations had acquired a small number of assault landing craft and had begun converting larger vessels on which to transport them and the troops they were intended to disgorge.

The largest of these transport vessels were three fast twin-screw cargo liners built for the Glen shipping line in 1939, intended for trade to the Far East. Before the war began the Admiralty had taken note of the potential of these fast new ships for naval operations and they were quickly commandeered when hostilities broke out.[27] The three Glen ships were named HMS *Glenearn*, *Glengyle* and *Glenroy*. Converted in stages, by early 1941 they were fully operational as 'Landing Ships, Infantry'. They could cruise at 18 knots, carrying 12 assault landing craft, two motorised landing craft and over 1000 troops to land from them, although the complement of landing craft on each vessel allowed only around 400 to be disembarked from them in one flight. Later modifications doubled their craft-carrying capacity. In the months that followed, Combined Operations built up a small fleet of assault ships and transports.

In October 1940 HMS *Glengyle* arrived in the Clyde to embark the full strength of No.4 Commando, one of the units formed by volunteers from the Army's Southern Command. No.4 arrived by train from their billets around Weymouth in Dorset where they had been carrying out preliminary training. At this stage in her conversion *Glengyle* could carry only ten assault landing craft. These nevertheless were a new and welcome sight to the Commandos who at Weymouth had been making do with rowing boats, motor launches and a pair of borrowed Royal Navy cutters.[28] *Glengyle* did not have far to sail; a short voyage took No.4 Commando out of the Clyde, north of Arran by the Sound of Bute, and north-east up into Loch Fyne.

At 41 miles Loch Fyne is the longest of the Scottish sea lochs, reaching deep into Argyll. It was, and is, a great source of herring and seafood, and along its shore are beaches of varying character. On the western shore a few miles south of the eighteenth-century planned village of Inveraray, a new Royal Navy shore station had just opened. HMS *Quebec* was No.1 Combined Training Centre, the first of the locations where sailors, soldiers and even airmen would come to learn together the art of assault from the sea. It had the right conditions, it was easily reached by sea after rail journeys to the Clyde coast, and it was far away from danger and enemy eyes. More than 40 such centres opened in the west of Scotland and south of England in the following three years, as Allied forces prepared amphibious landings in North Africa, Italy and France. But for long HMS *Quebec* and the plethora of camps and smaller installations that lined either side of the loch, was the foremost of them, a thriving centre of activity with a flotilla of training vessels. All manner of military units would find themselves there, exiting from a variety of landing craft and splashing through the waters of Loch Fyne.

The third element of Combined Operations was also on hand. Soldiers at the Combined Training Centre might find their exertions accompanied by air support or compounded by mock air attack from aircraft of a specialised unit of the Royal Air Force.[29] In January 1941 the 1441 Combined Operations Development Flight was formed. It was based at RAF Abbotsinch (now Glasgow Airport) until a new airfield was made ready at RAF Dundonald near Troon in Ayrshire. The unit flew a variety of fighter and twin-engined aircraft to bring a third dimension to the exercises around Loch Fyne, simulating attacks on landing craft and beach areas, laying smoke screens and carrying out low-level reconnaissance flying. Redesignated 516 Combined Operations Squadron in April 1943, the unit also trained visiting air crew to develop their understanding and experience of operational flying of this kind.

When No.4 Commando arrived in autumn 1940 all this was just beginning. They, and other special service units that followed, had to learn from scratch, indeed they had to work out for themselves, the practicalities of how to get on and off ships and landing craft, and onto beaches of all kinds. With them was James Dunning who, as a commissioned officer from 1943, was to become an instructor (and later a historian) of Commando training techniques:

> All this took time to organise; even sorting out the timings and routes from mess decks to boat stations took both time and practice. Nevertheless, drills were worked out and recorded, for this was not just for No.4, but also for those that were to follow us. In this and the subsequent landing drills we were the 'trail-blazers' – and such procedures tended to be very repetitive and irksome.

Nor did the training task end once landings were accomplished and troops mustered at the loch-side road:

> The terrain around Inveraray was ideal for the 'onshore' training the troop leaders had in mind. Great stretches of uninhabited hillsides and wild moorlands, interspersed with fast-flowing rivers and streams, provided testing challenges – no need for man-made obstacle courses there; Mother Nature had already done that job.[30]

Also part of the original set-up at Inveraray was a Beach Signals Section, assembled from army signalmen picked out from units of the Royal Corps of Signals by their commanding officers. One such was 2nd Lieutenant Hilary King who, in addition to the challenges of amphibious training common to all, was concerned with the technical difficulties of waterproofing and precisely tuning radio sets for seaborne operations:

> Much of the training at Inveraray (by day and night) consisted of rapid disembarkations from the Glen ships, or their ALCs and MLCs complete with rigorously prepared individual man-loads of equipment, on to the foreshore of the 'enemy-held territory' of Upper Loch Fyne between Strachur and Cairndow – followed of course by the instant establishment of complicated radio communications to, from, and between beaches .... The role of the Beach Signal Party (consisting of the Army's Beach Section and their Navy colleagues for ship-to-shore networks), as worked out with Major Cole, was to have the advance party with the first wave of the assault, in the first landing craft to hit the shore. Then, while the assaulting infantry swept inland, the Beach Signal Party would stay on, or very close to the beach, setting up the ship-to-shore communications while the next waves of the assault came ashore, together with lateral communications with any flanking beaches where landings were also taking place.[31]

Getting troops ashore was only half the battle after all. The complexities of beach organisation and communication would engage the attentions of Combined Operations planners for some time to come.

* * *

At the end of January 1941 HMS *Glengyle*, *Glenroy* and *Glenearn* lay off the Isle of Arran, *Glenearn* already carrying a Beach Signals Section from Inveraray and a small Royal Marines element. The ships had arrived to embark 'Force Z', an assemblage of No.11 Commando, a party of Courtney's canoeists and, lately arrived on the island, Nos 7 and 8 Commando and one Troop from No.3 Commando. These last had been in training at Inveraray and home-town bases on the Ayrshire coast at Largs and Girvan. The destination on this occasion was not another Scottish training centre, but Suez in the Middle East, from where 'Force Z' was to be deployed on raiding operations in the eastern Mediterranean. Unbeknown to all but a select few, the Arran-based training of No.11 Commando had been already intensified with a view to early deployment on active service in a projected raid to capture the Italian island of Pantellaria, off the coast of Sicily. This ambitious plan had not come to fruition, postponed and ultimately cancelled for want of available naval and air support. Instead, targets in the Dodecanese islands of Greece were identified as acquisitions that would strengthen the British hand in the region, and enhance the security of the British power base in Egypt.

'Force Z' departed Arran with the mission of an assault on the Italian-held island of Rhodes. With news of their objective came a new force codename, *Layforce*, a reference to their overall commander Colonel Robert Laycock. With them as an intelligence officer was a recent recruit to special service whose fictional chronicles of life in a Commando unit continue to have currency, reflecting how much more successful he was a writer than a Commando. Evelyn Waugh was already a celebrated novelist when he arrived at Largs in Ayrshire as a Commando staff captain. His caustic humour and tendency to condescension quickly made him enemies, including his former Oxford contemporary Lord Lovat, present on Arran as a staff officer representing Admiral Sir Roger Keyes' Combined Operations headquarters. Lord Lovat was not a good enemy to make and Waugh suffered at his hands, with assistance in the preparation of practical jokes coming from Lovat's cousin, David Stirling. Incompatibility between the Waugh life view and the Commando ethos colours the peppery account of shambolic proceedings in the west highlands and calamity in the Mediterranean given by Waugh in his semi-autobiographical novel of 1955, *Officers and Gentlemen*.[32] As to his factual recollections, Waugh summarised his time on Arran without sympathy in a personal memorandum later published with his own diaries:

> The plan of training was for each Commando to go ashore alternately for two weeks while the other did training on Holy Island and Arran. The boat training consisted of packing into ALCs which the military seemed to consider an esoteric art requiring great practice, and letting the naval officers make a nonsense of the navigation. Again and again they ran boats aground and let them get left by the tide.[33]

The story of *Layforce* in the Mediterranean was indeed one of frustration and failure, although there were successes. By the time *Layforce* was ready for deployment from Egypt, reinforced by Commando units raised from British forces in the Middle East and trained *in situ*, German offensives in Greece and North Africa had changed the strategic picture entirely. Although one raid was launched against the Italian-held North African port of Bardia by No.7 Commando (designated 'A' Battalion of *Layforce*) and supported by Courtney's canoeists, the deteriorating strategic position meant that much of *Layforce* was directed into emergency defensive duties as part of regular formations. It was an unfortunate echo of the situation that had earlier befallen the Independent Companies in Norway. As 'C' Battalion of *Layforce*, No.11 Commando made up part of the garrison of Cyprus while the rest of the Commando units were reinforcing the defenders of Crete. In this deployment the Scottish Commandos were fortunate, since in confused and chaotic retreat from the German airborne invasion of Crete all but a quarter of the three other *Layforce* battalions were left prisoners on the island.

In early June the Scottish Commando was allotted a task closer to the role it had worked towards on Arran. British and Australian regular forces were poised to advance into the French colony of Syria, where the Vichy French regime was co-operating with the enemy in the provision of strategic bases and airfields for German and Italian use. Barring the British invasion route north from Palestine was the Litani River, which runs into the Mediterranean north of Tyre in present-day Lebanon. No.11 Commando, or 'C' Battalion of *Layforce*, was given the job of landing on three beaches on the enemy side of the river and securing crossing points over which 25th Australian Brigade could then advance unhindered. The password for the conjunction of the Commando force and the main advance was to be 'Arran'.

The Litani River raid did not go entirely to plan, and the Commandos paid a heavy price for its success. Bad weather at sea meant the landings were delayed by some hours and the element of surprise was lost. With the Commando split into three, two of the parties encountered fierce resistance over the course of a full day as they fought to secure gun positions commanding the Kafr Bada bridge over the Litani. The third group, led by the lately promoted Major Geoffrey Keyes, somehow landed south of the river in error. Undeterred, Keyes led a small party across the Litani in a single small-boat and captured an enemy position on the other side. The efforts of the Commandos were not enough to stop the French from blowing the bridge just before the Australians reached it; but their action did allow the Australians to engineer a successful night crossing by pontoon. The cost to the Commando was 123 casualties, nearly a quarter of its total strength, with commanding officer Lieutenant-Colonel Pedder who had pushed them so hard on Arran among the dead. Geoffrey Keyes was left in command as acting Lieutenant-Colonel at the young age of 24. In a letter home he acknowledged the lengths Pedder had gone to in training his unit:

> My lot arrived in the wrong place rather late and light, and consequently got hell, but we succeeded in our object and got across, which should have been unnecessary had we arrived in the right place. My cavaliers took a bad knock though everyone was splendid. We certainly showed the other chaps how, and even they admitted it. The remainder got on alright and did a grand job all over the place, and P.'s training really showed its worth. They made hay there and caused great disorganisation.[34]

With the disaster that had befallen the rest of *Layforce* in Crete, the strong performance of 'C' Battalion at the Litani River was not enough to save the remnants of *Layforce* from disbandment. But for what remained of No.11 Commando there was still to be one more operation. By direct appeal to the Prime Minister, Laycock managed by October 1941 to gain authority to reconstitute a single Middle East Commando unit. It would comprise those from *Layforce* who wished to remain, and new elements such as the recently formed 'L' Detachment Special Air Service created by

Major David Stirling, late of *Layforce* and No.8 Commando. Volunteers were called for while 'C' Battalion was returning from its Cyprus base to Alexandria to prepare for dispersal. Demoralised by the fate of *Layforce*, and unclear exactly what was intended for the new Commando, many chose to go elsewhere. But Keyes stayed on, commanding a Troop which, with a preponderance of former 'C' Battalion men in its ranks, insisted on calling itself No.11 Commando. It quickly received its first mission: a raid on targets near the coast of German-held Libya.

As part of a plan to support a British counter-offensive in North Africa, the raid was directed against installations in the Cirene area, including buildings at Beda Littoria believed to be the headquarters and house of the overall enemy commander in North Africa, General Erwin Rommel. The plan to kill Rommel was audacious and, as it proved, misdirected. On 10 November 1941 the Commandos attempted to land by rubber dinghies from two submarines. Heavy seas meant that several could not get ashore and the operation had to be scaled down from the start. The picture was then confused further by information from local British intelligence contacts indicating that Rommel's house was in fact at Sidi Rafa. On the night of 14 November Geoffrey Keyes led a party in an attack on the Sidi Rafa house, which proved to contain none of the enemy more senior than two staff officers. In the course of searching the house and killing four of the occupants, Keyes was mortally wounded.

Worse followed. For those who returned to the beach the heavy seas made withdrawal by dinghy to the waiting submarines impossible. When the enemy caught up with them, the Commandos were forced to break into small groups and make for distant British lines. Only two succeeded, one of them the original *Layforce* commander Colonel Laycock who had supervised the overall landing operation. The remainder were either killed or captured. Lance Corporal Leslie Stables was one Commando who was taken prisoner. The silk map by which he attempted to find his way to safety is one of his possessions preserved today in the Regimental Museum of the Royal Scots. With it, also carefully hidden and preserved through four years of captivity, is his No.11 Commando black hackle.

For his gallantry in leading the operation at Sidi Rafa, Lieutenant-Colonel Geoffrey Keyes was posthumously awarded the Victoria Cross. It later emerged that neither the headquarters at Beda Littoria nor the house at Sidi Rafa were places visited by Rommel more than occasionally, and that on the night of the raid Rommel was actually in Rome. Frustration and grief over the outcome of the raid might nevertheless have been tempered by the knowledge that, despite setbacks, one of its principal targets was reached and engaged. Had the intelligence proved correct, the Commandos might very probably have achieved their objective.

* * *

When *Layforce* departed Arran in January 1941, they had left behind other Commando units training hard around Loch Fyne, and at new home bases nearby in Argyll and Ayrshire. At the end of 1940 Nos 3, 4 and 5 Special Service Battalions, comprising Nos 4, 7, 3, 8, 5 and 6 Commandos, relocated to billets at Girvan, Largs and Helensburgh and passed through No.1 Combined Training Centre in turn. In their home bases they continued their speed marches, weapons and tactical training on land, and their small-boat work and landing exercises at sea. The canoeists of 101 Troop meanwhile moved from Arran to a new mainland base on the shore of Loch Leven around Ballachulish and Glencoe. From there they proceeded to the Special Training Centre's boat station at Dorlin where work was leavened by opportunities to shoot and fish on the local estates within reasonable limits agreed with the factors and keepers.[35] By November the canoeists were on their first real reconnaissance mission, assessing beaches and enemy defences for a forthcoming raid on a German gun battery at Houlgate on the Normandy coast.[36]

From the Commando units in Scotland came the first larger-scale raid launched against a European coast. In March 1941 detachments of No.3 Commando and No.4 Commando sailed from Scapa Flow for Operation *Claymore*, a raid on ports in the Lofoten Islands off the north-west coast of Norway. With them went two former members of the instructing staff at the Special Training Centre Lochailort: Commander Geoffrey Congreve in post as the Senior Landing Officer, and Lord Lovat attached to No.4 Commando as an observer for Combined Operations headquarters. Though modest in its objectives and in the extent of action against the enemy, the Lofotens raid was an unqualified success. Production facilities with stocks of fuel and fish oil used in the production of explosives were destroyed, local men anxious to escape the German occupation and serve in Norwegian forces in exile were brought away, prisoners were taken, important coding information was extracted. But the more significant effect was a moral one. British raiding forces had successfully returned, if only fleetingly, to the vicinity of Narvik from where the earlier British expedition had been forced to evacuate in haste only months earlier. After months of training, during which the majority of Commando volunteers had seen no action, this was a timely antidote to a feeling of disillusion that was beginning to take hold among them. The raid's success was widely publicised, and hailed by the home press much as Churchill had intended.

The Commando idea was firmly entered into the popular consciousness. Unlike the activities of MI(R), Commando training and operations were not a matter of secrecy. Information was strictly controlled and, as at Lochailort, private photography was not permitted.[37] But action-filled images of Commando exercises in Scotland were captured by War Office official photographers early in 1941 and released for publicity purposes. Among them is a seminal photograph showing men of No.2 Commando wading ashore from a Landing Craft Personnel (Light), on what is probably Loch Fyne. First out of the craft is Major Jack Churchill who, if the photograph is examined closely, can be seen to be carrying a sword. No relation to the Prime Minister, Churchill was one of the most charismatic of the early Commando volunteers. A pre-war regular officer with the Manchester Regiment, he had rejoined from the Reserve, and won the Military Cross in the 1940 campaign in France.

One of Churchill's passions was for archery, in which sport he had represented Great Britain in the 1939 World Championships in Oslo. On active service in France he was reputed to have accounted for at least two of the enemy by the silent means of bow and arrow. English by birth, Churchill was Scottish by inclination; his first love was the bagpipes, a skill in which he was adept. He would play the pipes on exercise and, later, did the same on operations. With pipes, longbow or highland basket-hilted sword, Churchill was one much-decorated individual who represented a fusion of military traditions and the innovative and newly aggressive attitude that was held to epitomise the Commandos. He, like many of those around him, was quite in his element in the highland setting.[38]

While all this was going on at Inveraray, No.9 Commando, No.11 Commando's original Scottish partners on Arran, languished a little longer at Whiting Bay before moving to Criccieth on Tremadog Bay, North Wales, handily placed for the mountains of Snowdonia. But two of the Troops from No.9 were no sooner in Wales than they found themselves sent back to the west highlands. They arrived first at the former MI(R)

small-boat school at Dorlin House to spend two weeks under the instruction of Commander Vyner's naval staff. It was then on to the Special
Training Centre Lochailort. Early in 1941 the Commandant of the Special
Training Centre had been asked to report 'fully, strictly, and frankly' on
all officers and NCOs attending the course and on Commando Troops and
detachments sent for collective training there. This was perceived as a
informed means of comparing the training standards within different
Commando units:

> These reports, which will have been compiled by officers who
> have had opportunities of seeing and studying representatives from
> all Commandos, should form a valuable guide for Commanding
> Officers and should provide a useful means of judging their training.[39]

One of the No.9 Commando detachment was another former Independent Company officer, Captain Ralph Cameron, who later recorded
his impressions of their 1941 procession through the highland training
centres:

> Training at Lochailort was more rigorous than at Dorlin House.
> However, in his initial address, Colonel Stockwell emphasised the
> need for mental as well as physical ability: 'Your brains must not go
> to your boots.' Accordingly the officers were put to study and pre-
> pare the exercises which were later carried out. The other ranks were
> introduced to tougher assault courses and were instructed in more
> advanced unarmed combat. The stay at Lochailort ended with a
> three day exercise in and about Loch Awe, a physical exercise for
> which we had been preparing and to test mental ability. It was – as
> were most such exercises – also an endurance test and trial of diet.
> The diet was prescribed by Surgeon Commander Murray Levick
> R.N. who had been on Scott's 1912 expedition. The gross amount
> weighed two pounds. From memory, the principal food was oatmeal
> ($^1/_2$ lb), army biscuit, sugar, salt, a little bully beef or pemmican and
> dried fruit. And a few cigarettes, one to be smoked at the conclusion
> of a meal. We covered some fifty miles of rough going and most
> participants had food left at the end being too tired to do more than
> suck at a dried apple or apricot which had been included in the diet.

In summer, No.9 Commando as a whole, with other Commandos and some infantry units, participated in large-scale landing exercises at Inveraray, which Cameron felt 'were probably of greater benefit to the staff than the troops involved'. In fact these exercises were intended to be demonstrations of the viability of Commando operations overall. Despite the success in the Lofotens, other small raids launched thus far had produced little by way of significant operational worth and the Combined Operations set-up faced persistent criticism from among senior Army officers. The summer training culminated in a still larger exercise with naval support where troops embarked in the Clyde for landings at the Scapa Flow naval base in Orkney.[40] The exercise was not a great success, a disappointment compounded by the presence of HM King George VI as an observer, who Cameron remembers 'nearly stepped on me'.

With no major operations on the horizon, No.9 Commando moved to Galloway and into billets at Castle Douglas and Kirkcudbright. In the autumn they and all the other Commando units in Scotland each supplied some 40 volunteers for a new training course. This composite course was to be led by Major R. J. F. (Ronnie) Tod, Commanding Officer of No.9 Commando, an original Independent Company Officer and already a veteran of two small reconnaissance raids.[41] Its location would be one of the holding centres requisitioned the previous spring for the use of MI(R): Achnacarry, ancestral home of the Camerons of Lochiel. Achnacarry had been allotted a permanent staff as a Holding Centre for the Special Training Centre under the command of Major J. C. M. T. O'Donovan, formerly adjutant under Stockwell at Lochailort.[42]

The officer chosen to command the extra training volunteers from No.9 Commando was Captain Cameron:

> This course lasted about four weeks. Major Tod insisted upon disci-
> pline, shooting and marching. These were principles from which he
> never deviated. The assault courses, severe as they may have been,
> were essential trials of strength and fitness, but not superior to skill-
> at-arms. The marching in Battle Order included 10 miles in two hours
> and 7 miles run-and-walk in one hour. The 20 mile march was at
> normal infantry pace. There was some elementary instruction in the
> use of small canvas boats.[43]

Those who passed through these early Achnacarry training courses (or who, as Cameron notes, did not, were found to be unsuitable and returned to their original units) were the forerunners of some 25,000 men who would go through Achnacarry after it became, early the following year, the main centre for all Commando training.

* * *

For all the Commando forces assembled in great haste during the second half of 1940, 1941 was supposed to have been the year in which their raids would fall against German-held coasts with growing effect. Whereas in 1940 the priorities of home defence had frustrated the scope of special operations, the threat of invasion had since abated with victory in the Battle of Britain and had all but disappeared with the German invasion of the Soviet Union in June 1941. Still, despite progress in equipment and training, Combined Operations had instead been engulfed in the eastern Mediterranean in the greater military reverses that had been suffered, and against western European coasts had yet to achieve much of great substance. Furthermore, opposition to the organisation of Combined Operations and to the Commando idea itself was strengthening among the Chiefs of Staff. The Army in particular, in the shape of General Sir Alan Brooke, Chief of the Imperial General Staff, felt that the raiding role could better be directed within the conventional structures of the field army, and that in acting independently Combined Operations was doing little more than squandering resources.[44]

By way of evidence the anti-Commando theorists could cite a raid on the Arctic island of Spitzbergen mounted in August 1941. The destruction of Spitzbergen's coal mines was successfully achieved by a raiding force comprised not of Commandos but of Canadian infantry troops who had trained for their mission at Inveraray. With only 'pinprick' successes to point to, Admiral Sir Roger Keyes' position in defending the independence of Commando forces was weak. In September 1941 Winston Churchill agreed to give the Chiefs of Staff greater influence in planning and resource allocation for special operations. Rather than accept this effective demotion, Keyes resigned. His replacement was Vice-Admiral Lord Louis Mountbatten, a member of the Royal family and, until promoted to the appointment, a Royal Navy Captain who had recently commanded a destroyer in the Mediterranean. Mountbatten's job as Chief of Combined

Operations was to reshape Commando organisation and objectives in full co-operation with the three services, towards landings on a significantly larger scale than had proved practicable thus far. The highlands of Scotland were to feature strongly in his plans.

The year at least ended with a flourish. One further small-scale raid against Houlgate on the French coast, and involving 100 men of 9 Commando, failed to produce an actual landing. However, as the new Combined Operations regime fully took hold, weightier operations against Norway were quickly embarked upon. Since returning from the Lofotens Raid, No.3 Commando had been in billets at Largs in Ayrshire. In early December it provided troops for a second, more daring assault on northern Norway. Joining them were a small medical detachment of No.4 Commando from further down the Ayrshire coast at Troon, a party of canoeists from 101 Troop, and part of the strength of No.2 Commando then based at Weymouth. The target on this occasion was the northern Norwegian port of South Vågsøy, and the small island of Måløy which dominated the approaches to the port from the Vågs Fjord. Stiff resistance was expected from the German garrison at South Vågsøy.

The attack was preceded by a diversionary return to the nearby Lofoten Islands on Boxing Day; the main landing the following morning was supported by a substantial naval force that bombarded Måløy and was given air cover by the Royal Air Force flying from Wick and Shetland. Present with No.3 Commando was Major Jack Churchill, who piped out 'The March of the Cameron Men' as his landing craft raced towards Måløy. For the first time Commando forces in Europe engaged in sustained fighting. At a cost of 76 casualties the Commandos cleared the enemy from the streets of South Vågsøy, destroying shipping, dock installations and fish-oil processing factories. More than 100 prisoners were taken back to Scapa Flow, along with more willing voyagers in the shape of some 70 local men who volunteered to join exiled Norwegian forces stationed in Scotland.

As for the Lofotens, publicity was one of the raid's purposes. On this occasion a film unit from the War Office captured dramatic footage which was quickly edited into newsreel for the instruction and inspiration of British cinema audiences. Over a triumphant commentary, 'The Vaagso Raid' played real and swiftly restaged scenes of Commandos in action, and the encouraging sight of burning buildings, the coralling of German prisoners and their Norwegian collaborators.[45] Less content with the results of the raid was the Norwegian government-in-exile, who saw less purpose in the exercise and correctly anticipated reprisals against the local population by the German occupiers. Nevertheless, Vågsøy represented a significant mark of progress for the Commandos who at last had obtained proper material support and were beginning to be better prepared and equipped. In addition to their general preparations, the Vågsøy force enjoyed the benefit of pre-planning using detailed models of the town and the opportunity to rehearse the landings together at Scapa Flow immediately before embarkation.[46]

* * *

With their public profile heightened by this latest success in Norway, the UK-based Commandos returned to further training and life in their civilian billets. They might have hoped to enjoy a little of the mystique that came with their growing reputation as something maverick and dangerous, but an image of uncompromising toughness was harder to maintain in places where the men themselves were part of everyday routine. The Commando presence in the small towns of Argyll and Ayrshire was something of a constant from 1941 to 1943. Stripped of any air of mystery they were to be remembered there with affection rather than adulation. The friendly reception from local families was more than a matter of the daily cash allowance that each Commando soldier had to spend on food, accommodation and entertainment.[47] Returning 'home' each night when not on special training schemes or operations, the Commandos could become, temporarily at least, part of the life of local communities in places like Ayr, Helensburgh and Girvan. One such interlude was recalled by Henry Brown, Orderly Room Staff Sergeant of No.1 Commando stationed at Irvine on the Ayrshire coast from May 1941 until the summer of 1942, where he shared a billet in a large house on Waterside:

> It was in fact the manse and home of the Reverend and Mrs James Wishart, a very charming couple indeed, and for well over a year this manse of the Wilson Fullarton Church became for me, and for Norman Tasker our senior medical corporal, a second home .... The Wisharts often held musical evenings in the upstairs lounge at the Manse, and when they discovered I possessed a fairly respectable

tenor voice I was often called upon to entertain them. This eventually led to me singing items from oratorios at the evening services at the Wilson Fullarton Church fairly regularly, which brought about many glowing reports in the local Irvine Press.[48]

For some families, their lodger could be even more of a novelty than the British Commando soldier. In early 1942 a number of Dutchmen, serving with the Princess Irene Brigade of the Dutch Army in exile, volunteered for Commando service and were divided between the Commando units at Largs, Troon, Rothesay and Dunoon. Brahm Levi was one of their number who went to No. 3 Commando, he and his wife having earlier escaped from Holland, and the Nazi persecution of Dutch Jews, in a rowing boat. For more than six months Levi was the paying guest of a family in Largs, of whom May D. Murray was a 16-year-old daughter:

> He didn't talk much about that journey, but after interrogation he joined up and was decorated by Prince Bernhard of the Netherlands and he was very proud of this. Eventually he came to Largs with the Commandos and coped with the rigorous training; as a schoolgirl I watched them jump from the Pier fully kitted; leave from the railway stations on special missions, 'blacked up' and in combat gear. Fortunately Brahm – as we all called him – came back safely. He was a charming, courteous fellow, desperate to please my mother and grateful for anything she did for him.

Two years later, after the Allied invasion of north-west Europe, the family was distressed to hear from Levi's wife that he had been killed in action back on Dutch soil, shot by a sniper within 13 miles of his home village.[49]

As already had been found in the small communities of the west highlands, the atmosphere of conviviality and spirit of welcome from the locals was occasionally tested to the limit. The combination of soldiers off duty and strong drink could be a combustible one: where explosives were added to the equation, it could be very dangerous indeed. Damage was usually accidental, but not always so. Among many stories recounted of Commando high jinks in home bases, one tale recorded by Lord Lovat is a guide to the rest, and concerns an officer of engineers with No. 4 Commando at Troon, summarily dismissed one day early in 1942 for minor misdemeanours:

That same afternoon, smarting with resentment, he drew, without authority, all available high explosives from the quarter-master's store, loaded them into a truck and proceeded to blow up the most conspicuous landmark in the neighbourhood: a tall factory chimney, some 100 feet high, in a disused brick kiln behind the town. There was hell to pay .... Ayrshire was indignant.[50]

In spite of lapses such as these, and because the Commandos lacked the traditional local connections whereby many Regular Army units were recruited, recognised and supported, there were also gestures of 'adoption' from civil authorities. Acknowledging their national identity as one of the Commandos raised in Scotland, No.9 Commando was presented in 1941 with a Scottish saltire flag by the Lord Provost and citizens of Glasgow.[51] Feelings of kinship also ran in the opposite direction. For much of 1942 the men of No.9 Commando were in billets at Rothesay on the Isle of Bute before they departed for operations in the Mediterranean. From their extensive campaign of raiding in Italy and Greece during 1943-44, one remarkable souvenir survives: a German flag captured by No.3 Troop during the Anzio operations. The flag is decorated with drawings of Commando insignia, including a representation of a black hackle, and with the names of the men who captured it. Above the central swastika device 'No.9 Commando' is emblazoned; below it is the legend 'Rothesay's Own'.[52]

But possibly the strongest material legacy of the Commando presence in that part of the country was an unwitting gift from the bonnet-makers of Ayrshire. Early in 1942 the officers of No.1 Commando concluded that the appearance of their unit, with its hotchpotch of regimental headgear and badges, should be put on a more uniform footing. A beret was decided upon. Referring to the colours in their (unofficial) unit shoulder flash, they settled upon green. No.1 Commando's first green berets are believed to have been supplied by an unidentified firm in the burgh of Irvine. Another version of the story places the supplier in Ardrossan. Whatever its precise origin, No.1 Commando's green beret innovation would shortly afterwards be adopted as the uniform headdress of all Commandos and, as such, a symbol of the élite status of the trained Commando soldier.[53]

*   *   *

Although during 1941 Commando training in Scotland coalesced around Loch Fyne and the Clyde, the training centres of the west highlands were still much in demand. Small groups of officers and non-commissioned officers (NCOs) from each Commando continued to be sent periodically to the Special Training Centre Lochailort for intensive instruction, revising techniques, and reiterating the standards that were to be instilled in the men under their command. When in February 1942 Lieutenant Stuart Chant of No. 5 Commando arrived at Lochailort, it was the third occasion that he had been there in two years. Chant harboured no doubts as to the value of his previous experiences in the place he and his comrades dubbed 'Hell's Glen':[54]

> The impact on us of this specialist training and of these feats of endurance was extraordinary. Even the humblest and smallest soldier quickly developed into a man 'twice his height', as it were, who thought nothing of hardships which would have seemed impossible to him and his mates a few weeks before arriving in that lonely part of Scotland.

The occasion of his third visit was, however, to more immediate and specialised purpose than the familiar Lochailort course tailored towards the general requirements of Commando students:

> Once again we were living there in the cold Nissen huts scattered amongst the shrubs and rhododendron bushes in the grounds of the castle. Once again we paraded each morning in the half-light of winter.
> But this time there was a difference: instead of the physical train-ing and test of endurance we were now being initiated into the hand-ling of more sophisticated explosives and destruction than hitherto. We enjoyed blowing up dead trees and large slabs of mountainside, but it did not cross our minds that this portended our being ear-marked for duties of a different kind; and after weeks of this train-ing we returned to our respective Commandos around the coasts of Scotland and England.[55]

Leaving Lochailort once more, Lieutenant Chant took away with him some unauthorised snapshot photographs of his No. 5 Commando comrades 'very, very cold', and an Ordnance Survey map of the area marked up with landing sites and routes of march in South Morar.[56]

The nature of Chant's next training destination began to suggest that something was afoot. At the port of Burntisland in Fife, he and his selected No.5 Commando comrades were reunited with other parties drawn from Nos. 1, 3, 4, 9 and 12 Commando whom they had already met during their latest stint at Lochailort. The group spent some days conducting mock demolitions of the small dock installations at Burntisland before moving to Cardiff for similar efforts on a larger scale at Barry docks. From Cardiff they graduated to theoretical destruction of the giant King George V Dock at Southampton. The period of specialised demolitions work at Lochailort proved then to be one stage in preparations for one of the most audacious Combined Operations raids of the war: the destruction of the port of St Nazaire on the north bank of the Loire, six miles inland from the French coast. The dry dock at St Nazaire was the only harbour on the Atlantic coast with the capacity to service the battleships of the German surface fleet, the much-feared *Tirpitz* in particular. The purpose of the raid was to deny the enemy that important facility.

The spectacular raid of 28 March 1942 began with the dock entrance rammed at full speed by the Royal Navy destroyer HMS *Campbeltown*, packed with explosives on a delay charge. Commando demolitions teams then landed from the ship and from motor launches proceeding up river, to destroy other dock and submarine installations. Although he was wounded on the run up the river, Chant and his team successfully destroyed their target, the harbour's main pumping station. Wounded a second time, Chant was one of more than 100 Commandos captured, when re-embarkation into the small craft of the naval flotilla proved impossible. The raid was costly, with a British death toll of 169, but the dry dock was successfully put out of action for the rest of the war. This was assured when *Campbeltown*'s load of high explosives finally detonated on their nine-hour charge, spectacularly interrupting German efforts to photograph and parade Commando prisoners, including Chant, as evidence of the raid's failure.

Confused information about the extent of the damage done made an immediate positive assessment difficult, and the planners were conscious of the numbers killed or captured. Nonetheless St Nazaire was the major success Combined Operations had been striving towards for well over a year. Among numerous decorations awarded to the participants were two

Victoria Cross awards to Commandos.[57] Although small reconnaissance and sabotage raids were to continue against European coasts and in other theatres thereafter, the tactical approach was thenceforth to 'think big', using Commandos as storm troops in the major Allied landings being planned now that the United States was in the war.

With such greater things in mind, Mountbatten and his deputy, Brigadier Charles Haydon, were rethinking the process of Commando training. A greater throughput had to be achieved, since larger operations were going to demand greater numbers of special service troops. Two new courses of action were decided upon. One was to expand the size of special service forces by raising new Commando units. Rather than draw further volunteers from the Army (and so raise the ire of the War Office by further denuding field army formations of their most eager soldiers), the bulk of the new Commandos would be drawn from the Royal Marines, the specialist ship-borne soldiers of the Royal Navy. The second initiative was that Commando training would no longer be left in the hands of individual Commando units, and that every new Commando soldier should go through a standard formal induction of intensive training at a centralised location. The free-form days of special operations training and its innovative instigators were finally and entirely at an end. The location chosen for the course was a new Commando Depot at Achnacarry in Lochaber, the former holding wing establishment of STC Lochailort.

Despite their long tradition of amphibious operations, the Royal Marines had thus far been standing rather on the sidelines of Combined Operations, left to look on whilst the Army Commandos improvised the seaborne raiding role which Royal Marines might reasonably have felt was theirs by right. Priority had gone to maintaining fleet-borne forces for the protection of warships, and preparations to equip and protect advanced naval bases. The creation in 1940 of a Royal Marine Division of fully equipped and trained battalions as a Strike Force was a step towards offensive operations, but by early 1942 this had produced little by way of action. While the Army Commandos went to work on the smaller raids, Combined Operations Command kept the Marines in hand for larger operations that seemed never to come to pass. Although Royal Marines provided small raiding forces for operations in the Mediterranean during 1941, much of the Division spent that year at the Combined Training Centre on Loch Fyne, training and waiting.

The transformation of the Royal Marine Division into Royal Marine Commandos began in February 1942 with the creation of 'A' Royal Marines Commando, a unit of volunteers drawn from across the Division.[58] Following selection and further training at the Royal Marines depot at Deal, the Commando spent April at HMS *Dorlin*, the Moidart boat station recently transferred from STC Lochailort into the control of the Royal Navy. At Dorlin the Commando conducted its own training in boatwork, fieldcraft, and landing exercises extending to a west-coast landing far to the north in Wester Ross, preceding a cross-country march and attack on defended targets at the east-coast town of Dingwall.[59] After further training on the Isle of Wight, in August the Royal Marines Commando joined Nos 3 and 4 Commando as the special service elements of an amphibious raid in force against the French port of Dieppe.

This was a full-scale combined operation, spearheaded by specially trained Canadian infantry. It was designed as a test for the invasion of north-west Europe that must come if the Allies were to win the war and towards which Allied commanders were already planning. Dieppe was to be held for a day, its harbour facilities and defences and a nearby airfield destroyed while the Royal Marine Commandos captured a stock of German landing craft kept in the harbour. The raid was a disaster. The Commando forces involved were fortunate to be operating on the fringes of the main attack and so avoided the worst of the catastrophe. The operation was weakened from the start, after plans for a preliminary bombardment from the air were dropped for fear of French civilian casualties. After German intelligence picked up that something was afoot against Dieppe, the beach defences were manned and ready. Amidst carnage on the beaches the attack was aborted, but not soon enough to prevent 4000 of the 6000-strong assault force being left behind dead or as prisoners. The two Army Commando units had notable but isolated successes attacking gun batteries on either flank of the landing. As tragedy unfolded on the main landing beaches, the new Royal Marines Commando had to abandon its efforts to get ashore.

Chastened by the Dieppe experience, Combined Operations Command was stung by another disaster a month later in a failed raid on Tobruk involving Royal Marine landing forces and a supporting Commando infiltration across the North African desert.[60] With confidence in the value of medium-scale raids ebbing away, strategic planning for combined operations increasingly looked to the long-term in building up forces that could successfully conduct a major landing with the naval and air support that had been lacking at Dieppe. On the horizon was an amphibious invasion of Vichy-French colonies in North Africa. A little beyond it yet were major landings in Italy, the need for actions in the war against Japan in south-east Asia where so much British held territory had lately been lost, and, at some stage in the future, the landings that would open a 'Second Front' in north-west Europe. In the interim, smaller raiding operations were nevertheless to continue.

As part of the preparations for what must come, over the 18 months following Dieppe the strength of the Royal Marine Division would provide seven new Commando units, with a further one added from scratch thereafter. Ultimately integrated into Special Service Brigades alongside Army Commando units, they were each allocated their own identities numbered 40-48, beginning with the original 'A' unit, recovering its strength after losses at Dieppe, as 40 Royal Marine Commando. These new Commando units were therefore pre-existing, trained Royal Marine battalions converted as a whole, but shorn of their transport and heavier weapons. Taken out of their barracks, they were introduced to the self-supporting Commando way of life in civilian billets. During 1943 the landladies and families of Ayr, Troon and Castle Douglas would welcome them while they underwent further training in their new role at the Combined Training Centres that now peppered the Firth of Clyde, and at the new Commando Depot at Achnacarry.

Elements from the first Royal Marines Commando (later 40 RM Commando) had gone through the full Army Commando course at Achnacarry in April 1942.[61] However, first up for the Royal Marines 'conversion' training there by unit were 41 RM Commando whose Troops arrived in turn for a two to three-week course in the early weeks of 1943.[62] Thereafter Combined Operations Command decided that, notwithstanding the extended training they had already been through, new and serving Royal Marine Commandos were not going to be exempt from the requirement to pass through the central training course. In order to be recognised as Commando soldiers, each Marine was to undergo mandatory further training under the supervision of the Army. The remainder of the Royal Marine Division's Commandos found that they, like new intakes to the Army Commando units, were going to have to go to Achnacarry.

The decision rankled a little among senior ranks of the Royal Marines. Their concern was not over the abilities of their men to pass the course, but touched on the implied interference between one service and another. Training by the Army was a hard thing for these men of the Royal Navy to take; harder yet for a force that had seen its traditional sea-raiding speciality usurped by those who were now set to be judges of their men's fitness for the role. Furthermore, Royal Marine officers were required to train at Achnacarry alongside their men under Army instructors, a situation that could be construed as undermining their authority. Mindful of the sensitivities, the commandant at Achnacarry took care to set out the command situation in advance. A mildly condensed version of the standard course was specially tailored for Royal Marines Commando conversion. The Achnacarry diet of individual training was mixed with a version of combined Troop training which maintained the integrity of the command structure within each unit. The pill was sweetened a little more when training instructors recruited from the Royal Marines became a permanent feature of the Achnacarry staff.[63]

*   *   *

By the time the Royal Marine Commandos began to arrive in succession, Achnacarry had been in full swing for over a year. Its reputation for toughness was already established. There, in February 1942, at the seat of Cameron country in Lochaber, Major O'Donovan, late of the Special Training Centre Lochailort, had departed his Achnacarry command for a new staff appointment at the War Office. He left the newly designated Commando Depot in a state of readiness for the arrival of its new commanding officer. Selected by Haydon for the task of training Commando soldiers to order, Lieutenant-Colonel Charles Vaughan was a First World War veteran who, before becoming a commissioned officer between the wars, was a Regimental Sergeant Major in the Coldstream Guards. Vaughan volunteered for Commando service in 1940, offering his experience in an administrative capacity. Immediately prior to his appointment to Achnacarry he had been Acting Commanding Officer of No.4 Commando with Lord Lovat as his second-in-command. A Londoner, steeped in the traditions of the Brigade of Guards, Vaughan was not exactly at home in the west highlands. But he knew plenty about discipline and a good deal about fighting, and he understood exactly the philosophy of Commando warfare. The regime Vaughan created at Achnacarry welded the innovations of Lochailort and the training programmes developed by Commando units since 1940 with a rigorously efficient Regular Army approach. His was a structured system that brought pressure and scrutiny to bear upon the individual man in training. Using the established Commando principle of 'Returned to Unit', Vaughan's staff put together a course that weeded out those who did not meet the standard required.

The other side of the coin was the extension of respect to those who stayed the distance, who were admitted into the ranks of the Commandos as trained men. An essential in the Achnacarry regime was the implicit recognition that training was what made the Commando soldier. The trainee was there to learn the skills that would make him an effective special service soldier on operations; but the training was also an end in itself. The volunteer was to be tested for his physical and mental fitness as an individual. As before, training would be ongoing in a Commando soldier's service, but from March 1942 onwards the would-be Commando soldier was not a Commando proper until he had passed the Achnacarry test. From late 1942 trainees finishing the course and achieving this coveted status received a material affirmation of their graduation by the presentation of a green beret, by then the universally worn Commando head dress. As Royal Marine Lieutenant Richard Baxter understood at the commencement of his course: 'We knew Achnacarry was the place where you became a Commando or didn't. If you completed the course successfully then you got a green beret. Otherwise you were put into something else. At that time the alternative was landing craft ....'[64] For Army Commando volunteers, the alternative remained the dreaded 'Returned to Unit'.

Before any berets were handed out, the trainees had to endure five weeks of the most demanding military training that could be imagined for them.[65] As had been the practice at Lochailort, there was no thought of gentle introduction. Immediately on arrival by train at Spean Bridge, each new intake was marched at speed from the station, across the Protected Area checkpoint at the Caledonian Canal swing-bridge below Loch Lochy, and up the hill to Achnacarry, a good eight miles in total. At the entrance to the camp the new arrivals were greeted by the unsettling sight of mock graves dug into the ground and marked with crosses, each bearing a warning. The trainee was thought likely to remember not to 'show himself on the skyline' and other such rejoinders when he saw the consequences of negligence written on a grave marker.

First sight of the imposing early nineteenth-century estate house was a little different to that which greets visitors today, as the expansive lawn before the house was then under occupation by Nissen huts and a crudely formed parade square. The castellated Achnacarry House itself served as headquarters, officers' mess and other staff accommodation. The huts before it provided more basic accommodation for those fortunate enough not to be put up in tents, as well as indoor training facilities for activities such as unarmed combat instruction and 'milling' – no holds barred boxing bouts of a single round. North and west of these utilitarian and comfortless structures were obstacle courses at low and high level. The latter was the 'Tarzan Course', a test in rope-climbing and swinging from trees that incorporated the natural barrier of the River Arkaig. Across the Arkaig was a bridge made from toggle ropes over which trainees were required to cross at speed. This exercise was a prelude to learning how to make and rig such a bridge themselves. Nearby, a further novel method of river crossing had been devised. Christened 'the Death Slide', this was a single rope fixed high in a tree on one side of the river and close to the ground on the opposite bank. By precarious means of a toggle rope looped over the fixed rope and held one end in each hand, trainees whizzed down across the Arkaig. To the unlucky came the added frisson of explosive charges being detonated in the water below them.

West of the house were shooting and grenade ranges and mocked-up timber buildings featuring pop-up targets. Whereas at STC Lochailort the primary purpose of these devices was to test individual reflex pistol shooting, at Achnacarry these were principally employed to teach the skills of street-fighting where Commandos might have to work together to clear the enemy from houses one by one. South of this zone was an area of rock outcrops leading back to the waterfall of the Allt Creag Innis nam Bo, where instruction in rock-climbing progressed from elementary scrambling and rope-work to three-man haulage of casualties and equipment. To learn the technique of abseiling, in the traditional and precarious manner of looping rope around back and shoulder, the novice climbers might also repair to the high walls of Achnacarry house itself:

> Another thing I remember about my time in Achnacarry was that we abseiled down the wall of the castle. And when I see people abseiling now with their harnesses and carabiners and everything like that I think they are doing a cushy job. We didn't have all that. You put the rope between your legs and round your body and round and onto

your arm and you abseiled like that. What slowed you down was the friction and you could feel it. But we managed. That was quite a thing.[66]

East of the house towards Clunes, where Lochiel and his family had sought refuge and oversight of their property, was the stretch of Loch Lochy where elementary seamanship was practised. The craft employed ranged from canoes, dories and cutters, to the 'Landing Craft, Assault' from which amphibious landings were rehearsed along the shore south of the boat house at Bunarkaig, or launched thence towards the opposite shore. The most testing of these was the much anticipated and little relished 'Opposed Landing', an exercise conducted through a carefully constructed maelstrom of live machine gun and mortar fire, controlled explosions and flares, designed to acquaint students as closely as possible with the extremities of a real amphibious operation against defended beaches: 'Big event today. We are making a landing with opposition by the instructors. They are using live cartridges which whistle past our ears while mines explode around us, in the water and on the beach. For some it is the Baptism of Fire.'[67]

A typical opposed landing scheme ran the scenario of an attack on an enemy target, where a Troop landed from one flight of four canoes with 50 minutes to get to shore, engage the target and withdraw again by boat.

Around the perimeter of the Achnacarry demesne ran a circuit of road along which the trainees would frequently pound. The northern stretch of this route, below a heavily wooded slope, was the Mile Dorcha or 'Dark Mile'. This was rather a misnomer for the sweating Commandos concerned, since in actuality their Dark Mile run was a circuit of some five miles in total. And yet this test, to be completed at first within an hour then progressively whittled down to 50 minutes, was a relatively gentle one. On frequent occasions the speed marches demanded of trainees were cross-country day expeditions that might take them as far as the 4406-foot summit of Ben Nevis near 20 miles distant. And the exertions did not necessarily end on return to base, as forced marches, long or short, could be followed immediately by digging in, shooting and drilling tasks.[68]

From their Achnacarry base, Commandos in training would range far and wide in all directions, on navigation, survival and tactical exercises. These schemes tested skills taught in the main camp area, such as map-reading and cooking in the field to the length of dispensing with mess tins and roasting food on spits or baking it in clay. Tactical exercises would also be 'fought' close to the main camp. One such, in regular use in 1945, provided the scenario that a training troop was to approach an enemy position just beyond Achnacarry blocking a theoretical advance along the south shore of Loch Arkaig to Inver Mallie. A two-phase attack by sub-section against enemy bunker positions followed, with two-inch mortars firing high explosives and smoke to screen movement.

An early published evocation of the atmosphere at Achnacarry came from the pen of John S. Gibson, a Commando volunteer from the Royal Corps of Signals. A lieutenant in No. 1 Commando from 1943, Gibson was later to become a noted historian of the Jacobite campaigns of the seventeenth and eighteenth centuries, a chapter of Scottish history with which the west highlands, and Achnacarry itself, were intimately connected. The young Commando officer sensed this link to the past even amidst his exertions:

> For the first week of my stay at Achnacarry, by some fluke of the weather, the sun shone bright every day from cloudless skies. I was introduced to a sporting gentlemanly life in which one was invited by the nicest chaps in the army to run long distances in full kit and to attempt some frightening rope crossings of the fast-flowing Water of Arkaig. Our dozen recruits and instructors had the freedom of the Castle and the glen. Everything was in delightful contrast to the torpor of garrison duty in Yorkshire.
>
> Then the rain came, persistent, heavy. Many recruits arrived. As was the invariable rule, they lost whatever rank they bore; each was allotted an identical forty square feet of a Nissen hut floor. The officers, crammed in Castle bedrooms, were little better off, and officers and men alike – even General M——y's A.D.C., who had volunteered for Commando service as a desperate expedient of escape from his job – all sat late in the July twilight polishing brass and cleaning equipment.
>
> At all hours the glen echoed to the bangs and crumps of exploding grenades. At night-time, flares bursting at tree-top height would throw a lurid light on loch and hill, while tracer fire, red and orange, sped across the water to splash beside the incoming boats of the attack.
>
> But, in my recollection, we spent most of our time in the alternate

hells of river-crossing and speed-marching – this last a march covering over seven miles of road in less than sixty minutes. So we doubled across the meadows at Gairlochy, where Claverhouse reviewed his highlanders in the Jacobite war of 1689, and grim and sweaty we pounded up the hill above the Spean Water, where Keppoch's Mac-Donalds ambushed the Royal Scots of the 'Forty-five. These historic braes of Lochaber seemed a barrier to our thoughts. The only things of importance in the world were to complete the speed march and survive the swaying rope-crossing above the swirling Water of Arkaig.[69]

If not every trainee heard echoes of Jacobite lore in the Lochaber surroundings, the Achnacarry permanent staff responded to the highland setting, and not just by occasional lapses into poaching. One of the sobriquets by which Lieutenant-Colonel Vaughan was known was 'The Laird of Achnacarry', and in tribute to the real owner of the establishment, their host, Vaughan's staff wore a patch of Cameron tartan on their berets. A Depot pipe band was formed, with pipers who doubled as a demonstration Troop to show trainees how the various training exercises ought to be done. When new intakes approached camp on their long march from Spean Bridge, the pipe band greeted them and accompanied them on the last stretch. At the end of the course the newly qualified Commandos departed in the opposite direction, once again to the sound of the pipes.

The course demanded a great deal of all trainees. Some found it a desperate, draining experience, and in their exhaustion drew their psychological focus down to nothing more than surviving the rigours of each day and getting through to its end. Others actively enjoyed it, felt the benefit of the physical demands made upon them, and appreciated the novelty of the setting. And underneath there was an understanding of the purpose behind the pain:

> One of the things about the training at Achnacarry was you felt that you were really being stretched and taught important things. It was a serious place, a lot of fun, but you were seriously being taught and trained things that would possibly save your life. And enable you to be a much more effective soldier.[70]

It was a deadly serious place, because on top of the pain and fatigue there was risk. As at Lochailort the combination of live firing exercises, demolitions, small-boat work, amphibious landings and struggles with the elements out in the hills, meant that there were fatalities: wounds, drowning, exposure. The frequency and intensity of live firing exercises, including mortar fire, heightened the danger. Figures for accidental deaths and injuries do not appear to have survived. On anecdotal evidence they were not so frequent as to be routine, but it was understood that they could and would happen. Instructors' notes on safety precautions commenced with an expression of general principle:

> No unnecessary risks will be taken but at the same time it must be remembered that we are training for war and that if any degree of realism is to be reached the chances of accidents occurring cannot be completely eliminated.[71]

The Achnacarry course proceeded on a basis not unlike that at nearby Lochailort, but with emphases and refinements reflecting how the Commando role in 1942 had developed away from the small-scale guerrilla warfare first espoused by MI(R). Fieldcraft, demolitions and unarmed combat were all still practised, but with them came an even greater stress on fitness, together with more developed tactical training for assault landings and sustained engagement with the enemy. It was a system aimed at creating an assault force that could spearhead aggressive operations in strength, working in tandem with regular formations in combined operations, and if necessary at greater length to contribute to conventional land-based offensives. The instruction embraced progressive training approaches that were gaining influence across the field army, and, crucially, applied experience acquired by Commando units both on operations and in organising their own training in the two previous years.

At root however, much that was done there had its origins at the original Special Training Centre. The 36-hour 'scheme' in the hills, culminating in a night attack that ended the Achnacarry course, was pure Lochailort. Unarmed combat instruction derived from Fairbairn and Sykes methods was taught as part of the physical training programme by Commando PT instructors, along with the obstacle courses and rope work.[72] The first weapons training officer was Captain P. N. Walbridge, imported directly from Lochailort. He continued to demand the highest standards of marksmanship and familiarity with weapons, the Commando repertoire including the Bren light machine gun (Bren Mark 1 automatic rifle), and the 'PIAT' rocket projector which was superseding the Boyes rifle as the anti-tank weapon of choice for light forces. Some elementary teaching in medium machine gun and mortar firing was also given, a departure from the lighter weapons upon which the Lochailort course tended to concentrate. But the rifle and bayonet, the Thompson sub-machine gun and the Sten sub-machine gun were all present. Weapons carried by allies and enemies remained in the syllabus. Demolitions training continued to feature, although this constituted a reduced element from Lochailort days since small-scale sabotage had largely passed into the hands of agencies other than the Commandos, and specialist training for operations was available elsewhere among the highland training centres and beyond.

The array of fieldcraft talent that had assembled at Lochailort in 1940 successfully enhanced existing military knowledge in this area, and their methods were refined for Commando tactical purposes by a new group of instructors. Teaching fieldcraft at Achnacarry, Captain James Dunning could draw on the skills of one direct recruit from the Special Training Centre, Sergeant Davidson of the Lovat Scouts, who was joined by a Sergeant McClelland of the Seaforth Highlanders, another highlander versed in the ways of the ghillie:

> As a role model Davidson was ideal. His movement in the hills was that of a hunter as he eyed the skies and smelt the wind. Then when he spotted his quarry, be it a beastie or a group of trainees, his rifle seemed to be an integral part of him as he slithered effortlessly to the ground to take cover and take up a firing or observing position, his eyes never leaving his quarry. I often used him as an example of how it should be done. All I needed to say was: 'Just watch him and see how to do it ....'[73]

Another influence in the lecture room or in the field was polar explorer George Murray Levick, though the Achnacarry approach to fitness and endurance diverged somewhat from his own. As a medical officer, Captain John Forfar of 47 Royal Marine Commando took particular interest in Surgeon Commander Murray Levick's recommendations while undergoing Achnacarry training late in 1943:

Murray-Levick had a simple formula for cold acclimatisation – 'live constantly just off the shiver and you will get accustomed to lower and lower temperatures'. He knew all about the Achnacarry course and agreed that it tested will power and the ability to stand excessive physical demands, hardship and stress and was valuable from that point of view, but he did not agree that that it was the right way to achieve physical fitness. He considered that continuous arduous training without adequate rest and with limited amounts of sleep checked the development of fitness and considered that if a well-trained fit man (most 'Achnacarrians' were such) lost weight as a result of further training, that training was being applied too acutely. Many 'Achnacarrians' did lose weight. Murray-Levick advised that the highest standards of physical fitness could only be achieved by the progressive increase in physical activity over a larger timescale than the duration of the Achnacarry course allowed, and with adequate rest.[74]

The Achnacarry production line turned out Commando soldiers from early 1942 until the end of the war and beyond, first as the Commando Depot and from December 1943 as the Commando Basic Training Centre. Through its gates came a steady supply of raw material that occasionally included special intakes other than Army volunteers and Royal Marines. One such was an influx of volunteers from the Metropolitan Police, 500 men brought forward to help reinforce special service troops early in 1942. Without any previous military training, the London policemen made highly acceptable Commando material and earned the admiration of the Achnacarry staff.[75] Vaughan offered the pick of them to No.4 Commando based at Troon, where they were gratefully accepted by second-in-command Lord Lovat who came back for more after Dieppe: 'First class material, with discipline and a good education behind them .... These stout bobbies were to exert considerable influence as non-commissioned officers. Some rose quickly from the ranks.'[76]

Not far behind the policemen came parties of French trainees, men recruited for the Free French Commando Troop, the 1er Compagnie Fusilier Marin, by French naval officer Phillipe Kieffer.[77] Their first Achnacarry-bound contingent arrived in March 1942 and included a number of men released from military detention for the purpose. In time the Free French were joined by volunteers from the exiled forces and individuals of numerous nations that were formed together into nationality-based Troops of No.10 (Inter-Allied) Commando. As with their British counterparts, the exiles saw in Commando service the prospect of a rapid route into action against German occupying forces in Europe. The enemy occupation of their homelands, and in many cases personal experience of living under it and escaping from it, naturally increased the sense of urgency with which they approached the prosecution of the war.

French naval gunner Maurice Chauvet's extraordinary journey of escape from occupied Paris took him to West Africa, a Spanish detention camp, Portugal, Casablanca, and final arrival on British soil at Greenock on the Clyde, an odyssey of 879 days. Chauvet's memoir of his service with a French Commando Troop records his experience of the Achnacarry course where an agonising foot complaint put his accession to Commando status in jeopardy. Facing rejection if he gave in to the pain, the crucible of Chauvet's personal struggle was a 15-mile speed-march which he forced himself to finish with a swollen bleeding foot:

> That day, with my blood-soaked sock before me, I had surpassed my limitations and, without knowing it, I had become a Commando.[78]

In the wake of Kieffer's Frenchmen came volunteers for the Dutch, Belgian, Norwegian, Polish, and Yugoslav Troops of No.10 (Inter-Allied) Commando, with smaller numbers of Czechs, Danes, and individual representatives of other nations. Among the overseas intake were a number of men officially designated as enemy aliens. They were bound for No.10 Commando's mysterious 'X-Troop', consisting of refugees from Germany and Austria, many of them Jews, with a smattering of anti-Nazi dissidents from other hostile nations such as Hungary. Facing torture and execution if they were captured on operations, they trained and served under assumed identities.[79]

The training regime at Achnacarry quickly attracted the attention of allies of rather a different origin. During 1941 the Military Intelligence Department of the United States War Department had already carried out a study of British Commando forces with a view to creating something of their own on similar lines.[80] In the first weeks of 1942, following American entry into the war, US Marines began to form into Raider Battalions for amphibious actions in the Pacific, and planning began for an American Commando-style force to operate in the European and North African theatres. The 1st U.S. Ranger Battalion formed in June 1942 in Northern Ireland, where US forces were stationed as a precaution against any German invasion of neutral Eire. Volunteers from American infantry and armoured divisions stationed in the province first completed a training and selection process at Sunnylands Camp, Carrickfergus. The Americans eschewed the 'Commando' name and instead adopted the 'Ranger' title that recalled auxiliary troops who fought for the British against French forces in North America during the Seven Years' War of 1756-63. The twentieth-century version, which grew to two battalions, became familiarly known as 'Darby's Rangers' after their commanding officer Lieutenant-Colonel William Darby, who led them into action during the major Allied landings in North Africa in November 1942 and in Italy thereafter.[81]

Although they kept their American tactical doctrine and equipment, the first 600 US Rangers learned the Commando trade at Achnacarry during July 1942. Students and teachers made a strong impression on one another, as initial wariness grew into mutual respect. If a little fun was had at their expense, and at their discomfiture over the privations of the camp as much as the rigours of the course, it was observed and appreciated that the American version of special service troops rose to the challenge of their weeks in Lochaber.[82] Without further delay, a select group of 51 Rangers went straight into operational training with British Commando units preparing for the Dieppe raid. The first American casualties of the European war were six US Rangers killed on the beaches of Dieppe.

Successful negotiation of the obstacles and exercises of the Achnacarry course was not quite the end of the Rangers' Scottish experience. Sent next to Combined Operations training on the sea lochs of Argyll, they proceeded thereafter to civilian billets in the east coast city of Dundee where they were to undergo further training alongside No.1 Commando. Scotland saw comparatively little of the wartime influx of American soldiers which remains such a strong element of British popular memory of the Second World War; but for three weeks in September 1942 the people of Dundee experienced their own friendly invasion when the US Rangers arrived in their homes. As happened in the seaside towns of the west, the locals quickly got over the initial shock; and when the Rangers left, crowds turned out to the railway station to see them off to their next destination – Corkerhill outside Glasgow. They left Dundee a little depleted in number. In mock attacks on coastal defences along the

Angus coast, two US Rangers were wounded, one mortally, in a live-firing accident.[83]

Less glamorous perhaps than the Americans of Darby's Rangers or the exiles of European nations, but no less determined to do well at Achnacarry, were men of the Home Guard in Scotland. Private J. Ferguson of 'C' Company Edinburgh Home Guard was one of 20 men from Home Guard units of Scottish Command who were put through a bespoke version of the course during July 1943. To those acquainted today with the great insect scourge of the highlands in late summer, one of his salient memories of his week in camp will be familiar:

> When we went to bed, having drawn our blankets, it was some little time before we could get to sleep, as there were millions of midges about. These insects proved very troublesome during the following week, so much so that a special issue of ointment was made (without effect) and men on parade were allowed to take a pace forward for the purpose of slapping their bodies where affected by bites.

Ferguson's day-by-day account of the experience records how the Achnacarry syllabus was condensed and crammed into the Home Guard training platoon, for whom one day's instruction could cover as many as eight subjects: *viz*, physical training, toggle-rope bridge-building, bayonet drill with gas masks on, unarmed combat, rock and cliff-climbing, opposed landing, fieldcraft, assault course. The Home Guardsmen were also given the opportunity to test themselves against Commandos in training during a final day's exercise in the hills above Glen Mallie to the south of Loch Arkaig, with satisfying result for Ferguson and friends:

> At the same time as the Home Guard Platoon left in the morning a Commando half-troop had gone out on a similar trip, but only for twelve hours. They had been given the task of ambushing us should we cross their path, but on reaching the head of the pass between Glen Mallie and Glen Loy forward scouts of our party spotted smoke from their fires some distance down Glen Loy. They were quite evidently still in bivouac, so our Captain led us very carefully down the hillside, using the bed of the stream as cover, and finally took up good position behind a dyke. This gave fine observation along the road up which they had to come. Some time later their scouts came

up, passed us, and were very nicely nipped by Burnet and someone else while we held back until the main body, all unsuspecting, walked right into our fire; the upshot being full marks to the Home Guard.[84]

Achnacarry's reputation as the height of toughness and effectiveness in military training was established by word of mouth, as tidings of the Herculean labours of the course spread through the armed forces and beyond. But it also enjoyed a public profile proceeding from official efforts to present the Commando image before the public. Shadier goings-on at nearby STC Lochailort featured only once in the press: *The Times* headlined 'WITH BRITISH GUERRILLAS. MEN TRAINED TO INDIVIDUAL ADVENTURE', a report carefully concealing as much as it revealed, with details of the name, location and precise purpose of the training centre conspicuous by their absence.[85] Achnacarry, however, featured in official photographs released to the press in 1943, in newspaper stories, newsreels and finally in a full-length feature film released by the Admiralty in 1945. 'Commando – the Story of the Green Beret' followed one Commando soldier through his training at Achnacarry, Wrexham and St Ives, with long sequences shot on location. The leading man was fictional, but those training around him were the real thing. Achnacarry Commandant, Lieutenant-Colonel Charles Vaughan, even made a brief personal appearance presenting green berets to Commandos on completion of their course.[86]

The Admiralty film followed the line of much of the public information released about the Commandos from late 1942 in stressing their disciplined and professional approach based on intensive training. The ruthless and unsavoury side to their genesis, the facet which generated public fascination in the first months of their creation, was largely absent; there was no longer any trace of Churchill's 'reign of terror'. The change of emphasis reflected the more positive war situation, and the broader purposes to which special service forces were being directed in consequence. It was also a response to the extent to which the enemy had already digested the original Commando message. One outcome of raiding operations during 1942 was a reaction from German High Command against the methods of their British Commando foes. After the Dieppe raid the Germans discovered the bodies of a dozen of their own men whose hands had been tied before they were killed. Only weeks later the German garrison in the occupied Channel Islands made a similar discovery after a British raid on the Island of Sark by the Small Scale Raiding Force.[87] The shooting of bound prisoners, even if as a consequence of attempts to escape, provoked understandable outrage. The strength of enemy feelings became apparent when deportations and other reprisals were enacted against the civilian population of the Channel Islands.

In the darker days of 1940 that gave birth to the Commando idea, the bitterness of the German reaction might have been taken from the British perspective as welcome evidence that raiding activity was having the desired effect on enemy morale. In the changing war situation of late 1942, it looked unnecessary, counterproductive even. Unknown to British intelligence at the time, the enemy had taken its grievance further. On 18 October 1942 Adolf Hitler issued a personal Führer Order to the headquarters of the German Army to the effect that prisoners from Commandos and other sabotage units of British or Allied forces captured during raids were to be summarily executed. This was not to apply to those captured during large-scale attacks or major assault landings, but death was to be the immediate fate of all prisoners from sabotage and raiding parties irrespective of whether or not they were carrying arms or wearing uniform.[88] Although the order was not adhered to in every case of capture thereafter, it cost many men their lives.

The hard line against British raiding forces did not, however, mean that the German Army itself eschewed the use of commando-style tactics. Projected raids by highly trained 'Brandenburger' special units formed part of the Operation *Seelöwe* (*Sealion*) plan to invade the British mainland in 1940, and these operations were intended to include infiltration behind British lines by Brandenburgers wearing British uniforms. In the event, following the cancellation of *Seelöwe*, only a single German commando attack was carried out on British soil, later acknowledged by a senior British Commando officer as 'one absolutely splendid raid carried out by the Germans from the Channel islands ... we were rather jealous of it, it went very well indeed'. This is believed to have been an attack against a radar station on the south coast of the Isle of Wight, launched from the occupied Channel Island of Alderney in 1941.[89]

* * *

Achnacarry was the means by which Commando soldiers were shaped, and the bar by which they were measured, but emerging needs for more specialised roles spawned two further Commando training centres in the Scottish highlands during 1942. The first was just outside the Argyll village of Ardentinny, at the mouth of Glenfinart on the shores of Loch Long, another sea loch giving out to the Firth of Clyde. One of the weaknesses exposed in the failure of the Dieppe raid was an insufficient level of organisation and communication on the landing beaches. It had previously been recognised that the role of the Royal Navy at the sharp end of a major Combined Operation could not simply end when Commando or other assault forces were delivered from their landing craft on to the beach. After an attack went in, the beachhead would necessarily remain crucial. The beach had to be secured and made safe from obstructions and hazards in order to be clear for subsequent attack waves who, as they disembarked, would need intelligence about progress and enemy dispositions. The beach also had to be made ready to receive the wounded and enemy prisoners back towards evacuation and, if necessary, to accommodate a withdrawal by reloading landing craft from the beach.

To these ends the Royal Navy formed dedicated Beach Parties, whose special training took them to the Combined Training Centres at Loch Fyne, the coasts of Ayrshire and Dumfriesshire, and the Isle of Arran, to exercise in conjunction with the Army. An important element in beach organisation was communication between naval and military elements. The requirement was tackled early in 1942 by forming specialised Royal Naval Beach Signals units at Combined Signals Schools at Inveraray and a new naval shore establishment near Troon, HMS *Dundonald*. Beach Signals training from late 1942 was also carried out at HMS *Dorlin*, where at least one unit heard lectures on survival from Surgeon Commander Murray Levick.[90]

Despite the importance of this beachhead interface between naval and military forces, and a notable success in the operation to capture the Madagascar port of Diego Suarez in May 1942, the new Royal Naval Beach Parties were not at first a popular branch of the service. Naval officers and ratings were reluctant to give up seagoing status for what appeared to be a support unit for the Army. Combined Operations Command decided to develop and better organise the beach co-ordination role, and quickly recognised that the function had to be made more attractive to volunteers. To emphasise their fighting status and importance in landing operations, where indeed they might be first onto the beaches, Mountbatten suggested that the Beach Parties should be seen to enter the magic circle of special operations by being renamed Royal Naval Commandos.[91] While this change to organisation and image was being enacted, the Royal Navy Beach Parties at Dieppe faced the exacting and terrifying reality of controlling beaches as a landing operation unravelled around them. On the beaches where opposition was heaviest, the sailors persevered in their tasks of organisation and evacuating the wounded, whilst themselves sustaining casualties under heavy fire. As the Canadian and British assault infantry were forced to retire and defend themselves on the beach, the men of the Beach Parties fought beside them. A third of the manpower of more than 200 naval personnel who landed were left behind as casualties or prisoners.

The Dieppe experience firmly underlined that the beach role was a fighting one, and one that needed a capability and versatility similar to that expected of Army Commandos. The Beach Parties were to be re-organised into Royal Naval Commandos comprising ten officers and 66 ratings, under the command of a Principal Beachmaster, a Royal Navy officer of commander or lieutenant-commander rank. This establishment was deemed sufficient to deliver an infantry brigade in a landing craft assault and perform all the functions a changing situation could require of it.[92] Twenty-two such Royal Naval (RN) Commando units were to form, each assigned an alphabetical designation usually expressed using the services' phonetic alphabet. The RN Commandos were recruited in part from officers and ratings who volunteered specifically for the job, but also through drafting men who had volunteered for Combined Operations duties in general or by compulsory drafting of RN recruits direct from entry training. The last to be formed, 'W' or 'William' RN Commando, was recruited entirely from the Royal Canadian Navy and its Volunteer Reserve.[93]

To support this new organisation the RN Commandos were allocated a holding base and training centre of their own, HMS *Armadillo* at the edge of Ardentinny on Loch Long. Headquarters and wardroom were in Glenfinart House, since demolished. The main accommodation was a nearby forestry camp built as a relief measure during the economic depression of the 1930s in an area to the west of Glenfinart Bay called 'The Grotto'. This timber camp was supplemented by new Nissen hut structures until it could hold up to 600 all ranks. All RN shore stations were required to carry a ship's name. The choice of *Armadillo* in this instance is reputed to derive from the involvement of Assistant Training Officer

Lieutenant Roger Wake who chose the location and, to help enliven the surroundings, offered to bring along a stuffed armadillo lying neglected at his parents' house. History records, however, that the armadillo in question never arrived, and it must be noted that other Combined Operations shore stations of the day carried names of similar inspiration, such as HMS *Manatee* on the Isle of Wight and HMS *Brontosaurus* at Castle Toward on the Clyde. The name might therefore have brought this piece of taxidermy to mind.[94]

RN Commando training at HMS *Armadillo* naturally placed emphasis on the arts of landing craft disembarkation and re-embarkation, crossing and clearing barbed wire and beach obstacles, and the other skills especially required for the beachhead role. But much of the specialised and collective training of the beachhead Commando was inculcated at other Combined Training Centres after completion of his individual training at Ardentinny.[95] In its general approach to individual fitness, endurance and adaptability, *Armadillo* took its lead from the toughening and testing ethos of Achnacarry. The camp at Ardentinny had its own assault courses and ranges, and the hills above Glenfinart became the scene for the customary Commando diet of endurance marching, fieldcraft, weapons-training and rock-climbing. Close combat and shooting on the Fairbairn-Sykes principle also featured. A swim in full kit across Loch Long from Ardentinny to Coulport on the eastern shore was another element of the course, one that might be followed by a long march in wet clothing back to Ardentinny, north around Loch Long and Loch Goil.[96] Photographs of RN Commandos in individual training differ from those of their Achnacarry counterparts principally in the dark sailor's caps worn by the naval trainees, a last vestige of naval uniform worn with their army battle dress uniforms and personal equipment.

At some stage in up to 14 weeks of individual training, RN Commando trainees were likely to find themselves at Achnacarry itself, where a completion course was devised for their benefit condensed from the full Achnacarry syllabus down to 143 training sessions of 40 minutes' duration.[97] At the end of this further examination, the sailors who lasted the course received their green berets and Fairbairn-Sykes Commando knives from Lieutenant-Colonel Vaughan, just as their Army and Royal Marine counterparts did. As facilities at *Armadillo* developed, the Navy's reliance on further training at Achnacarry diminished, but Vaughan and his staff were frequent visitors to Ardentinny, observing and advising.

For RN Commandos who completed their individual training without recourse to Achnacarry, Vaughan arrived to present green berets and knives at *Armadillo*'s own passing out parades. With their training heightened in this way, and their consequent status as fully-fledged Commandos affording them greater visibility and respect within the Combined Operations structure, RN Commandos became an essential component working with Military Beach Groups in the larger assault landings that were conducted in North Africa, Europe and Burma from late 1942.

Like the Royal Navy, the Royal Air Force (RAF) adapted some Commando methods in order to contribute to Combined Operations on the greater scale. In January 1942 the RAF formed a number of small Commando units of its own. The job of the RAF Servicing Commando Units was to ensure front-line air cover for an invasion force by landing and advancing with it to man temporary airstrips and captured enemy airfields. The units would fuel, service and re-arm aircraft in these front-line airfields and, if necessary, fight to defend them from enemy counter attack. This was a role the RAF concluded required a select force trained along Commando lines. Like the RN Commandos, the RAF Servicing Commandos wore army battle dress with Combined Operations shoulder badges in addition to their own insignia. Fifteen units of around 150 officers and men formed in total, and contributed successfully to invasion operations in the Mediterranean, north-west Europe and the Far East.[98]

For those Servicing Commando Units formed in the UK, training involved an introductory 'toughening' course held on RAF bases, but overseen by instructors borrowed from the Army Commandos. Those airmen who passed the first stage proceeded to the Combined Training Centre at Inveraray to learn how to work with the landing craft in which they and their equipment would arrive on invasion beaches. Two weeks of work on Loch Fyne progressed to landing exercises with a final stage of rehearsals on the Ayrshire coast at Troon. Unlike their RN counterparts, the Commandos of the RAF did not develop their own special training centre.[99]

The Ardentinny version of Commando training served to make one further RN contribution to landing operations. Something akin to the Army Commando canoeists begun by Courtney on Arran, the Combined Operations Pilotage Parties (COPP) were small teams of canoe specialists deployed from early 1943 to conduct clandestine reconnaissance of enemy-held beaches from small craft as part of planning for landing operations. The COPP units brought together men from the Army and the Royal Navy. In addition to their boat training, each individual 'COPPist' had to pass through Commando training before allocation to a COPP. The soldiers went to Achnacarry; the sailors to four weeks at HMS *Armadillo*.[100] COPP work was highly specialised and hazardous. In the eyes of Combined Operations Command, the training regime developed at Ardentinny had achieved parity with its celebrated mentor in Lochaber.

* * *

The second specialist Commando school to open in the highlands in 1942 served rather a different function. Far removed from the beaches of Argyll, this was established in December at the eastern edge of the Cairngorm mountains, at Braemar on the River Dee. Its purpose was to train Commandos for operations in Norway, and to enhance Commando know-how in winter warfare generally. No further operations on the scale of the 1941 Lofoten and Vågsøy raids were in the pipeline; but while the main focus of planning was moving elsewhere, the intention was to keep the German garrison in Norway in a high state of alert by way of small raids that would disrupt and destroy valuable industrial resources where possible. In the autumn of 1942 a small sabotage party drawn from No.2 Commando and two Norwegian NCOs attacked and damaged a power station at Glomfjord in the Narvik area. The team landed from a submarine, then undertook a difficult approach to its target across mountainous winter country. For those who escaped capture after the attack, an epic journey to the Swedish border was their route to safety.[101] With a view to directing further similar attacks against German air bases in Arctic Norway, Mountbatten considered that operations of this kind required a greater degree of specialisation and so ordered the creation of 'North Force' to train for the role. A Troop from No.12 Commando was already based at Lerwick in Shetland, and this force was strengthened by the local knowledge and winter experience of a party drawn from the Norwegian Troop of No.10 Inter-Allied Commando. In addition, an entirely new unit was raised as No.14 Commando. Only two Troops strong, and consisting of small-boat and skiing specialists, No.14 Commando was led by Scottish mountaineer and former STC Lochailort instructor Lieutenant Colonel E. A. M. (Sandy) Wedderburn.

At this point the War Office was already at work developing mountain warfare capability outside the field of special service and Combined Operations. Despite experience of a campaign fought in the foothills of the Italian Alps during the First World War, the practice of mountain warfare in the British Army had never developed much beyond the long-standing imperial mountain artillery units deployed on the frontiers of India. In August 1941 the Prime Minister ordered that at least one infantry division should be trained in the mountain role. In order to meet this considerable undertaking, the War Office turned to some of the leading pre-war British mountaineers who had been offering advice in this area of potential operations since the beginning of the war. Among them was the Himalayan climber and celebrated mountaineering author F. S. (Frank) Smythe, who since 1939 had been working for the War Office on the design of winter clothing and equipment. Brigadier Robert Laycock, Commander of the Special Service Brigade, therefore asked Smythe to create a new winter training centre for the Commandos and gave him a free hand to choose where it should be. Smythe settled on the same range of hills that the Army was already using to train its mountain troops.

At that time Frank Smythe was, in a literal sense, the world's top mountaineer, in that he had been higher on a mountain than any other man. In his summit attempt with Eric Shipton during the 1933 British Everest Expedition, Smythe was stopped only by deteriorating snow conditions and unacceptable risk to solo climbing at 28,100 feet, less than 1000 feet from the summit. This was only the height of a mountaineering career of Himalayan and Alpine ascents and ski-tours that Smythe shared with a wide readership through his numerous popular books. During the 1920s Smythe briefly served in the RAF and it was in the rank of squadron leader that he based himself at Braemar on Deeside as the commanding officer of the new Commando Mountain and Snow Warfare Training Centre.

The Cairngorm mountains above Braemar do not have the extensive ridge systems and abundant rock-climbing challenges sought out by Wedderburn in his earlier Commando climbing courses on the Cuillin of Skye, on Ben Nevis, and in Glencoe. But the expansive granite uplands of the Cairngorms offered great remoteness, treacherous snow gullies among the corries of the great hills, and the most challenging weather conditions to be found in the United Kingdom. In winter the wind and snows over the exposed high ground are at times Arctic in character. In summer, with little warning, conditions on occasion can be much the same. Here more than anywhere, winter snow cover is likely to be found. In topography, flora and weather, the Cairngorms gave a training area as closely equivalent to Norwegian terrain as was available. With great distances to be covered across high plateaux, and few natural aids to navigation, this was potentially an ideal setting in which to rehearse long cross-country patrols on foot and ski.

To the north-west of the range, the infantry and artillery units of 52nd (Lowland) Division were well into their work to become one of the Army's new mountain formations. Smythe chose to base his Commando centre on the eastern side, at Braemar and along Glen Clunie. To serve as headquarters, he set in train the requisition of the Fife Arms Hotel, one of the large Victorian resort establishments that dominate the village of Braemar. As a further base, he took over a shooting lodge belonging to the Invercauld estate. No longer standing, the lodge was five miles south of Braemar down the Clunie Water, beyond which the road rises to over 2000 feet. While he waited for the property requisition process to be completed, Smythe scouted out the hills and corries to inform a general scheme of training. In this reconnaissance he had the guidance of Lieutenant W. M. Mackenzie, recruited from the instructional staff at Achnacarry. Mackenzie had been an officer in No.2 Commando, arriving by way of the 5th Scots Guards ski battalion. As one of the leading lights in the Scottish Mountaineering Club, and with a particular interest in skiing, he knew the Cairngorm terrain.[102]

Using personal contacts and a War Office list of recommended mountaineers compiled by fellow Himalayan climber Noel Odell, Smythe recruited more mountain and skiing expertise for his instructional staff.[103] The Chief Instructor was to be Major John Hunt, a Regular Army officer and experienced Alpine and Himalayan climber. After the war, Hunt's climbing career would culminate in leadership of the successful British and Commonwealth Everest Expedition of 1953, but one of his qualifications for the Braemar role in 1943 was that he was already, at his own instigation, running 'toughening' courses in the mountains of North Wales for 20th Armoured Brigade.[104] Among those brought in to assist Hunt at Braemar were fellow Alpine Club member Captain David Cox, and the polar explorer and ornithologist Lieutenant David Haig-Thomas.[105] Together with Mackenzie, these pre-war mountaineers first trained a cadre of under-instructors, and prepared to receive their first intake for North Force.

By the time Braemar was ready to receive Commandos for training, North Force consisted of two troops of No.12 Commando and a party from the Norwegian troop of No.10 Inter-Allied Commando. Only a handful of skiers from Wedderburn's No.14 Commando were involved, joined by some intelligence-gathering specialists from No.30 Commando.[106] The first trainees to arrive at Braemar were two Troops from No.12 Commando. Unfortunately, the anticipated skiing conditions failed to materialise. Only for a week or two did sufficient snow gather to allow a little skiing on the slopes of Glas Maol and the Devil's Elbow down into Glenshee; images of their efforts were captured by Smythe whose talent for photography illustrated his own mountaineering books. Smythe's pictures show staff and trainees wearing the hooded smocks and trousers in windproof material that he had earlier helped the War Office to procure for its mountain troops. The woollen 'cap, comforters' beloved of Commandos are shown still to be in favour, and all are carrying their personal loads in Bergen rucksacks. On and off skis, cleated boots either of standard army 'ammunition' issue or of specialist mountaineering design, were worn with short puttees fitted over the top to keep the insides clear of snow.

In the absence of deep snow, training was conducted on foot over rocks and wet heather in the strength-sapping hold of high winds, which seemed hardly to abate over weeks. On one occasion the winds caused the slightly-built commanding officer a little trouble in front of his No.12 Commando charges:

> We had set off from Derry Lodge, each man carrying some 70 lb. of food and equipment with the intention of camping for a week by Loch Etchachan. In Glen Derry it was merely blowing the usual gale, but when we turned the corner into Corrie Etchachan we encountered a hurricane. As we mounted the slopes towards the loch the fury of the storm grew and veritable tornadoes of sleet and hail swept down the glen. I was ahead prospecting for a suitable camping site, and behind me was the leading section, which was commanded by a certain cockney sergeant, one of those humorous grumblers that for generations have been the backbone of the British Army .... Of a sudden a gust whirled me off my feet and flung me violently down on a rock several yards away. As I lay recovering my wind, which had been knocked completely out of me, I saw the section in single

file manfully toiling up towards me. Then came another gust which lifted every man off his feet. As they slowly struggled upright there was a momentary lull and in it I heard the voice of the sergeant: "'e can 'ave 'is Everest, every ———— inch of it!'[107]

Navigation, rations, load-carrying, and high bivouac, were taught in sessions during these trips and, as elsewhere, the courses concluded with a full-blown tactical exercise over a number of days where live-firing and explosives were employed.

All told, the Braemar experiment was not a huge success. Bad luck with the weather meant that although conditions were extreme enough to give a grounding in arctic warfare, the Commandos made no advance on skis. The previous winter there had been snow a-plenty on the Scottish hills, and No.3 Commando had managed an essay in skiing in the hills above Killin in Perthshire as late in 1942 as March.[108] The winter after the Braemar episode brought sufficient snow for 52nd (Lowland) Division to train on skis and snowshoes in major exercises across the Cairngorms. But as the winter days of early 1943 lengthened into spring, the impetus of 'North Force' melted away with the shortage of night cover for special operations, though not before several minor actions against targets in southern Norway had been launched from the Shetland base. For the Braemar staff there was a sense of frustration that the six weeks available to each course was not sufficient to instil the necessary competence in mountain navigation and survival. Guided by his conviction that 'the secret of success in mountain training is to teach the men to enjoy it. It must never be allowed to become a toughening course – that is the worst possible psychology', Smythe took a gentle approach and sought to impart his love of mountain country by leading long treks through the hills. Chief Instructor John Hunt complemented Smythe's unwillingness to conform to a narrow military approach to the task, by instilling the level of physical rigour expected of Commando training.[109]

Its future role unclear, the Commando Mountain and Snow Warfare Training Centre persevered at Braemar through spring 1943, with intakes from Nos 1 and 4 Commando who were sent as part of their general training programme. In May the Centre was wound up and the staff transferred from the Scottish highlands to a new base at Capel Curig in North Wales to devote themselves to teaching Commandos rock-climbing. The North Wales training school endured little longer than its progenitor at

Braemar, and in December 1943 it moved to St Ives in Cornwall to concentrate on cliff assault from the sea under the command of former Braemar instructor Major Geoffrey Rees-Jones. Among those it had already introduced to the Welsh crags in the intervening months was the whole strength of the Lovat Scouts. Lord Lovat had not forgotten his family regiment, and in late 1942 he went the length of direct personal appeals to the King and the Prime Minister to see the Scouts put to the sort of role he felt they merited.[110] Lovat received a sympathetic hearing, but no place could be made for the regiment either as a Commando, or as a battalion of the mountain-trained 52nd (Lowland) Division. At last the Lovat Scouts were designated a special high-mountain unit, a role which soon afterwards took them to another training centre directed by Smythe, this time in the Canadian Rockies.

*　*　*

Braemar was the last of the wartime Commando training centres to open in the Scottish highlands. During 1943 Allied strategic planning was concentrating around the great objective of a major landing on the coast of France. It had been decided that if Commandos were not to be reduced or disbanded altogether, their future must lie in expansion towards the role of assault infantry, landing from the sea at the spearhead of major attacks, leading river crossings, and operating on the flanks of infantry formations.[111] It was this decision that had brought the additional RM Commandos into being and into training at Achnacarry. The need for small raids continued through 1943 and a series was launched against the French coast with the purpose of obtaining information about enemy defences and the suitability of possible landing sites. But from January 1944, as the planned invasion drew close, small raiding was largely discontinued on the grounds that provoking further strengthening of enemy defences in response would be counterproductive to the main operation.

With the additional capacity given by the entry of the Royal Marines, the Commandos were ultimately to form into four Special Service Brigades each made up of at least four Commando units.[112] Each Brigade was organised and equipped to fight in co-operation with conventional infantry and, henceforth, not necessarily to withdraw after an attack. In their incarnation as assault infantry, Commandos landed on the shores of

Tunisia, Sicily and the Italian mainland before 1943 was out, forming into 2 Special Service Brigade for further action in Italy and the Balkans. 3 Special Service Brigade departed the United Kingdom in November 1943 for action in Burma, which culminated in intense fighting against the Japanese after landings in the Myebon peninsula in January 1945. Then 4 Special Service Brigade landed on the Normandy beaches from 6 June 1944 and fought through northern France to the River Seine, before re-grouping for amphibious landings on the Dutch island of Walcheren and sustained engagement along the River Maas into 1945.

Also landing on the Normandy beaches was 1st Special Service Brigade which successfully neutralised its 'D-Day' targets before pushing inland on the eastern flank of the general advance along the River Orne, and resisting heavy counter-attacks. Withdrawn from this front, the Brigade's subsequent campaign in Germany saw its troops involved in assault crossings over five rivers before finally reaching the Baltic in May 1945. Commanding the Brigade until he was wounded six days after D-Day was Brigadier Lord Lovat, famously accompanied by the music of his 'personal' piper. This unofficial position with Brigade headquarters was taken up by former member of the Achnacarry demonstration troop, Piper Bill Millin. The imagery of the Scottish clan chief leading Commandos into action to the sound of the pipes is part of the abiding iconography of D-Day, not least thanks to its featuring in the Hollywood screen adaptation of war correspondent Cornelius Ryan's classic reportage, 'The Longest Day'.[113]

The story of the major Commando operations of the Second World War has been told in detail elsewhere in unit histories and general studies, and forms no part of this brief account of their Scottish training.[114] But Achnacarry endured as the Commando Basic Training Centre supplying the trained manpower the Commandos needed to sustain their solid performance in this role.[115] Rehearsals for operations continued at the established Combined Training Centres, and over temporary training areas which in Scotland included a sweep of the Moray coast where No.4 Commando exercised with the Royal Navy and 3rd British Infantry Division in the run-up to the D-Day landings. But if the effective and courageous performance of the Special Service/Commando Brigades in action from late 1943-45 was a vindication of their years of hard training in the Scottish highlands and other parts of the United Kingdom, fighting of this kind was also something rather removed from their 1940 inception as raiders and guerrilla fighters. So different had their role become that, despite the undoubted achievements of the brigades during 1943-45, those within the Army who doubted the necessity of maintaining a separate organisation for the specialised Commando function remained unconvinced.

Those who felt that a normal infantry unit ought to be capable of conducting all but the most specialised of small raiding operations included some of the most senior and successful British soldiers of the war, such as Field Marshal Viscount Slim who masterminded the British victory in Burma. Of the strategic value of special service units, including the 'Chindit' long-range penetration columns that contributed to the Burma victory, Slim was, and remained, sceptical:

> Any well-trained infantry battalion should be able to do what a commando can do; in the Fourteenth Army they could and did. This cult of special forces is as sensible as to form a Royal Corps of Tree Climbers and say that no soldier, who does not wear its green hat with a bunch of oak-leaves stuck in it, should be expected to climb a tree.[116]

Leading figures in the Commandos could counter that an infantry battalion organised, trained and equipped for Commando warfare would in consequence be weakened in doing its infantry job: competent at one or the other perhaps, but excellent at neither.[117] But the feelings against the Army Commando organisation won the day. At the end of the war, the Chiefs of Staff of the armed services decided that the Commandos' amphibious strike role should carry forward with the Royal Marines and not the Army. The Royal Marines were to form three Commando units on a permanent footing for peacetime service, defined by the officer commanding the Corps of Royal Marines as 'a lightly equipped infantry unit, with a minimum administrative tail, trained for cliff and assault landings on different natures of beach. They may be employed in raids, on special tasks in a major assault – such as the capture of a flank coastal battery, as at Dieppe – or in the seizure of a port.'[118] Despite the efforts of the departing Chief of Combined Operations Major-General Robert Laycock to preserve them, the Army Commandos were no more.[119] The Commando Basic Training Centre at Achnacarry closed down with them and its function was taken over by the Royal Marines Training Group at

Tywyn on Cardigan Bay in Wales, forerunner of the Commando Training Centre at Lympstone in Devon which functions today.

Notable from the perspective of the present study, those who held against the maintenance of Commando forces as part of the Army numbered among them one former commanding officer of the Special Training Centre Lochailort. Lieutenant-Colonel J. P. O'Brien Twohig succeeded Lieutenant-Colonel Stockwell at Lochailort in April 1941. From his observations there, and from his experience of more orthodox infantry operations, he contended that the manner of organising Commandos outlasted its usefulness beyond the initial period in 1940 when small raids were the only offensive operations possible:

> ... instead of forming a magnificent training and battle school for junior leaders of the field army, the Commandos hardened into a specialised unit which demanded the best of the field army and returned nothing but its rejects. Intentionally or otherwise it developed into a 'shock troop' unit, something on the German pattern, but remained organised on British civil billets and incapable of looking after itself in the field for any length of time.[120]

Twohig's emphasis towards improving the training standard of the orthodox infantry battalion did not, however, mean that the two had been, or had to be, mutually exclusive. In the course of the war there was a useful cross-fertilisation of training innovation between special service and more orthodox warfare. Realistic battle training of the type pioneered at STC Lochailort flourished, not just in the Commando and Combined Operations organisations, but in numerous battle schools that from 1941 sprung up to serve formations of the field army. Indeed, so far was British tactical training invigorated across the Army that in late summer 1942 the War Office decided that the Special Training Centre Lochailort had outlived its usefulness. The Big House at Inverailort closed its doors on the Army for the last time on 20 August 1942 amidst highland ceremony and a send-off from the local population.[121]

It was not yet time, however, for the Cameron-Heads to resume occupancy of their ancestral home. The training facilities vacated by the Army were instead handed directly on to the Admiralty. Forthwith, and until the end of January 1945, the Royal Navy ran the centre as HMS *Lochailort*, a training school for naval cadet-ratings who were to be officers 'in Combined Operations ships and craft only'. HMS *Lochailort* existed for longer than the Special Training Centre, and it is from this second incarnation that interior evidence of the wartime occupation of Inverailort survives today.[122] If the administration, staff and purpose of the Centre changed in 1942, there was nevertheless a notable degree of continuity in its methods. HMS *Lochailort* was not a place for specialised naval training. It was essentially a toughening centre, a test of individual mettle of the cadet-ratings. Many of these had yet to serve at sea and little was done at Lochailort on the water; the syllabus was a familiar one of running, climbing, river-crossing and physical training using the existing facilities, natural and man-made. If the cadet-ratings passed the test, they went on to learn their landing craft trade elsewhere as newly commissioned officers.[123]

Habits established in the experimental days of summer 1940 died hard at Lochailort. Nevertheless, after providing the prototype for Achnacarry and foreshadowing the growth of tactical training for battle throughout the army, STC Lochailort was eclipsed by the changing circumstances of the war and by evolution in the special service and field army organisations that had to fight it. The original impetus at Lochailort in the MI(R) days of Mayfield, Stirling and Lord Lovat had been towards small-scale guerrilla warfare and sabotage operations. These skills had since been carried forward as part of the Commando repertoire, albeit an element whose relative importance diminished as the war progressed. But the priority of MI(R) had been towards the support and encouragement of resistance organisations in foreign countries under enemy occupation. Although MI(R) gave birth to Lochailort with this objective still very much in mind, as early as July 1940 responsibility for planning and operations in this area were passing to a new agency into which MI(R) was later absorbed. This was Special Operations Executive (SOE), a clandestine organisation that functioned separately from the Combined Operations structure and reported directly to the government.[124] SOE had its own precise requirements and developed a sophisticated training structure to suit. Its function required officers who could survive on their own initiative in hostile territory, win the confidence of local resistance movements and train them to carry out sabotage raids. To train new officers for this highly individual and dangerous work, SOE looked anew at the west highlands of Scotland, and established itself just a few miles up the road from Lochailort.

NOTES TO PART TWO

1. D. Gilchrist: *Castle Commando* (Edinburgh: Oliver & Boyd, 1960), pp. 3-4.
2. Speech to the House of Commons, 13 May 1940. W. Churchill (ed.): *Never Give In. The Best of Winston Churchill's Speeches* (London: Pimlico, 2003), pp. 204-206).
3. Cabinet records, National Archives, Kew, CAB 120/414.
4. Ibid.
5. D. Reitz: *Commando* (London: Faber & Faber, 1932). Clark's account is in Defence Committee records, National Archives, Kew, DEFE 2/4.
6. The term 'Commando' was applied both to a formed Commando unit and to an individual Commando officer or soldier. For clarity, 'Commando unit', 'Commando officer' and 'Commando soldier' are used wherever appropriate in this text.
7. Interview with Tommy Macpherson, Imperial War Museum Sound Archive, 17912, Reel 1, 1998.
8. John S. MacKay: transcript of interview with the National War Museum, 13 February 2003.
9. R. Laycock: 'Raids in the Late War and their Lessons', in *Journal of the Royal United Service Institution* [RUSI Journal], November 1947, pp. 534-35. CQMS was a Company Quarter-Master Sergeant, a fixture of conventional infantry organisation. The author of this outline study was Major-General Robert Laycock, Independent Company Commander in 1940, leader of the Commando force despatched to the Middle East in 1941 and, from late 1943, Chief of Combined Operations.
10. Memorandum of Major General R. H. Dewing, Director of Military Operations and Plans, 13 June 1940, War Office records, National Archives, Kew, WO 193/384.
11. Layock: op. cit., pp. 530-37.
12. War Office records, National Archives, Kew, WO 26/11
13. 'Commando Training Instruction No.1', War Office records, National Archives, Kew, WO 33/668.
14. 'Special Service Brigade Spring Training Instructions 1941', Montanaro Papers 3, 101/G/2, Trustees of the Liddell Hart Centre for Military Archives, King's College London.
15. John S. MacKay: op. cit.
16. J. Dunning: *It Had To Be Tough. The fascinating story of the origins of the Commandos and their special training in World War II* (Durham: Pentland Press, 2000), pp. 42-43.
17. Quoted in E. Keyes: *Geoffrey Keyes* V.C., M.C. *Croix de guerre, Royal Scots Greys, Lieut. Colonel 11th Scottish Commando* (London: George Newnes, 1956), p. 137.
18. This exercise was conducted by 'X' Organisation of the Marine Naval Base Organisation, which experimented with the landing of guns over improvised piers. It was the forerunner of the original combined operations development establishment at Fort Cumberland, Eastney. See J. Ladd: *The Royal Marines 1919-1980* (London: Jane's, 1980), pp. 46-47.

19. Interview with Tommy Macpherson, Imperial War Museum Sound Archive, 17912, Reel 1, 1998.

20. This and previous two quotes: John S. MacKay: op. cit.

21. 'No.4 Commando's original badge', Notes in *The Bulletin of the Military Historical Society*, vol. 44, no. 173, August 1993, pp. 50-53.

22. In June 1941 this tune was renamed 'Colonel Pedder' in memory of No.11 Commando's commanding officer, killed in action during a raid in Syria.

23. John S. MacKay: op. cit.

24. Captain Geoffrey Keyes, quoted in E. Keyes: op. cit., p. 145.

25. Ibid., pp. 145-46. Carley floats were simple rubber life rafts, part of the life-saving equipment of most vessels.

26. '101 Troop Training Programme', Montanaro Papers, 3 101/G/2, Trustees of the Liddell Hart Centre for Military Archives, King's College London.

27. The Glen Line was acquired by Alfred Holt & Co. in 1936, but continued under the Glen name. Information on the three Glenearn class ships kindly supplied to the National War Museum by Mr W. Grant of Oban War & Peace Museum.

28. J. Dunning: *The Fighting Fourth. No.4 Commando at War 1940-45* (Stroud: Sutton Publishing, 2003), p. 9.

29. From January 1941 this was 1441 Combined Operations Group, based first at RAF Abbotsinch (now Glasgow Airport), then at RAF Dundonald. In April 1943 the expanded unit was redesignated 516 Combined Operations Squadron.

30. This and previous quote from J. Dunning: op. cit., 2003, pp. 19-20.

31. Unpublished memoir courtesy of Mr Hilary King CBE, Isle of Luing, per Mr W. Grant, Oban War & Peace Museum. 'ALCs' were Assault Landing Craft, 'MLCs' Motorised Landing Craft. Major Eric Cole, Royal Corps of Signals was the training instructor of B1 (Beach) Signal Section.

32. E. Waugh: *Officers and Gentlemen. A novel* (London: Chapman and Hall, 1955).

33. M. Davie (ed.): *The diaries of Evelyn Waugh* (London: Wiedenfeld and Nicolson, 1976), pp. 492-93.

34. Quoted in Keyes: op. cit., p. 181.

35. Standing Order by Captain G. C. S. Montanaro concerning game shooting and fishing, 17 June 1941, Montanaro Papers, 3 101/G/2, Trustees of the Liddell Hart Centre for Military Archives, King's College London.

36. Two of the four canoeists were captured during this operation. The next month much of 101 Troop was absorbed into No.2 Special Boat Section, a specialist raiding and beach reconnaissance unit led by Courtney that operated independently of the Commandos as part of the seaborne counterpart of the SAS. See G. Courtney: *SBS in World War Two. The story of the original Special Boat Section of the Army Commandos* (London: Robert Hale, 1983), p. 94.

37. Such prohibition was not, of course, always and universally followed, but those photographs of the original Special Training Centre that do exist are essentially amateur snapshots.

38. Imperial War Museum Photograph Archive, H 14597. Information about Colonel Jack Churchill courtesy of Mrs R. Churchill and Mr M. Churchill.

39. 'Special Service Brigade Spring Training Instructions' (1941): op. cit.

40. Exercise *Leapfrog* was intended to test a plan for landings in the Canary Islands, one of several options for amphibious operations against Atlantic Islands that were considered during 1941, without result.
41. Later Brigadier commanding 2 Commando Brigade in Italy and Greece.
42. Information from Major O'Donovan's son Tim O'Donovan, who lived and went to school locally while his father served at Lochailort, Inverlochy and Achnacarry. His boyhood photograph and scrap albums are a source of rare images of the Special Training Centre Lochailort.
43. This and previous quotes concerning Lochailort and Inveraray from Major R. A. C. Cameron MC DCM (Greece) MA in a letter to the National War Museum, 17 March 2002.
44. See, for example, his diary edit notes for 25 September 1941: '... I remained convinced till the end of the war that the commandos should never have been divorced from the army in the way they were. Each division should have been responsible for maintaining a divisional battle patrol capable of any commando work that might be asked of it.' A. Dabchev and D. Todman (eds) *War Diaries 1939-1945, Field Marshal Lord Alanbrooke* (London: Phoenix Press, 2002), p. 185.
45. Gaumont British News Issue 835, 'The Vaagsø Raid', Imperial War Museum Film and Video Archive, MGH 21.
46. J. Ladd: *Commandos and Rangers of World War II* (Book Club Associates, 1978), p. 34.
47. Officers received double the amount, which allowed many the choice of living in small hotels.
48. Unpublished memoir of Mr Henry Brown OBE, Ruislip, per Mr E. Allan of Irvine.
49. Letter of May D. Murray of Largs to the National War Museum, 27 July 2002.
50. Lord Lovat: *March Past* (London: Wiedenfeld and Nicolson, 1978), p. 229.
51. Later placed with the Commando Memorial in Westminster Abbey.
52. Now in the collection of the Clan Cameron Museum, Achnacarry.
53. J. Ladd: op. cit. (1978), pp. 169-70.
54. S. Chant-Sempill: *St Nazaire Commando* (London: John Murray,), p. 7.
55. Ibid., p. 10.
56. Items now in the possession of his son Lieutenant-Colonel the Honourable Ian Chant-Sempill.
57. A further three Victoria Crosses were awarded to Royal Navy officers for their part in the raid. Lieutenant Chant, No. 5 Commando, was awarded the Military Cross, which he received following repatriation from captivity on medical grounds in 1943.
58. The designation 'Royal Marines Commando' was originally used within the unit before the plural was dropped, and the term 'Royal Marine Commando' became for a time standard to all those formed.
59. J. Beadle: *The Light Blue Lanyard. Fifty Years with 40 Commando Royal Marines* (Worcester: Square One, 1992), pp. 8-10.
60. This was Operation *Agreement*, where the Commando forces that attacked Tobruk from the landward in advance of the amphibious landing were drawn

from remnants of 'Layforce' including former 'Scottish' Commandos. Most of the raiding force was taken prisoner, including Privates Allardice and MacKay quoted above.

61. The Achnacarry trainees from 40 RM Commando included 'T' Company, separated from the rest of the volunteers and allocated for operations in the Far East aboard the special service vessel HMS *Fidelity*. All 51 men of 'T' Company lost their lives when the *Fidelity* was torpedoed off the Azores (30 December 1942).

62. R. Mitchell: *They Did What Was Asked of Them. 41 (Royal Marines) Commando 1942-46* (Poole: Firebird Books, 1996), pp. 22-25.

63. Ministry of Defence records, National Archives, Kew, DEFE2/1134.

64. Lieutenant Richard Baxter, 45 RM Commando and instructor at the Commando Mountain Warfare Training Centre, St Ives. Film interview with the Reverend Richard Baxter OBE recorded for the 'Commando Country' exhibition, National War Museum, 2006.

65. The full training course originally devised ran for twelve weeks, but soon after this was condensed to a maximum of six weeks in most cases.

66. Baxter: op. cit.

67. M. Chauvet: *Commando Games. Training sketches for my fellow commandos and the little boys of England, 1943*, unpublished typescript with watercolour, pen and ink drawings. National Army Museum Department of Fine and Decorative Art, acc. no.8607-16. Amateur artist Chauvet was then serving as a Corporal in No.4 Commando.

68. This description of the layout of training at Achnacarry is based on that supplied by Major James Dunning's leaflet 'The Commando Trail', compiled for Lochaber Limited, Fort William and Lochaber Tourism Limited, and Lochaber District Council, supplied by the Clan Cameron Museum at Achnacarry. Description of the training syllabus is based on Dunning's *It Had To Be Tough*: op. cit., pp. 102-25 and the document 'Commando Basic Training Centre, Instructions and key to programme of work for intakes for Commandos, 14th July 1945', Commando Association papers, National Army Museum Department of Documents, 9203-218-2. The latter represents a final refinement of the Achnacarry syllabus for intakes training in advance of posting to the war against Japan.

69. J. Gibson: 'Commandos of Achnacarry' in *Scotland*, no. 63, May 1952, The Scottish Council (Development and Industry), pp. 11-12.

70. Baxter: op. cit.

71. 'Commando Basic Training Centre, Instructions and key to programme of work ….': op. cit.

72. Dunning: op. cit. (2000), pp. 115-16.

73. Ibid., p. 117.

74. J. Forfar: *From Omaha to the Scheldt. The Story of 47 Royal Marine Commando* (East Linton: Tuckwell Press, 2001), p. 14.

75. Dunning: op. cit. (2000), pp. 111-12.

76. Lord Lovat: op. cit. p. 281.

77. Later expanded to 1er Bataillon Fusilier Marin, distributed as two Troops of No.10 (Inter-Allied) Commando and one Troop attached to No.4 Commando.

78. Translated from M. Chauvet: *It's a long way to Normandy. 6 juin 1944* (Paris: Jean Piccolec, 2004), p. 141.

79. I. Dear: *Ten Commando 1942-45* (London: Leo Cooper, 1987), pp. 5-8.

80. The study was published as the pamphlet 'British Commandos', Military Intelligence Special Series 1, US War Department, 9 August 1942.

81. Darby was killed in action in Italy in April 1945.

82. Gilchrist: op. cit., pp. 74-95.

83. M. King: 'Rangers: Select Combat Operations in World War II', Leavenworth Paper no. 11, Combat Studies Institute, US Army Command and General Staff College, Fort Leavenworth, Kansas, June 1985.

84. J. Ferguson: 'Commando Exploit, July 1943', in *The Watch on the Braids. The Record of an Edinburgh Home Guard Company 1940-44* (Edinburgh: William Blackwood, pp. 146-53).

85. *The Times*, 8 May 1941, preserved in a file of cuttings kept by MI(R) and its successors. MI(R) papers in Special Operations Executive records, National Archives, Kew, HS8/260.

86. 'Commando – the Story of the Green Beret': Imperial War Museum Film and Video Archive, ADM 7072. Official photographs from the Imperial War Museum Photograph Archive.

87. The Small Scale Raiding Force raided across the English Channel during 1942 from a Motor Torpedo Boat. Its command responsibilities were jointly to Combined Operations and Special Operations Executive. In late 1942 it came under the command of Lieutenant-Colonel W. J. Stirling, formerly Chief Instructor at STC Lochailort.

88. Führer Order No.003830/42g.Kdos. OKW/WST translated in C. Messenger: *The Commandos 1940-46* (London: William Kimber, 1985), pp. 159-60.

89. Laycock: op. cit., p. 538.

90. D. Lee: *Beachhead Assault. The Story of the Royal Naval Commandos in World War II* (London: Greenhill, 2004), p. 49.

91. A. Cecil Hampshire: *The Beachhead Commandos* (London: William Kimber, 1983), pp. 46-47.

92. Ibid., p. 59.

93. E. Finley and E. Storey: 'Royal Canadian Naval Beach Commando "W"', in *Military Illustrated Past & Present*, no. 58, March 1993, pp. 34-45.

94. Lee: op. cit., p. 46.

95. Combined Operations file, 'Function and status of HMS *ARMADILLO* and training procedures for Naval Beach Commandos' in Admiralty records, National Archives, Kew, ADM1/12629.

96. Hampshire: op. cit., p. 61.

97. Ibid.

98. 'Servicing Commandos for Combined Operations', Jan-Mar. 1942, Air Ministry records, National Archives, Kew AIR9/641. See also J. Davies and J. Kellet: *A History of the RAF Servicing Commandos* (Shrewsbury: Airlife, 1989).

99. 'Servicing Commandos: Training Dec. 1942-May 1943, Air Ministry records, National Archives, Kew AIR39/118. See also T. Atkinson: *Spectacles, testicles,*

fags and matches. The untold story of the RAF Servicing Commandos in World War Two (Edinburgh: Luath Press, 2004), pp. 25-27.

100. I. Trenowden: *Stealthily By Night, The COPPists. Clandestine beach reconnaissance and operations in World War* II (Crécy Books, 1995), pp. 107-14.

101. Two officers captured after the raid became the first to be executed under the Führer order. Layock: op. cit. p. 537.

102. F. S. Smythe: 'Some experiences in mountain warfare training', in *The Alpine Journal*, vol. LV, no. 272, May 1946, pp. 233-40.

103. 'Personnel with mountaineering and skiing experience, Dec. 1939-Sept. 1943', War Office records, National Archives, Kew, WO193/21. Captain Noel Odell was a member of the British Everest Expedition of 1924 serving in late 1941 on the staff of the Future Operations and Plans branch of the War Office. This followed a brief stint as an instructor at STC Lochailort and a period on attachment to No.5 Commando at Falmouth advising on cliff assault techniques.

104. Hunt papers, Trustees of the Liddell Hart Centre for Military Archives, King's College London. See also R. Clark and E. Pyatt: *Mountaineering in Britain. A history from the earliest times to the present day* (London: Phoenix House, 1957), pp. 227-28.

105. Haig-Thomas later became an officer in No.4 Commando. Serving as a liaison officer to airborne forces, he was killed in action after parachuting into France in immediate advance of the D-Day landings.

106. No.30 Commando specialised in collecting papers, technical equipment and prisoners from enemy naval vessels, headquarters and installations.

107. Smythe: op. cit., p. 237.

108. Recorded by official photographer Lieutenant W. T. Lockeyear, Imperial War Museum Photograph Archive, H18098.

109. J. Hunt: *Life is Meeting* (London: Hodder and Stoughton, 1978), pp. 63-64. Hunt returned to the Cairngorms shortly after the Braemar centre's closure for some recreational climbing. A fall from Mitre Ridge of Beinn a' Bhuird in July 1943 left him with minor injuries.

110. Lord Lovat to the Prime Minister, 5 October 1942, in file 'Home Forces: location of divisions; employment of the Lovat Scouts; strength of the Dover garrison', Cabinet records, National Archives, Kew, CAB120/237.

111. Messenger: op. cit., pp. 241-43.

112. From late 1944 the Special Service Brigades were renamed Commando Brigades.

113. C. Ryan: *The Longest Day. June 6, 1944* (London: Victor Gollancz, 1960), pp. 176-77. The film adaptation produced by Darryl F. Zanuck was released in 1962. Piper Millin himself played the role. Millin published his own account in 1991, as B. Millin: *Invasion* (Lewes: Book Guild, 1991).

114. For an overview, see in particular Messenger: op. cit., 1985 and Ladd: op. cit., 1978.

115. The Commando Basic Training Centre at Achnacarry was disbanded with effect from 29 May 1946. War Office records, National Archives, Kew, WO379/115.

116. Field Marshal the Viscount Slim: *Defeat Into Victory* (London: Cassel, 1961), pp. 455-58.

117. Laycock: op. cit. pp. 530-31.

118. General Sir Dallas Brooks: 'The Royal Marines', *Journal of the Royal United Service Institution* [RUSI Journal], vol. XCIII, May 1948, no. 570, pp. 256-67.

119. Combined Operations file 'Disbandment of the Commando Group: Order of the Day', in Ministry of Defence records, DEFE/2/1325.

120. J. P. O'Brien Twohig: 'Are Commandos Really Necessary?', *Army Quarterly*, 1948, pp. 86-88. Twohig, like his predecessor, left Lochailort to take command of an orthodox infantry battalion. His successor, Lieutenant-Colonel Howard, was the last of four commanding officers.

121. Lieutenant-Colonel A. F. Austen MBE BEM: 'The Special Training Centre Lochailort, Inverness-shire, a Personal Memoir', Royal Signals Museum Archive, Ref. 936.4, p. 43.

122. I am most grateful to Miss Mackintosh, resident at Inverailort, for permission to view the inside of the house.

123. P. Lund and H. Ludlam: *The War of the Landing Craft* (London: W Foulsham & Co., 1976), pp. 81-91. See also 'Combined Operations: HMS LOCHAILORT' Admiralty records, National Archives, Kew, ADM1/14003.

124. The function was vested in a bureaux first designated SO2. See Part Three.

PART THREE

The Road to the Isles
SPECIAL OPERATIONS EXECUTIVE

> I thoroughly enjoyed that period of training. I can remember a splendid commanding officer called James Young who had two very simple principles and that was that young officers had to be able to dance an eightsome reel and drink a half bottle of whisky – and be on parade to climb mountains the next morning. It was really pretty strenuous stuff.

CAPTAIN PATRICK HOWARTH'S memory of one of Special Operations Executive's (SOE) paramilitary training schools in the Scottish highlands reflects the rather blithe tone in which the staff of that organisation were sometimes given to express its work, in deadly earnest though they were.[1] SOE's staff recruitment profile, inherited from the card-index and word of mouth approach of MI(R), lent its activities a certain rarefied atmosphere. The nature of its undercover work in enemy-occupied territory meant that success relied heavily on the individual ability and resourcefulness of its officers. Service in the field with SOE could be a leap into the unknown, quite literally on occasions when officers were dropped by parachute into occupied countries to make first contact locally. Organising and encouraging resistance networks was a job that required the officer to work on his (or her) own, or with a very small team, and to win the confidence of strangers to a sufficient degree that they could be directed into actions of great danger. SOE therefore prized individuality in a way that might have been frowned upon in more formal military circles.

For operational service in the field SOE recruited an extraordinary collection of volunteers. Many came from the British armed forces, others were brought in directly from civilian life on account of language skills or other aptitudes. Some were young and untested; others were experienced servicemen. Behind them was an organisation replete with men of international reach through the worlds of business, diplomacy and espionage.

Besides its British nationals, SOE oversaw the training and deployment of volunteers from the nations of occupied Europe, either as individuals or as small units of trained soldiers from Allied armies-in-exile stationed in the United Kingdom.

Somehow this eclectic grouping had to be made ready for operational objectives that were diverse and complex in themselves, and in the execution of which few in the organisation had any great experience at the outset. To such ambitious ends SOE developed an elaborate and flexible system of training, designed to test potential operational officers and teach them everything they might need to know in order to carry out and survive their mission. One aspect of this programme, particularly important for those without previous military experience, was 'paramilitary training' on guerrilla warfare lines. This would combine instruction in some of the skills pioneered at STC Lochailort with an individual toughening programme of the sort that the Commandos were developing. For all the reasons that brought MI(R) to Lochailort in the first place, it made sense to concentrate much of this element of SOE training in the Scottish highlands. By 1943 more than a dozen small highland properties were operating as Special Training Schools for SOE in conditions of high security and secrecy.

Much as was the case for the Commandos, SOE emerged in response to the extremity of the military situation that Britain faced in summer 1940, and took the form it did partly thanks to the personal patronage of Prime Minister Winston Churchill. As an entirely new organisation, throughout its short life SOE sailed a difficult course between the sensitivities of the British government's Secret Intelligence Service and the concerns of the conventional armed forces that resistance activity could be of little help, and potentially a hindrance, to military objectives. SOE began its existence as something of an accommodation between the competing claims of the Foreign Office and the War Office for primacy in the field of subversion and sabotage activity and, as a hybrid, was placed outside the control of either. In late July 1940 the heads of a constitution was agreed by the government, making a 'Special Operations Executive' tasked with activity in subversion, propaganda and planning, directly responsible to the Minister of Economic Warfare, Dr Hugh Dalton. Liaison with the armed forces and other government departments was a priority from the beginning and SOE's room for independent manoeuvre would never in practice be assured. The influence of the military Chiefs of Staff on its operations grew as the war progressed. Nevertheless, on 21 July 1940

Dalton was personally enjoined by the Prime Minister to 'go and set Europe ablaze'.[2]

The elements from which SOE was forged were three-fold. First was 'Section D', a small branch of the Secret Intelligence Service controlled by the Foreign Office. Set up in 1938, Section D had been tasked with much the same objectives as those MI(R) began studying within the War Office shortly afterwards. Section D placed its emphasis on influencing sabotage activity inside Germany and in neutral countries by gathering intelligence and nurturing anti-Nazi political contacts. But in examining potential sabotage methods and equipment at the same time, its work in the first year of the war extended into areas that paralleled the remit of MI(R). The second element was therefore those functions of MI(R) that remained in July 1940 after its earlier creations, the Independent Companies and the Special Training Centre Lochailort, passed into the control of Director of Military Operations at the War Office. The third SOE function was inherited from a small department of the Foreign Office known as 'Electra House', concerned with influencing public opinion in enemy and neutral countries by means of propaganda in all available media. SOE retained a role in the last of these only until August 1941, when the propaganda function moved to a new independent Political Warfare Executive.[3]

British military thinking developed in response to the German victories of 1940 placed a greater emphasis on the future importance of resistance activity than would later be realised. As long as the British empire was fighting without a powerful ally, and as long as Germany maintained its alliance of convenience with the Soviet Union to the east, there was no tangible prospect in the short term of defeating Germany by a land invasion of the European continent. While home soil and the Empire was defended, the British strategy for war in Europe (raiding operations aside) was to be one of naval blockade, air bombardment, and the encouragement of resistance movements in the countries that Germany had conquered. The optimistic view was that the flames of resistance could be fanned to such effect that in time it would be possible to defeat German occupying armies by the insertion of a relatively small British invasion force. More pragmatic was the awareness that resistance activity would at least keep the enemy under pressure and so less dangerous until such times as major offensive operations could be conducted, hopefully in a future alliance with the United States. Speaking after the war, the Director of Special Operations Executive summarised the original purpose of SOE's organisation and the scale of the challenge it faced. This was Major-General Sir Colin Gubbins, who joined SOE in November 1940 as its Director of Operations and Training with the rank of Brigadier:

> Here was the problem and the plan, then: to encourage and enable the peoples of the occupied countries to harass the German war effort at every possible point by sabotage, subversion, go-slow practices, 'coup de main' raids, etc., and at the same time to build up secret forces therein, organised, armed and trained to take their part only when the final assault began. These two objects are, in fact, fundamentally incompatible: to divert attention from the creation of secret armies meant avoiding any activity which would attract German attention; to act offensively entailed attracting the special attention and efforts of the Gestapo and SS and the re-doubling of vigilance on their part. Not an easy problem, but somehow the two had to be done.[4]

The task was moreover a delicate one and not one that could be rushed into, for there were sensitivities in dealing with the exiled governments of the countries concerned. More immediately, there were the obvious dangers of compromising what resistance organisation might already exist in occupied countries by blundering into their midst. An organisation had to be developed that could deliver people, arms and explosives into occupied territory without attracting attention, and that could maintain clandestine communications with agents successfully introduced into resistance networks. Above all, personnel had to be properly prepared for operational service. There was no sense in sending under-prepared and untrained men to what might be their death. Training, as Gubbins noted, was therefore 'of the utmost importance'.[5]

As SOE began to formulate its plans for training in late summer 1940, Colin Gubbins was still in his War Office post developing and commanding the GHQ Auxiliary Units. With new men in senior positions in SOE, Gubbins was one of only a few from the original staff of MI(R), or indeed from Section D, who would actually work for the new organisation. However, before Gubbins' arrival, two other officers with MI(R) backgrounds transferred directly across to SOE and immediately began the work of studying the training requirements and making recommendations. Major F. T. (Tommy) Davies, assisted by Major J. S. (Jack) Wilson, suggested a scheme whereby training would be split into three stages. Preliminary schools would vet potential agents and give elementary training in fitness and military skills. This step successfully completed, students would move on to Paramilitary schools 'where they would be instructed in demolitions, weapons, minor tactics, combined operations, as well as the necessary intelligence methods (forward reconnaissance, topography, field security) and communications'.[6] The paramilitary step would also include parachute training, since this was foreseen as the most common means of delivering men and materials behind enemy lines.

After the paramilitary stage, students would move on to Finishing schools corresponding to their nationalities. Each 'Country Section' through which SOE operations were being organised would run one or more Finishing school of its own. These would give instruction in security, enemy military and secret service methods, and the local conditions that applied in the students' future destination. Their training completed, students would be held in readiness at their Finishing school or sent to other holding camps. As a final step before deployment on an operation, individual agents would receive a briefing on the specifics of their task at another property in London operated by their 'Country Section'.[7]

This system worked out on paper was designed with security very much to the fore. Students would be given information about the nature of their future work only as it became necessary. Different stages in the system would be kept entirely separate, as would different groups of students. Just as for the students, staff at the training schools would be told only as much as they needed to know in order to do their job, to process their charges and pass them on to the next stage. What was needed by way of accommodation was not one or two concentrated training centres on the lines that Lochailort or Achnacarry would develop, but a sizeable number of small independent properties where students could live and learn in discreet groups without attracting too much local attention. SOE's work was secret. Its nature, its very existence indeed, was not to be divulged to civilian or military authorities except at the highest level. For the paramilitary stage a general reference to 'Commando training' would give suitable security cover. The Commandos were not a secret and so might stand as sufficient explanation for what would be going on in the SOE schools without need to divulge any specifics to neighbouring communities or military authorities.

1. Colin Gubbins (centre) with Hugh Dalton on a visit to Czechoslovak forces in the United Kingdom, 1941.

(IMPERIAL WAR MUSEUM)

2. Ernest Van Maurik, SOE paramilitary instructor: '... none of them knew what they were being trained for, nor did any of us, but as far as they were concerned if it led to the opportunity of having a bash at the Germans, so very much the better.'

(E. H. VAN MAURIK)

3. Soldiers of 1st Independent Polish Parachute Brigade on exercise in the Perthshire highlands near Dunkeld, 1944.

(MR STANISŁAW KORZENIOWSKI)

4. and 5. Heydrich assassins Sergeants Ján Kubiš (left) and Josef Gabčík, 1941.

(CZECH NEWS AGENCY)

6. Surgeon-Commander George Murray Levick heading for the beach at Arisaig, 1941.

(TIM O'DONOVAN)

7. Ensign Violette Szabo, whose SOE training in 1943 included the paramilitary course at Inverie.

(IMPERIAL WAR MUSEUM)

8. Christmas card sent by Herbert Brucker to fellow American OSS wireless operator Jean Guiet. Both men trained at Meoble Lodge.

(NMS)

9. Meoble Lodge in South Morar, one of the SOE Group A Paramilitary Schools.

(NORWAY'S RESISTANCE MUSEUM, OSLO)

10. The staff at Inverlair, February 1944. Major Aonghais Fyffe is at the centre of the front row, C. S. M. Thomson is beside him fourth from right. Lance Corporal Purisiol is at extreme right of the back row.

(MR JAMES U. THOMSON/MAJOR A. A. FYFFE)

11. Linge Company men advance through timber structures erected close to Glenmore Lodge.

(NORWAY'S RESISTANCE MUSEUM, OSLO)

12. Linge Company demonstrate railway sabotage for HM King Haakon of Norway, second from left, and HRH Crown Prince Olav, fourth from left, on a royal visit to Glenmore Lodge.

(NORWAY'S RESISTANCE MUSEUM, OSLO)

13. Lieutenant-Colonel Jack Wilson, right foreground, with the 'Heavy Water Raid' saboteurs celebrating in Oslo after the liberation of Norway, 1945.

(NORWAY'S RESISTANCE MUSEUM, OSLO)

14. The post-war naturalist and author Gavin Maxwell on joining SOE in 1941.

(SOE ADVISOR, FOREIGN & COMMONWEALTH OFFICE)

15. Major David Parsons (third from left), commandant at Inverie, with French and US officers, 1944.

(IMPERIAL WAR MUSEUM)

16. Assault course at the Highland Fieldcraft Training Centre Glenfeshie, 1944.

(NMS)

17. Highland Fieldcraft Training Centre students on exercise in the Torridon mountains, 1943.

(NMS)

18. Sculptor Scott Sutherland at work on his Commando Memorial.

(THE HONOURABLE HUGH FRASER)

19. Lord Lovat, on the extreme right, looks on at the unveiling of the Commando Memorial by HM Queen Elizabeth the Queen Mother, 27 September 1952.

(THE HONOURABLE HUGH FRASER)

*   *   *

The job of requisitioning, organising and staffing these new training schools was not one that could be completed overnight. SOE quickly established its first training school at Brickendonbury Manor in Hertfordshire, formerly used by Section D as an espionage and sabotage school.[8] But with paramilitary training to organise, the thoughts of the two former MI(R) officers in charge naturally turned north to what was already being developed at the Special Training Centre Lochailort. SOE wished to make as early a start as possible to its work in occupied Europe, and to avoid complete operational inactivity during the inevitable hiatus while the organisation was put on a proper footing and its agents trained. It therefore looked to support efforts towards the aid of one conquered nation where there was a prospect of early action.

Poland's rapid defeat and subjugation at the hands of Germany and the Soviet Union in 1939 had not prevented large numbers of Polish servicemen from escaping to fight another day. The Polish Army regrouped in France, but there saw its hopes for a rapid liberation of the homeland dealt a further crushing blow when German invaders once again swept all before them in the summer 1940. Those Polish units that managed to escape the onslaught in France more or less intact were evacuated to British ports. The War Office concentrated the new arrivals in Glasgow, then directed them to holding areas in Lanarkshire. By mid-July there were some 17,000 Polish soldiers in the United Kingdom, almost all of them in Scotland.[9] This was a substantial resource of trained military personnel, with an autonomous command structure. It could and would stand as an ally in the defence of the United Kingdom; but at the same time the Polish government in exile in London was dedicated to the cause of Poland's liberation by the quickest possible means.

Senior Polish Army officers in London had high expectations of the willingness and ability of the Polish people living under occupation to organise, resist and even defeat the enemy. The conception of a secret Home Army had been aired even before Poland fell, and was discussed with Gubbins during the British Military Mission to Poland in September 1939. During its time in France, the Polish government established secret wireless communications with a growing resistance network inside Poland. Now the Poles wanted to begin actively supporting their Home Army (Armia Krajowa) as quickly as possible. If their British hosts could provide aircraft, supplies and facilities for training, they would do it themselves. While they negotiated with SOE and the British Chiefs of Staff for these precious resources, the Poles set about selecting and training men to parachute into Poland.

From its very first days the Special Training Centre Lochailort envisaged a role for itself in training foreign nationals for special operations. Now there was someone to train. Inverlochy Castle near Fort William had already been requisitioned and set aside for MI(R) use. Through liaison between the Training Bureau of the Polish Army and the War Office, and with the nascent SOE training organisation looking on with approval, Inverlochy was made available to Polish forces as a guerrilla warfare school. It took form as the 'Allied Wing' of the Special Training Centre under the command of Major David Stacey, reporting to the Commanding Officer at Lochailort. The administrative staff would be British, as would most of the instructors, but the Poles would also have their own instructors on the staff headed by one Captain Antoni Strawiński of the Polish Engineers.[10]

In early autumn 1940 the 4th Cadre Rifle Brigade of the Polish Army was stationed at Eliock in Dumfriesshire. On 2nd September the Brigade's commanding officer Colonel Stanisław Sosabowski was directed by the Polish Chief of General Staff to select a small group of his best commissioned and non-commissioned officers for special training. These men were the first to go to Inverlochy, among them Captain Władysław Stasiak:

> After the briefing Captain Strawiński showed us the tents where we were to live. The tents did not look encouraging. At this time of the year on the west coast of northern Scotland, almost at the foot of the highest peak in the Scottish mountains – Ben Nevis – it was cold and the Scottish rain that we already knew well was falling. The cynics say it starts raining when it stops snowing and it only stops raining when it starts snowing again. The tents stood on a damp field near a stream, where we were to wash. Hot water, even for shaving, was never mentioned. Luckily, inside the tents wooden floors were laid. It was little comfort but at least we did not have to lie directly on the damp ground.[11]

At the conclusion of a four-week guerrilla course of Lochailort design, the men returned to their Brigade in Dumfriesshire. Although they did not know it at first, their course had been a trial run for the first stage in a training and selection process designed for men to be sent to the aid of the Home Army in Poland. This was the first of 13 Polish courses that would pass through Inverlochy until its closure in spring 1942.[12] Each course numbered between 20 and 48 students and the Inverlochy staff grew to 37, 15 of them Polish.[13] Permanent instructors detached the short distance from Lochailort included the marksman Lieutenant Cyril Mackworth-Praed and the mountaineer Captain Ashley Greenwood. Shortly after Lieutenant-Colonel Stockwell took over command of the Special Training Centre, Major Stacey was replaced as Inverlochy commandant by Captain J. C. M. T. O'Donovan, with a remit to tighten up administration as had already done at the parent school. There seems to have been some tension between British and Polish elements at Inverlochy, but Captain Strawiński maintained a considerable degree of autonomy in directing and refining the content of the course.

Inverlochy did not teach parachuting, but gave some preparatory theoretical and physical instruction in advance of the practical training the men would shortly be receiving at Ringway airfield near Manchester. The principal concern of the course was to teach the guerrilla warfare skills the men were expected to need in order to conduct their missions inside Poland. The syllabus placed a heavy emphasis on demolitions, and on Strawiński's speciality mine-laying. Weapon-training, fieldcraft and un-armed combat were all covered. As was the practice with the parent course at STC Lochailort, visits to the British Aluminium Company's nearby plant were used as an aid to instruction in the techniques of industrial sabotage. Lengths of railway line were acquired so that railway sabotage theory could be applied in practice.[14] There was also teaching in the English language with reference to military communication, and a surviving set of manuscript course notes taken by 2nd Lieutenant S. R. Piekło features lessons on reading British maps.[15] At least one course extended its efforts to boat training at Dorlin House.[16]

Those Inverlochy students successfully selected to become parachutists and sent to the aid of the Polish Home Army as couriers, organisers and advisers, became what was known as the *Cichociemni*, 'the silent and unseen'. The origins of the name are obscure, although the term is believed to have come into usage during the training process and not in the field in Poland.[17] Rendered in the usual English translation its relation to the nature of clandestine warfare seems straightforward. However there are subtleties to this unusual Polish term. One possible if slightly tenuous explanation is suggested by Władysław Stasiak, who returned to his unit from the first Inverlochy course to face an inquisitive fellow officer. Stasiak was not permitted to satisfy his comrade's curiosity about what he had been doing while he was away:

> What were we doing? I told him that he should know that we have to 'sit quietly' and not say a word about the course because it is a secret. Then he said 'you fool, don't you even trust me? That is what you are, a quiet fool [*cicho-ciemniak*]'.[18]

Any nuance of teasing as suggested in this exchange did not, however, translate into what the term *Cichociemni* came to signify in Poland.

For the Cichociemni, Inverlochy was only the first step in their hazardous journey home. SOE's Polish Section developed a training network of its own based at Briggens and Audley End House in Essex and involving a number of other properties in the Home Counties. By late 1941 these had taken over much of Inverlochy's function as well as covering the 'preliminary' and 'finishing' aspects of the Polish version of the training scheme. Never formally under the control of SOE, the 'Allied Wing' of the Special Training Centre did strive to co-ordinate its efforts with the exclusively Polish schools run by SOE, and with the Parachute school at RAF Ringway, until STC Lochailort itself was run down and closed. Inverlochy doubled throughout its military life as a guerrilla warfare training school for regular elements of the Polish Army and, in theory if not in practice, for soldiers of other Allied nations.[19]

The mark of the trained Cichociemni soldier was a parachute qualification badge. This took the form of a Polish white eagle diving from the sky with talons drawn, and was worn above the breast pocket of the battle dress uniform. The badge was based on a drawing by Marian Walentynowicz, a book illustrator serving with Polish forces in Scotland. On the back was inscribed the motto 'TOBIE OJCZYZNO' ('For you, my fatherland').[20] The basic design spawned a later embellishment to denote combat service, and these badges were principally worn by soldiers of the 1st Independent Polish Parachute Brigade. This regular combat unit was formed from the 4th Cadre Rifle Brigade, by then stationed in Fife, whose commanding officer Colonel Sosabowski determined to form an airborne unit for the Polish Army.

To supplement the Ringway parachute school, Sosabowski's new Brigade opened its own preliminary parachute training centre at Largo House in Fife, and also ran a survival school in the forests of Dunkeld on the Atholl estate in highland Perthshire, where Cichociemni attended on occasion.[21] One officer from the 4th Cadre Rifle Brigade who attended both Inverlochy and the Dunkeld camp in the spring and summer of 1941 was Lieutenant Wiesław Szczygieł:

> In great secrecy, some of us were sent on a 'cloak-and-dagger' course in Inverlochy Castle near Fort William. Here we were back to the Nissen huts and washing in the freezing stream nearby (it was too far to the toilet block). At least the programme was interesting – training in 'reflex' shooting, use of explosives and booby traps, night exercises and climbing Ben Nevis. We were all sworn to secrecy as this was, as we later discovered, the preliminary training and selection for being sent for underground work in occupied Poland. Not all were selected for further secret training but this was the beginning of the formation of our future Parachute Brigade ....
>
> ... Our 'Sosab' [Sosabowski] was full of ideas: one of these was the establishment of a camp near Dunkeld for the purpose of training officers and officer cadets in fieldcraft and watercraft. As a sapper, I was posted there as a watercraft instructor on the river Tay. Back to life in tents and the rigours of the Scottish weather! On the whole I enjoyed the three months of rough living in one of the prettiest parts of Scotland. There was shooting, fishing, boating, river fording, mountain climbing, campfire cooking and when the skies opened, plenty of bridge in the tents.[22]

The men of Polish Parachute Brigade, with Lieutenant Szczygieł among them, would later drop into action in the Netherlands in the ill-fated Arnhem operation of September 1944. But the paratroopers never had the opportunity to fulfil their true purpose as envisaged by Sosabowski – a part in the liberation of Poland.

In 1940 SOE had the highest hopes for Poland, spurred by the determination and capability of the Polish forces in exile and the potential of its sizeable underground army. But a hard fate often awaited Polish agents, a mirror to the bitter misfortune and suffering of their country which did not end with the defeat of Germany. Of 316 Cichociemni who parachuted into Poland, over a third lost their lives.[23] Most of the fatalities came in action against the German Army, or in murder by the Gestapo after arrest. Some were killed in the Warsaw Rising of August 1944, when the Home Army emerged to liberate their capital just before the Soviet Red Army reached it and then stood back and let the insurgents be destroyed. Some of those Cichociemni who outlived the German occupation were later detained and murdered by the Soviet NKVD security police, as the Soviet Union took over from Nazi Germany as the occupiers of Poland.

* * *

While the Poles were pressing ahead with their own training programme in autumn 1940, Majors Davies and Wilson were putting their recommendations for a broader SOE training system into action. No other nation had the resources and manpower of the Poles at this stage, neither in the United Kingdom nor in their home resistance organisations, and activity in other occupied countries would have to rely much more heavily on what SOE could create. The system as planned required accommodation for Preliminary and Finishing schools, and these were found by requisitioning suitably secluded country houses in the Home Counties, with a cluster of Finishing schools on and around the Beaulieu estate in the southern New Forest of Hampshire. As SOE grew, further properties were taken over across southern England and the Midlands, so much so that SOE's attractive property portfolio apparently earned it the moniker 'Stately 'Omes of England' among staff and trainees. Parachute training would remain concentrated at the parachute school at RAF Ringway, where for security reasons SOE's students would be kept apart from military trainees in accommodation requisitioned for the purpose.[24]

For paramilitary training, SOE obtained agreement from the War Office that pending the identification, requisition and opening of SOE's own schools, small parties sent by SOE could receive training at the Special Training Centre Lochailort.[25] This was a temporary measure, and not ideal from the security point of view, but it sufficed while Davies and Wilson got on with creating what would become the 'Group A' Paramilitary schools in the west highlands (the Finishing schools were referred to as 'Group B'). The task of identifying suitable houses fell largely to Major Wilson, who already had some knowledge of STC Lochailort and had ideas about the training potential of the broader area. Jack Wilson had followed a successful career in the senior ranks of the Indian Police in Calcutta, from which he was familiar with surveillance and counter-subversion intelligence techniques. Returning to England during the 1920s he had taken up post as Chief Instructor of the Boy Scout Training Centre at Gilwell Park in Essex and was Director of the Boy Scout International Bureau. In 1940 he was serving in the Local Defence Volunteers when his background in police work and adventure training brought him to the attention of MI(R). Wilson was promptly recruited to help in directing the training of the Independent Companies. Wilson's London-based role involved liaison with STC Lochailort, and it was he who arranged for Lochailort instructors Freddy Spencer Chapman and Michael Calvert to take their skills to Australia.

When still working for MI(R) in early September 1940, Jack Wilson arranged to transform Arisaig House from its function as a holding centre for the Independent Companies into a constituted 'Military Intelligence Wing' of the Special Training Centre Lochailort, which by then had moved out of MI(R)'s control. He helped set up and run a small trial course there, bringing Major J. W. (Jimmy) Munn and Captain William Godfrey the short distance from Inverailort to command and instruct. Traces of the No. 5 Independent Company's deer-stalking activities, legitimate or otherwise, were still in evidence: 'Bill had to spend a week cleaning out all the pieces of dead "beasts" that the Special Company had thrown away in the shrubberies.'[26]

The proposed Military Intelligence Wing at STC Lochailort went no further than this first experimental course. But on joining SOE, Wilson already knew the area around Lochailort was suitable for its purposes and that at least one secure property was already available.

Wilson's first step towards creating the Group A schools was therefore to arrange transfer of Arisaig House and its small staff from the administration of STC Lochailort into the control of SOE. This was a substantial property that would do as a headquarters and administrative centre. Wilson and Davies then used it as a base from which to make a reconnaissance of the wider area, looking for further properties for smaller training schools. Sharing all of STC Lochailort's advantages, the Arisaig and Morar district was found to be entirely suitable. It had the right terrain and coastline, it was remote but served by a railway, and it was inside the Protected Area. Major Wilson also had confidence in the discretion of the local people:

We were going down Loch Morar in a small motor boat managed by a highland ghillie, long grey beard and all. I turned to him and said: 'Mac, we are going to bring a lot of foreigners up here and they are going to do lots of funny things. We don't want it talked about. Will you pass the word round?' There was a pause before the slow reply, 'Aye, we kept Prince Charles secret here'. Astounded, but very quickly, I said, 'Good, that'll be all right'. It took me quite a while to explain to Tommy Davies all that the reply affirmed and that all would be equally true 200 years later.

Others who served with SOE in the area recount similar allusions to local complicity in the flight of 'Bonnie Prince Charlie' in 1746.[27]

The boat trip on Loch Morar took Wilson and Davies to Meoble Lodge, a small shooting lodge on the River Meoble that runs between Lochs Beoraid and Morar. Part of the Meoble estate owned by Sir Berkeley Sheffield, Meoble could not be reached by motor vehicle but was less than a mile distant from a small pier on Loch Morar's south shore. Wilson decided it would do very well for SOE. He then settled upon Rhubana Lodge at the west end of Loch Morar, another of Miss Astley-Nicolson's properties let to a seasonal tenant. Proceeding up the Road to the Isles to Mallaig, Wilson took another boat across to the remote Knoydart peninsula where he found Inverie House suitable for requirements.[28] South again towards Arisaig, a smaller private house at Camusdarach above a beach on the west coast of Morar was earmarked and added to the list soon after.[29] The difficulties that wartime requisitioning placed upon the owners and tenants of properties were never a great concern for SOE and other government or military agencies. Awareness that Inverie was owned by Lord Brocket, a known pre-war Nazi sympathiser, might have eased any twinge of conscience felt by Wilson on this occasion.[30]

The government's Ministry of Works conducted the requisitioning of property on behalf of SOE, which was naturally reluctant to become involved at all with owners or their concerns. Where interaction was necessary, SOE presented itself under one of the organisation's cover names, the 'Inter Services Research Bureau' (ISRB). Later, in November 1941, government minister Hugh Dalton used the nondescript ISRB profile in responding to a complaint from Lord Brocket about his Knoydart houses made through his member of parliament. This concerned SOE staff's intention to remove furniture from Inverie House and a second of

Lord Brocket's properties, Glaschoille, to the west of Inverie Bay, which had also been requisitioned. Dalton expressed polite sympathy and agreed to keep furniture at Inverie. Upholding the decision to make more space at Glaschoille, he was however moved to observe in a covering memo: 'This young Lord appears to own a large number of alternative residences in various parts of the British Isles and I cannot believe that he is suffering undue hardship.'[31]

With the requisitioning in hand and SOE in possession of its new highland houses, there remained concerns about security. Location within No.1 Protected Area was not felt to be sufficient insurance. Through the headquarters of Scottish Command in Edinburgh, Arisaig House, Camusdarach, Inverailort, Inverie House, Meoble, Rhubana, and the former Independent Company holding centre at Traigh House, were all declared 'Protected Places' under Defence Regulations of the Emergency Powers (Defence) Act of 1939.[32] No one was permitted to enter within their boundaries unless in possession of a permit bearing the name of the house and issued under the authority of the commanding officer of that house. Possession of a Protected Area permit was not sufficient for admittance unless specifically endorsed in this way, and a permit for one house did not entitle the holder to enter any of the others. Anyone presenting himself for admission who could not produce the correct permit was to be detained for questioning.[33]

By December 1940 Brigadier Colin Gubbins had passed up likely opportunities of a senior Army command to transfer into SOE and was in overall charge of training. To this enterprise he brought a number of the instructors with whom he had been putting the GHQ Auxiliary Units, the British version of an underground army, into a state of readiness. Wilson was retained under Gubbins as training staff officer, based in an office near to SOE's London headquarters in Baker Street. Over the Christmas period of 1940 Gubbins escorted Minister Hugh Dalton on a visit to Polish forces stationed in Scotland and, on Christmas Day, to Lochailort and the new SOE establishment at Arisaig House. On Boxing Day Gubbins and his boss were driven around the area looking at other possible stations and found 'quite a number in the vicinity of Arisaig', presumably including those already marked out for use.[34]

Subsequent to this visit, further properties in the area were identified for requisition until there was scarcely a large house in the area not earmarked for SOE occupation. Garramor, second home of a Colonel

Liston of Edinburgh, lay just across the road from Camusdarach and was taken over as an annexe to it. Swordland Lodge was a property belonging to Mr Caldwell of Lockerbie and was six miles east along the north shore of Loch Morar. Like Meoble Lodge to the south of the opposite shore, Swordland could only be reached by boat or by way of a long hike. SOE wanted it principally to accommodate staff and students undergoing boat-work and ship sabotage training. Although parachute drop was the customary means of delivering SOE personnel into the field, small groups and individuals were also landed from the sea. The 'para-naval' training was run on Loch Morar and from the pier at Tarbet Bay on Loch Nevis, only a mile's walk to the north, where two yachts and a number of smaller craft were manned by Royal Navy crews. A little later Glasnacardoch Lodge, a mile south of Mallaig, completed the Group A estate, and was later to be used specifically as a foreign weapons training school.[35]

With the exception of the relatively grand Arisaig House and the sizeable Inverie House, these were quite modest private houses or small lodges, none of them anywhere on the scale of Inverailort House or Achnacarry as training establishments. At their fullest extent of develop-ment, attained during 1943, the Group A schools along the Road to the Isles and Loch Morar taken together could train up to 75 students simul-taneously. A small staff administered each school, the officer in charge at each reporting to the Group's overall commanding officer at Arisaig House. Between them the schools had 16 officer instructors and 26 non-commissioned officer instructors. The students were segregated according to the Country Section through which they had been recruited, but there was no permanent allocation of school to nationality. Any aspect of the Group A training syllabus might be taught at any of the schools, other than at Swordland/Tarbet and Glasnacardoch with their specific functions.[36]

Of course the houses themselves were only one part of the training experience. Although some had their own firing and demolitions ranges and areas in the immediate vicinity for other instruction, much of the training test was in the picturesque but unforgiving environment of the surroundings. Less than taken with the west highland setting, a former Dutch naval officer, recruited for SOE's Dutch Section during October 1942, described the course as it had then developed as 'an intensified commando course':

It was the kind given to ordinary soldiers but quicker and more thorough in every way. It took about eighteen hours spent in trains to reach our destination plus several hours in a motor boat. It was a wretched, barren countryside, thinly populated; rain fell from a heavy sky that never cleared completely. Though there were few people there were multitudes of sheep. It was a most depressing place.

We were to stay at a single-storied stone hut hidden among man-high bracken. Training became, if anything, even more strenuous. Our instructor was a lieutenant of a Scottish regiment, a hard fellow with spurious cheerfulness. He was tireless and his muscles bulged under his kilt. How he had managed to get so tanned in that climate we could never discover. At night we would crouch round the open fire, exhausted and soaked to the skin with rain.[37]

If this was a formative experience for resistance work, it was not however a mandatory one. Depending on the experience and previous training of individual SOE personnel, and the nature of the work they were engaged to conduct, it was entirely possible to be deployed on SOE operations without setting foot in the west highlands. Indeed, the Group A schools accepted 2479 students, as compared to 6810 trained by SOE in total. In time the Preliminary training element became more sophisticated, and from mid-1943 featured a central selection board to which students from all the Country Sections were subject. A number of specialist training schools, including one for wireless operators at Belhaven School, Dunbar in East Lothian, were also developed. Together, this mix of alternatives meant the Group A stage could often be bypassed. Wherever it was done, the training was intended not just as preparation, but as a test to weed out weakness and unsuitability. Of the total numbers trained through SOE's formal system in the United Kingdom, 1532 were rejected as unfit for operational service. No figure is given for the failure rate at the Arisaig group, but a similar rate of above 20 per cent seems likely.

* * *

The Group A complex took many months to establish, and in late 1940 SOE was in no position to wait for its full realisation. While still confined to use of Arisaig House and the borrowed facilities of STC Lochailort, the new Paramilitary set-up took its first two intakes of students during

January 1941. In contrast to most of those who arrived later, these students did not come from Allied nations under enemy occupation. One group of 16 was from Spain, whose government's position of neutrality was somewhat equivocal, and the second group consisted of five Italian nationals who were, technically, 'enemy aliens'.

SOE interests in Spain were two-fold. The organisation was already quietly putting out feelers within Spain to establish escape lines whereby SOE officers could be brought out of France across the Pyrénées mountains and returned to the United Kingdom via Portugal. But SOE had the second purpose in mind for the men sent to Arisaig. It was known that the German government was exasperated with the neutrality of the Franco regime it had helped to install in Spain. There appeared to be a distinct possibility that Germany might seek to dominate the Mediterranean by invading Spain and Portugal. The Spaniards at Arisaig were part of an SOE programme called *Sconce* intended to infiltrate resistance organisers into Spain should a German invasion come to pass. The men had been recruited from among exiled Spanish Republicans serving with the French Foreign Legion, and their brief spell of SOE training was split between Arisaig and the old Section D school at Brickendonbury.[38] Meantime, parties of Spanish-speaking British officers were going through the STC Lochailort course with the same objective. Wary of provoking the Spanish government into throwing in its lot with Germany, SOE was reluctant to intervene in any way before it was clear an invasion was definitely in the offing. No invasion came and so none of the men trained in guerrilla warfare in the west highlands reached any further than Gibraltar.

Of the first Italian students, a single man did go into action back in his native country. SOE operations in enemy, as opposed to enemy-occupied, countries were always likely to be more difficult. For obvious reasons, covert local support could not be relied upon to anything like the same degree. But SOE's intention at this early stage was to identify and prepare an anti-Fascist Italian who could act as interpreter and guide for a Commando attack being planned against the Apulia aqueduct in south-eastern Italy. This was Operation *Colossus*, an entirely new kind of venture in that the raid was to be carried out by a group of parachutists from No.2 Commando, recently renamed as 11th Special Air Service Battalion.[39] This would be the first British airborne military operation.

Of five Italian dissidents brought to Arisaig, three did sufficiently well in their makeshift guerrilla warfare course to pass on for parachute training at RAF Ringway where one, an employee of the Savoy Hotel in London named Picchi, was selected for the operation. Picchi agreed to guide the Commandos, despite the great risk his role would carry. Although wearing British uniform and carrying false papers, Picchi would be in particular danger should the raid not go to plan, or the party fail to make the hazardous cross-country escape journey to rendezvous with a British submarine off the Campania coast. The team landed by parachute on the night of 10 February 1941 and reached the aqueduct, but their demolition charges proved insufficient to destroy the target to the required degree. The whole party was captured soon after the explosion. Identified as an Italian national by his captors, Picchi was executed.[40]

At this early stage the Arisaig course undergone by the Spaniards and Italians was entirely based on the syllabus of STC Lochailort.[41] Elements of the Lochailort course were also introduced into the teaching of the Group B Finishing schools, combined with the Section D-derived training of Brickendonbury Manor and aspects of the security training used by the British Army's Intelligence Corps. The Arisaig-based courses condensed STC Lochailort teaching in fieldcraft, weapons, unarmed combat, physical training, navigation, raiding tactics, boat-work and exercises in the field, but refined these or introduced new elements to suit SOE purposes.

Physical fitness remained an important element underpinning the whole course, particularly as students might be recruits direct from civilian life who, prior to arrival in the highlands, would have experienced no formal military training beyond that received at the Preliminary stage. PT training included pre-parachuting exercises, preparatory to the forthcoming experience at RAF Ringway. Communications were a mainstay of SOE operations, so Morse code was given particular attention. There was also a concern with developing clarity in the preparation of plans, orders and reports. Again, this was a military discipline with which those from a civilian background would be less acquainted, and even for military-trained personnel the necessity of drawing up one's own operational plans from scratch was likely to be something new. A pro-forma was developed to aid the planning of small operations, considering all possible variables as a matter of course.

With first Arisaig Commandant Major Munn and Chief Instructor Captain Godfrey both former STC Lochailort men, there was initially some sharing of instructors with the 'Big House' at Inverailort. There is evidence that early SOE students received some of Fairbairn and Sykes' brand of close combat wisdom straight from the horse's mouth. French Country Section officer George Langelaan is one who records his encounter with one of the two. Langelaan describes the unnamed 'Shanghai Buster' who, assisted by a Japanese instructor, taught 'Murder made easy' skills which gave the students 'more and more self-confidence and a sense of physical power and superiority that few men ever acquire'.[42] But for security reasons, SOE sought to run its Scottish schools with the minimum of external involvement, and relied wherever possible on its own instructing staff trained within the system.

Paramilitary training instructors had to come from somewhere, however, and early in 1941 they were themselves being trained for SOE at STC Lochailort. To man its training schools SOE sought out young officers from Army units who had experience of instructing soldiers and, where possible, knowledge of a foreign language. Lieutenant E. H. (Ernest) Van Maurik of the Wiltshire Regiment was one such candidate recommended by his commanding officer. Lieutenant Van Maurik's main qualification was attendance at a weapons training course at the Army's Small Arms School at Hythe in May 1940, from which he had passed his newly acquired knowledge on for the benefit of his battalion. Despite disappointing SOE expectations on account of his name that he would be a fluent Dutch speaker, Van Maurik was conversant in French and German. Following an interview in London he arrived at Lochailort in February 1941. It was not until he had completed two weeks of the three-week STC Lochailort course alongside a number of the Spanish-speaking intake, that he was given to understand that he and a number of his fellows were being prepared not for operations but to become instructors themselves.[43]

On completing the Lochailort course, Lieutenant Van Maurik and fellow new recruit Lieutenant Harry Hale were taken off on a truck journey to an unknown destination. This turned out to be a trip of only 15 minutes' duration that ended at Arisaig House. The two new arrivals were given the briefest introduction to the nature of their work by the new commanding officer Lieutenant-Colonel Evans and chief instructor Captain John Bush before being informed that they were to start up and run courses for French-speaking students at Garramor, one of the properties recently requisitioned and as yet unoccupied. After only a few days of further instruction in demolitions work, the two were to draw up their course syllabus and see that the house and its surroundings were in a state of readiness to receive students within a matter of only a week or two. New ranges for pistol-shooting and demolitions work were prepared, the latter with lengths of railway track for teaching how to apply charges.

With visiting instructors from the other schools supplying weapons, unarmed combat, Morse code and foreign weapons instruction, it was left to Lieutenants Van Maurik and Hale and a small staff of NCOs to prepare and deliver all other aspects of the training, including demolitions:

> I had been taught the use of explosives at Lochailort. I had never done it before and after two or three weeks of fiddling about with explosives I had to teach people how to blow things up. And why we didn't blow ourselves up I do not know.[44]

Lieutenant Van Maurik also laid his own plans for fieldcraft and navigation exercises by reconnaissance trips over the hills of North and South Morar, easily reached from the house.

The Garramor staff greeted their first student intake with curiosity. Some wore the uniforms and badges of identifiable British regiments; others were in new uniforms with only 'General Service' insignia, indicating that SOE had probably had them commissioned into the Army direct from civilian life. The students were from SOE's French Section, mostly British but having a French parent or some other close connection to the country:

> They had been together as a group since joining a preliminary school in the South and their morale was high. As we revived them with a drink after their long journey from London they were curious as to what they would be subjected to in Scotland. They already knew that subsequently they had to face parachute training. I decided that they were perfectly ordinary, nice persons who accepted a task which only someone with their linguistic ability could perform and that they were determined to undertake it. I became convinced that they were out to learn all they could – after all their lives might depend on it – and that it was up to me to do all in my power to help them.[45]

Lieutenant Van Maurik's determination to give the best he could for his students led him afterwards to press for an opportunity to complete the parachute training to which his charges were all committed. He was later parachuted into France on operational service, to liaise with a resistance network around Nantua, who were to infiltrate him across the French-Swiss border for service with the SOE Mission in Berne.

*   *   *

Many of the students sent to Arisaig in the ensuing years were bound for operations in France. With a view to resistance support for any forthcoming Allied invasion, France was a priority area for SOE's work from early 1943 in particular. From the start the proximity of the country to the United Kingdom and its long coastline offered relative ease of delivery for supplies and personnel by air and sea. Would-be agents, or 'Joes' as they were known in SOE parlance, were either French themselves or British officers selected for their linguistic ability and other attributes. The former were recruited into an independent French Section ('RF' Section), run on behalf of General De Gaulle's Free French forces. French-speaking British officers were more directly controlled by SOE. They came into the orbit of the organisation's own French Section by a number of routes.

An example was one young Army officer recruited in early 1942, 2nd Lieutenant C. S. (Sydney) Hudson. In summer 1941 Hudson was detached from his battalion of the Royal Fusiliers to work with the GHQ Auxiliary Units in the east of Kent. Through this connection his knowledge of French and his overall potential was drawn to SOE's attention. Born and raised in Switzerland, Hudson was not only bilingual, but had taken advantage of the sporting opportunities of his youth to become proficient in skiing and mountaineering.[46] After passing an interview at which he was informed in general terms that the job on offer entailed parachuting behind enemy lines to aid resistance groups, and in which his own acceptance was assumed, Hudson passed through the three set stages of SOE's UK-based training programme. He found the paramilitary course at Meoble Lodge especially to his taste:

> What a time we had! Especially me – climbing in the hills, rock climbing, shooting with various weapons, demolitions, pretending to sabotage the railway from Fort William to Mallaig. Only occasionally did the thought occur to us that, perhaps in the rather near future, all this might be for real![47]

For Hudson the reality came in September 1942 when he parachuted into Vichy France only a few weeks after completing his Finishing training. This was the beginning of a very different war than the one he and the hundreds like him might otherwise have experienced. He was captured almost immediately after arrival in France, enduring more than a year in a French prison until he escaped in a mass break-out and managed to cross the Pyrénées into Spain. Not atypically, on reaching home Hudson volunteered for further operational service. He parachuted into France once more, in April 1944. At this stage, with the Allied invasion of France approaching, SOE efforts in providing direct aid and arms to resistance organisations was intensifying. Hudson worked with resistance forces in the Sarthe region, south of the Allied bridgehead established in Normandy after D-Day, until the American 3rd Army arrived. In May 1945 he was once again dropped by parachute on an SOE mission, this time into northern Thailand.

Undoubtedly, the aspect of SOE operations in France that is best known today is the organisation's willingness to deploy women as officers in the field. SOE relied heavily on female staff throughout its organisation as staff officers, clerks, drivers, wireless and cipher operators. But in the conviction that female couriers and wireless operators could do as effective a job as men, and might attract less attention from enemy security forces, SOE deployed more than 50 female agents within resistance networks in France where they faced the same risks as male officers, including interrogation and the possibility of execution if captured. Only a handful of the female officers were sent for paramilitary training in the Group A schools; most conducted the whole of their training in the Preliminary, Finishing and Specialist schools south of the border. But those who found themselves in the west highlands underwent the same training as the men.

Yvonne Rudellat was probably the first of these, only the third woman to be infiltrated into France by SOE. A French-born British subject in her mid-40s, Rudellat was working as a hotel receptionist when she was 'spotted' by French Section's recruiting officer, the thriller writer Selwyn Jepson. Rudellat arrived at the Group A complex in May 1942 where she excelled at shooting in the ranges at Garramor and, in spite of her advanced years relative to the majority of students, proved entirely competent in the physical aspects of the course. Evidently mindful of Rudellat's pioneering and potentially isolated status as a lone woman among male instructors and students, her recruiting officer Captain Jepson made the trip to Scotland to check on her progress and morale. Both were found to be entirely satisfactory.

Rudellat successfully completed her training and in July 1942 was landed by boat on the south coast of France to work as a courier to resistance networks in northern and central France. For eleven months she conducted her courier and liaison work and took part herself in sabotage operations, putting into practice the demolitions training she received at the Group A schools in Scotland. In March 1943 she was personally responsible for the destruction of two railway locomotives at Le Mans. Later that year she was one of a group intercepted by German troops in the village of Dhuizon in the Sologne and was badly wounded in an attempt to escape. Yvonne Rudellat was later discovered to have died in Belsen concentration camp shortly after its liberation by British troops in April 1945.[48]

During her training, Rudellat was accommodated at Garramor. Female students are also known to have been at the Paramilitary school at Inverie House in Knoydart. Among them was Nancy Fiocca (better known by her maiden name, Nancy Wake), a New Zealander living in France when the Germans invaded in 1940.[49] After three years of involvement in resistance activity, at her own instigation Fiocca crossed into Spain to avoid the attention of the Gestapo and reached the United Kingdom soon after. Recruited by SOE, she was returned to France by parachute drop in April 1944. In the interim she had been sent, like Yvonne Rudellat, as a lone woman, to the Inverie training school with a small group of Frenchmen, French Canadians and Poles, to Ringway, and on to one of the Beaulieu Finishing schools. By her own account Fiocca found the paramilitary course little to her liking or aptitude. One mishap occurred when on a boat trip from Inverie: 'An experienced deep sea fisherman had been detailed to teach us how to retrieve parachutes and containers that had fallen into the water.' In essaying this exercise, Fiocca fell overboard, was retrieved but laughed so much at her own predicament that she capsized the boat, consigning a fellow student, her instructor and herself once more to the sea: 'It was a case of swim or drown for everyone, including the poor fisherman. That's definitely one course I didn't pass.'[50]

Despite this and other difficulties, and her own fears of being rejected in consequence, Nancy Fiocca's extensive experience of real resistance work stood in her favour. The confidence shown in her by her French Section sponsors was more than borne out by her achievements during her second period in France. German demands for compulsory labour from Vichy France in February 1943 had led thousands of young Frenchmen to take to the mountains and forests to avoid the draft. From these 'Maquis' groups, SOE helped to organise guerrilla forces anticipating a forthcoming Allied invasion.[51] Working with the leadership of an underground Maquis army of more than 7000 men in the mountainous Auvergne region, Fiocca held the local rank of Captain and was frequently in action against the enemy. She later testified to the value of her Inverie training in preparation for such fighting work: 'We were instructed in the handling of explosives and grenades, weapons and silent killing. I had never held a revolver in my hand, let alone a Bren gun or a grenade, so this expert training was essential for me.'[52]

Nancy Wake/Fiocca's service with the Maquis was recognised in 1945 by the award of the George Medal. Her husband, Henri Fiocca, also a resistance organiser, was captured in October 1943 and executed eleven months later.

Also trained at Inverie, although not contiguously with Nancy Fiocca, was a young mother recently widowed by the loss of her French husband, who died of wounds sustained at the Battle of El Alamein. Violette Szabo was bilingual, born of an English father and French mother in Paris, and was working in London and bringing up her one year old daughter when, like Yvonne Rudellat, she came to the attention of Selwyn Jepson. It seems likely that Szabo's linguistic abilities had been noted during her earlier military service in the women's volunteer branch of the British Army, the Auxiliary Territorial Service. Surprised to be summoned for interview from quarters unknown, Violette Szabo nevertheless accepted the proposal that she be prepared for covert work behind enemy lines, her principal concern being that provision be made for her daughter.[53]

SOE arranged Szabo's commission into the First Aid Nursing Yeomanry, the official status given to the majority of female SOE officers.[54] After passing the new formal Students Assessments Board process at Winterfold, a country house near Cranleigh in Surrey, she arrived at Inverie House in September 1943. A series of detailed assessments of her progress there survive in SOE records. They are remarkable in demonstrating the detailed individual scrutiny to which instructing officers subjected their charges. On this occasion the officer in question found it hard to come to a conclusion about Szabo's potential, such were the apparent contradictions in her performance and personality which he found 'rather a puzzle':

After a certain amount of doubt, especially at the beginning of the course, I have come to the conclusion that this student is temperamentally unsuitable for this work. I consider that owing to her too fatalistic outlook in life and particularly in her work – the fact that she lacks the ruse, stability and the finesse which is required and that she is too easily influenced; when operating in the field she might endanger the lives of others working with her. It is very regrettable to have to come to such a decision when dealing with a student of this type, who during the whole course has set an example to the whole party by her cheerfulness and eagerness to please.[55]

French Section staff officers evidently had more faith in her, and a keen need for female agents. Despite the negative report from Inverie, Szabo was permitted to continue through the Group B stage and on to parachute training at Ringway, where she did well despite sustaining an ankle injury. Like that of her forerunner Yvonne Rudellat, the story of Violette Szabo's operational service in France has a disturbing ending. During her second mission to the Maquis resistance in the Haute-Vienne in June 1944, Szabo and two male resistance workers were intercepted at a German roadblock. Using the weapons training that she received at Inverie, Szabo held off SS soldiers for over half an hour until her Sten gun ammunition was exhausted, long enough for her comrades to escape. Like other captured SOE personnel, Szabo was interrogated and delivered to a concentration camp in Germany. In January 1945 Violette Szabo and two other female SOE officers were summarily executed. She was posthumously awarded the George Cross for her gallantry in resisting capture and her forbearance in captivity.

* * *

Across SOE there was great variation in the background and experience of students and thus a good deal of modification in the training they received. As well as British soldiers and civilians, Group A schools received intakes of trained soldiers from the constituted armies of Allied and occupied nations. The first were groups of soldiers from the exiled Czechoslovak Independent Brigade stationed in the United Kingdom. The first group of 20 arrived at Camusdarach to the care of Lieutenant Ernest Van Maurik and the new Garramor commandant, Major Young in July 1941:

As far as one could tell none of them knew exactly what they were being trained for, nor did any of us, but as far as they were concerned if it led to the opportunity of having a bash at the Germans, so very much the better. They enjoyed getting away from regimental life, they fired at targets as if they really believed they were Germans, they approached demolition training with the greatest gusto and all in all they had a darn good time. Nevertheless they maintained faultless discipline and never overstepped the mark.[56]

Between July 1941 and April 1943 twelve courses of soldiers despatched through SOE's Czechoslovak section underwent paramilitary training in Scotland: the first four courses at Camusdarach, the remainder a little further up the road at Traigh House, where a plaque now commemorates their presence. Local resident Mrs Barbara Salmon remembered watching one group arriving at Mallaig station. From one soldier, who spoke good English, she received a Czechoslovak 'V' for Victory badge as a greeting.[57] Typically these selected men were capable, highly motivated young non-commissioned officers who had already wielded the responsibility of training soldiers in the use of weapons and explosives. Two British conducting officers accompanied each course during its time at the Group A schools. A Czechoslovak officer, Lieutenant Antonin Petrák, was appointed temporarily to the Arisaig staff as interpreter and liaison officer.[58]

Like the Poles, special operations in Czechoslovakia were conducted with a considerable degree of autonomy, and the Military Intelligence branch of the Czechoslovak government-in-exile in London, not SOE, controlled communication with the underground movement in the Czech lands.[59] The Czechoslovak government was anxious to introduce clandestine representatives into resistance activity in the homeland, not least because it was aware that Soviet-trained Czechoslovak parachutists were already being dropped in from the east to liaise with communist resistance elements. The soldiers at Camusdarach and Traigh were being trained to form two types of parachute team: three-man units for general liaison with resistance forces, intelligence gathering and communications; and two-man units with specific sabotage missions. Those who successfully completed their paramilitary training proceeded to parachute training; and from there, depending on their mission, they progressed to communications instruction or further sabotage training at Brickendonbury Manor. Those finally confirmed as fit for operations then prepared for their respective missions at the Czechoslovak Section's holding centre, Bellasis, a country house in Surrey.

As the fate of some of Arisaig's women students underlines, resistance work in any occupied country carried a significant risk. For parachutists dropped to the countries of central and eastern Europe, the prospects were if anything even more daunting. Whereas SOE operatives in western European countries could be extracted by sea or, if necessary, attempt escape into bordering neutral countries, no such route of departure was open to men dropped into Poland or Czechoslovakia. Their commitment was open-ended; their service would last until their deaths or until their country was free. In September 1941 one course of students departing Camusdarach presented their instructor Lieutenant Ernest Van Maurik with a gift of appreciation, a copy of the book *Letters from England* by the celebrated Czech writer Karel Capek whose works had been black-listed by the Nazis. Of the 19 Czechoslovak soldiers who signed the title page of the book, ten later parachuted into their occupied homeland. Not one of the ten survived the war.[60]

A persistent factor to be taken account of in the planning of SOE sabotage activity was the threat of reprisals against local civilian popula-tions. This was a consideration everywhere, and a potential source of tension between SOE and home governments exiled in the United Kingdom; but again in central and eastern Europe the likelihood and scale of retribution was likely to be greater. It was certainly a risk understood by the Czechoslovak government leaders in London when they sanctioned the most audacious of their projects, Operation *Anthropoid*, the planned assassination of SS Obergruppenführer Reinhard Heydrich. Heydrich was the head of the German administration in the Czech lands, a favourite lieutenant of Adolf Hitler, and one of the most powerful men in the Nazi regime. As a target for elimination, he was certainly not a man to be mourned. Heydrich's record as 'Protector' of Bohemia-Moravia was one of shameful cruelty. If the plot to kill him was intended to proclaim to the world that Czechoslovakia was still a nation, and a nation still fighting, that emphatic declaration came at a high price.

On 27 May 1942 two undercover Czechoslovak soldiers waited on a quiet stretch of road in a suburb of Prague, armed with one Sten sub-machine gun and two bombs. Sergeants Ján Kubiš and Jozef Gabčík had parachuted into Bohemia on 28 December 1941, after completing the special training that began with the paramilitary course at Camusdarach that September. They were now anticipating the arrival of a German staff car in which they knew Heydrich would be travelling with only a light guard. The ambush they had set was the culmination of months of planning and activity involving several other parachutists who had trained in the west highlands of Scotland as part of their preparation. The opportunity their work created very nearly slipped by. As Heydrich's car rounded a corner, Gabčík stepped forward to fire and his gun jammed. While Gabčík stood helpless, Heydrich ordered his driver to stop and drew a pistol to fire at the apparently lone assassin. This fatal error gave Kubiš the chance to throw one bomb at the car. Although thrown inaccurately, the explosion against a rear wheel was enough to wound Heydrich and give time for both assassins to escape on bicycles.

Reinhard Heydrich died of blood poisoning eight days later, to the grief and fury of Hitler himself who demanded heavy retribution. As the German SS harried Prague in the weeks following, Kubiš and Gabčík were betrayed by a fellow agent. Surrounded in their hiding place in Prague's Karel Boromejsky Greek Orthodox church, the parachutists fought a gun battle with the SS before taking their own lives.

Among the dead in the church were two who had signed the book for Ernest Van Maurik at Camusdarach eight months earlier. A third from that training course, Lieutenant Alfréd Bartoš, was tracked down and killed a day later. The death of the assassins was not sufficient recompense in the eyes of the SS, however. From the day of the ambush, savage reprisals began throughout the Czech lands. Over 5000 Czechs died as a consequence of Operation *Anthropoid*, although it is possible that some of the deportations and executions that were ordered had been planned previous to the assassination. Most notorious was the eradication of the Bohemian village of Lidice, where the Germans wrongly believed Heydrich's assassins had received assistance. On 9 June the population of the village was rounded up. Women and children were deported; the men were executed on the spot. Lidice was burnt to the ground, the ruins bulldozed. The village of Ležáky, also implicated, was subjected to similar treatment.

As Czechoslovak President Eduard Beneš intended in ordering the mission, admiration for the spirit of resistance in his country, and sympathy over the ferocity of the German reaction, raised the stature of the Czechoslovak nation in the eyes of the Allies. But the scale of reprisals, the loss of agents and the damage to resistance networks built up since 1939, were all a serious blow to the Czechoslovak organisation working with

SOE support. It took a year for operations to recommence in the Czech lands. The Heydrich assassination was nevertheless a mark of the reach and impact that was within SOE's power to effect. Although the operation was ordered independently by the Czechs, SOE's training and infiltration organisations made it possible.

Reflecting the effectiveness of SOE's approach to security, the killing of Heydrich came as a surprise to all but a select few within the organisation. Training instructors especially were not expected to be in the know about the likely future deployment of their students. By then working as an Air Liaison Officer at SOE headquarters in London, Lieutenant Van Maurik received the news about the work of his former Camusdarach students, Gabčík and Kubiš, informally:

> In I think it was about June of 1942 I looked at the morning news-paper and there was a story that Heydrich, the so-called 'Protector' of Czechoslovakia who had in fact been just sending about two thousand people a month to their deaths in concentration camps, had been assassinated. And that morning a chap called Captain Hesketh-Pritchard, who I knew, came up to me and said, 'You've seen the paper this morning? Those are the chaps you trained'.[61]

* * *

In early 1942 a party of Danish volunteers arrived at Arisaig House for assessment by SOE. One of these Free Danes was Anders Lassen, whose boyhood of shooting and fishing in South Zealand equipped him in marksmanship and fieldcraft skills with which he excelled at the paramilitary training. Denmark had fallen to German military invasion in April 1940 but, with its armed forces emasculated, the country had been permitted to maintain its own government and a technically 'neutral' rather than occupied status. Danes who departed to fight against the *ad hoc* German domination of their country were compelled therefore to enlist in British forces as individuals, rather than in Danish units. From June 1941 SOE's Danish Section had been training agents for operations in Denmark.[62] These preparations took place against a background of tension between SOE's aspirations for sabotage operations and the cautious approach of resistance networks inside Denmark. Within the latter there was reluctance to commit to actions that might upset their chosen strategy of quietly building up capability towards aiding a future Allied liberation of their country when the time came.[63] SOE pressed ahead. Danish parachutists became more active from early 1943 and achieved substantial successes in railway and shipping sabotage, so much so that Germany was forced to take over the reins of power and garrison the country just as SOE intended.

But such progress was still in the future when Anders Lassen impressed his comrades and instructors at the Arisaig schools by stalking and killing a stag using only his knife.[64] Shortly after completing his paramilitary training, the Danish prodigy was singled out by SOE for recruitment into a new raiding force that had nothing to do with Denmark. This was a small multi-national party assembled to raid the coast of France from the *Maid Honour*, a 65-ton trawler based at Poole in Dorset. Diverted instead to a series of successful reconnaissance missions and attacks on the coast of West Africa, the *Maid Honour* force showed itself to be highly useful. On its return to England, the group was equipped with a Motor Torpedo Boat and formally constituted first as No.62 Commando, then as the 'Small Scale Raiding Force' (SSRF). During 1942 its activities bridged the gap between the covert operations in which SOE specialised and the larger raids which the Commandos had begun to concentrate upon. Reflecting this position, command of the SSRF functioned in co-operation between SOE and Combined Operations Command.

Another SSRF recruit was an old hand from the first days at STC Lochailort, Captain Peter Kemp, who with a colleague had since been waiting in frustration for operations to be commenced by SOE's Spanish Section. Such had been the hiatus in his own activity as a result, on joining the SSRF Kemp took the opportunity to return to the west highlands to get fit and update his sabotage training. There Kemp met one of the intakes of Czechoslovak soldiers whose attitude and ability impressed him, and a party of Spanish Republicans who appeared 'a villainous crowd of assassins' to this veteran of Franco's Spanish Foreign Legion. Kemp also formed a favourable impression of the paramilitary training he had helped to bring into being:

> The SOE paramilitary training centre was now at Arisaig, a few miles north of Lochailort. After reporting there we were sent to one of the outlying establishments, hard by the shores of Loch Morar. Here, under the direction of Major Young and the expert instruction of Captains Gavin Maxwell and Matthew Hodgart, we started a course

of hard and intensive training. Carrying tommy-guns and fifty-pound rucksacks we tramped across the hills in dense mist and darkness, trying to find our way by compass, stumbling over invisible obstacles, sinking into bogs and falling into gullies and ravines. On one of these schemes the Adjutant from Arisaig, an enormous Highlander, broke a leg and lay for six hours on a mountain top before he could be carried down.[65]

The Captain Maxwell encountered by Kemp, an old school friend, was one of the instructing staff who had been recommended for the Group A schools by virtue of a personal propensity for the outdoor life and an advanced knowledge of weapons. Lieutenant Gavin Maxwell of the Scots Guards arrived at Arisaig in January 1942, ill with a duodenal ulcer and therefore unfit for active service. He was serving as an instructor in sniping and camouflage at the Brigade of Guards School of Minor Tactics in London when he obtained entry to SOE through an old school friend, Captain Alfgar Hesketh-Pritchard, head of the Czechoslovak Section. Maxwell's aptitude for shooting and fieldcraft made him an obvious asset to the Training Section, but to qualify as an instructor Maxwell had first to go through the Arisaig paramilitary course and assessment himself. Despite his illness Maxwell received a positive report:

> This officer is a very good lecturer with an easy manner and has obviously had experience of lecturing. He is very good at fieldcraft and quite at home in this type of country .... He is a good organiser and a strong personality. The only doubt is regarding his health, but if this is not likely to break down we should have him in the area and he is himself keen to be posted here.[66]

Maxwell certainly was at home in the rugged country of the Rough Bounds. A grandson of the Duke of Northumberland, Maxwell's childhood and adolescence had been filled, between bouts of illness, by prodigious shooting expeditions on the moors of Galloway. At this stage in his life, the burgeoning love of wildlife and the natural world that would later inform his celebrated literary work was principally expressed through field sports.

Gavin Maxwell cut something of a flamboyant figure among the Arisaig staff, often donning the highland dress favoured by some of the instructors, and sporting a yellow Texan scarf with his battle dress blouse. Students remembered his party trick of extinguishing a cigarette on his bare knee, done without flinching ostensibly to demonstrate how to cope with interrogation after capture.[67] More conventionally, Maxwell's specialist knowledge of foreign weapons, taught from the collection he assembled at Glasnacardoch, made this subject a strength of the paramilitary course. Maxwell ended service with the Arisaig schools in 1944 as a major and commandant of Rhubana Lodge. Yet this was only the beginning of his association with that part of the world, where he had come to feel intimately involved even as he was disturbed by the death of friends and colleagues on SOE operations.

Immediately after the war, Maxwell struggled with a scheme to develop a shark fishery on the Island of Soay. This was an idea he hatched on wartime visits around the Point of Sleat onboard one of SOE's yachts, and to which he enlisted a fellow Group A instructor, the Newfoundlander Tex Geddes. From 1949 he began to live and write in an old lighthouse keeper's cottage at Sandaig on the Sound of Sleat, which he furnished by purchases from his friend of SOE days, Uilleamena MacRae of the Lochailort Inn. Sandaig became Maxwell's idyllic *Camusfèarna,* where the otter colony he created became the subject of his classic book *Ring of Bright Water* and its sequels, published to worldwide acclaim in the 1960s.

For Peter Kemp a year of dramatic but costly Small Scale Raiding Force incursions into enemy territory on the French coast and the Channel Islands came to an end in December 1942. Amidst concerns that its activity might hamper the more delicate operations of SOE's own clandestine organisation in France and the work of the Secret Intelligence Service, SSRF's commanding officer Major Bill Stirling took the unit to a new base in North Africa to conduct raids on Mediterranean shores. Kemp did not accompany his old Operation *Knife* and Lochailort counterpart, proceeding instead to service with SOE's Albanian Section. Under Stirling, the SSRF metamorphosed into the 2nd Special Air Service Regiment, expanding the SAS force created by his younger brother David. Anders Lassen, the Dane who brought down a stag single-handed back in Morar, won further decorations with the SAS, adding to those awarded for his part in SSRF's 1942 operations. In April 1945 he was killed during the Lake Commachio operation on the coast of Italy. For his outstanding bravery in an attack on German machine gun positions, Major Anders Lassen was awarded a posthumous Victoria Cross, the only foreign national to win the highest British gallantry decoration during the Second World War.

* * *

At the end of 1943 American voices began to be heard among the myriad foreign accents in the Arisaig Paramilitary schools. With Allied strategy for an invasion of north-west Europe by that stage into advanced planning, SOE was embracing a new approach to resistance organisation in France and the Low Countries that would work through co-operation between SOE and its United States counterpart. That such an organisation existed in the US at all was in no small part thanks to the pioneering work of SOE and its forebears. In August 1940, 14 months before American entry into the war, Colonel William Donovan arrived in the UK as a special envoy from the US President F. D. Roosevelt. Donovan's high-level enquiries about the British war situation brought him to meetings with the King, the Prime Minister, and senior military commanders. He also met British Intelligence chiefs including Colonel Colin Gubbins with whom he discussed the British approach to clandestine warfare.

On a second visit in December 1940, Donovan returned to tour a number of naval and military establishments. Following up his earlier interest in clandestine operations and guerrilla methods, Gubbins took Donovan to see what was being done at the Special Training Centre Lochailort and to tour the new Group A Arisaig complex. Donovan left convinced that the US needed a similar kind of organisation.[68] In this President Roosevelt gave him a free hand, and by the summer of 1942 Donovan was directing the Office of Strategic Services (OSS), a new agency reporting directly to the President with responsibility for special operations, secret intelligence and propaganda. The OSS became a powerful arm of the wartime US government, and although it was disbanded at the war's end its function was taken up in 1947 by a successor organisation, the Central Intelligence Agency (CIA).

Initially the Office of Strategic Services modelled itself on Britain's SOE and collaborated closely with it. OSS staff received training at an SOE establishment in Canada that has become known as 'Camp X', the Special Training School set up three miles west of Oshawa, Ontario in December 1941 with the chief purpose of providing this service to the Americans. The first students were senior figures in the OSS set-up, or were training to become instructors themselves. British instructing staff at Camp X included two direct exports from the west highlands. Captain Hugh Pelham-Burn was an explosives and fieldcraft expert who had taught at Arisaig after first serving in France with the Seaforth Highlanders, then joining the Royal Air Force as a fighter pilot. The second was unarmed combat instructor Major William Fairbairn. Leaving his former partner Eric Sykes behind to work for SOE, Fairbairn departed STC Lochailort in March 1942. After a period instructing at Camp X, Fairbairn went to work for OSS directly at its own training centre at Camp Greentop in the Catoctin Mountains, around 60 miles north-west of Washington DC. He brought with him all the methods propounded at Lochailort, including directions to construct a new 'Mystery House' range for reflex shooting.[69]

During 1942, with the United States now in the war, SOE and OSS worked up one collaborative scheme with the objective of injecting a new kind of special operations unit into occupied Europe. Together they would select and prepare a number of three-man teams to be dropped behind enemy lines. The teams were given the code-name *Jedburgh*, although any connection to the Scottish Borders town of that name was entirely random.[70] In each *Jedburgh* team would be one British or American officer, one officer from the recipient country, usually a Frenchman, and a sergeant wireless operator. Their function would be purely military; they would be soldiers, not specially trained civilians. Unlike agents from SOE's French Section, they were not intended to nurture resistance through extended preparations. They would be parachuted into France immediately after an Allied invasion with the immediate job of directing existing resistance forces towards targets previously identified for maximum benefit to the main invasion and advance. *Jedburgh* personnel would wear the uniform of their parent units, hopefully to avoid execution as 'terrorists' or 'Commandos' in the event of capture. By the time the *Jedburgh* scheme was hatched in 1944, French resistance potential had burgeoned, thanks partly to the phenomenon of the Maquis, who yet needed support. The *Jedburgh* strategy was modified accordingly in spring 1944, with a switch to introducing the teams some time before an Allied invasion, in some cases months before, and holding them in readiness all over France.

British officers and radio operators for *Jedburgh* service were sought throughout the Army, the latter largely from armoured regiments, and all were subjected to a formal assessment and selection process at two SOE properties outside London. From February 1944 the main centre for assembling and training *Jedburgh* personnel was Milton Hall, Peterborough, where the instructing team included Captain Eric Sykes, the other half of the broken Fairbairn-Sykes partnership, and American officers who had received training at Arisaig.[71] But before this interim arrangements devised by SOE's new head of training, former Arisaig commandant Colonel J. T. Young, included a preliminary paramilitary course at the Group A schools in Scotland. In November 1943 French volunteers for *Jedburgh* service also began to arrive at SOE's Arisaig complex. These were trained soldiers, several of whom were pre-war regular officers, and most of whom were recruited from the former Vichy French forces in North Africa that had joined General De Gaulle's Free French forces after the 1942 Allied invasion of North Africa.

The American *Jedburgh* officers were recruited by a broad sweep through personnel at US Army camps inside America. French speakers were sought in particular, but few true linguists could be found and the wider appeal extended to anyone interested in special duty overseas. Those who responded were informed only that their task would involve parachute training and that the work would be dangerous.[72] A personal interview process followed, not unlike the one that originally manned the British Commandos. Those who passed interview proceeded to Greentop Camp for an introduction to British Commando methods, including the silent killing and shooting lessons taught by Major William Fairbairn and his American counterpart Rex Applegate who had trained at STC Loichailort.[73] Formal psychological and psychiatric assessments applied by medical staff were another part of the course, a more scientific application of the 'weeding out' process that the British had been applying to special service volunteers by hard training and observation since 1940.

The first US phase of training and selection left 55 American *Jedburgh* officers still standing. In December 1943 they left Greentop Camp for New York and embarked aboard the converted liner *Queen Elizabeth* for one of its regular troopship crossings. After a five-day Atlantic voyage they arrived at Gourock in the Firth of Clyde and completed their journey by train the next day to the west highlands. The Americans were split between Garramor, Traigh House and Inverie. In a rare image record of staff at a Group A school, a series of photographs taken by Inverie commandant Major David Parsons includes American and French officers posted there temporarily, apparently as conducting officers and interpreters.[74]

The formal psychological testing undergone by American *Jedburgh* officers before embarkation was already being applied in the UK to all SOE volunteers, including the *Jedburgh* candidates. Dr William J. Morgan was an American psychologist who worked with SOE's Student Assessment Board at Cranleigh, Surrey, which from June 1943 operated in place of the Preliminary schools. The physical and psychological tests devised there became mandatory for all SOE and intelligence candidates, including those contributed by OSS. In time, a concern emerged that American candidates were being rejected by the Board too often, despite their prior training in the United States. Morgan was put forward as the OSS representative on the Board to help assess and interpret American behaviour patterns.

Morgan originally volunteered for service with OSS as a candidate for operational service, not as a psychologist, and was accepted on the grounds that he spoke fluent French and German. He reached as far as the UK before his qualifications as a psychologist caught up with him and he was seconded to work in the selection and training process. He did not lose sight of his original ambition, however, and on the pretext of gaining insight into what the men he was assessing would be going through, he managed to get himself put through the Arisaig group paramilitary course and on to parachute training at Ringway. At Arisaig he found acknowledgement from the instructing staff that the work of the Student Assessment Board had noticeably reduced the rejection rate at Group A: 'The instructors were grateful to us, because now they could spend their time training students rather than writing letters to London asking that dunderheads be dropped from the course.'

Struggling with an exercise that demanded a precipitous climb up an iron ladder perpendicular against a sheer rock face, and descent by a sophisticated version of the Commando 'Death Slide', he also perceived that the physical challenges set for students were really mental ones:

Every student, man or woman who came to the Scottish schools was strong and nimble and in the pink of condition. The rope-and-ladder exercise was to test nerve, not muscle. No student ever fell from the ladder or off the cliff, but several balked.[75]

The *Jedburgh* teams were only one aspect of co-operation between SOE and the American OSS towards the liberation of France. From

January 1944 overall efforts in special operations were co-ordinated by a joint Special Forces headquarters set up in London. Special Forces HQ preparations for Operation *Overlord*, the main Allied invasion, included the *Jedburghs*, and larger military striking units supplied by the British SAS and their American equivalents, the OSS 'Operational Groups'. But in the months before the invasion was launched, Special Forces HQ also looked to combine resources towards developing existing SOE resistance networks. With this purpose, American OSS personnel arrived for training at the Group A schools in Scotland independently of the *Jedburgh* arrangements.

Two such US students at the Arisaig group were OSS-trained wireless operators Jean Guiet and Herbert Brucker. Guiet was put through the course at Meoble Lodge, of which he later remembered in particular physical training with the manipulation of heavy logs, as favoured by the Commandos at Achnacarry, and fieldcraft exercises in rain-sodden open country:

> I learned covert movement across country (without log!) which I found difficult and frustrating due to lack of cover and concealment on the bare Scottish hills. I still remember crossing streams lying on top of ropes with one leg dangling down for balance and pulling one-self along. It worked far better that the OSS way of trying to hang by one's hands and swing especially with packs and equipment.[76]

Brucker also went through paramilitary training at Meoble, although not on the same course as Guiet. In May 1944 Brucker parachuted into France to form part of the resistance circuit code-named *Hermit* active around Blois on the Loire. Guiet was dropped further south, near Limoges, one night after the D-Day landings, forming one of the four-strong *Salesman* team that included Violette Szabo on her second, ill-fated mission. In 1945 Brucker and Guiet met for the first time while working together for OSS in China. It was only years later, when Brucker read R. J. Minney's 1956 biography of Violette Szabo, *Carve Her Name with Pride*, that he realised Guiet had also been in France. A Christmas card duly arrived at the Guiet household, drawn by Brucker to represent para-military training in 'England'. Its cartoon subjects included a struggling log-PT party.[77]

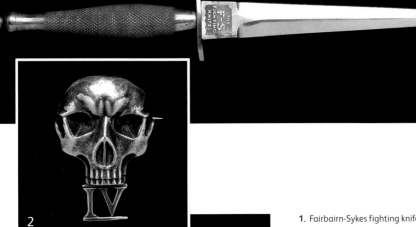

1. Fairbairn-Sykes fighting knife, first pattern, manufactured by Wilkinson Sword from a design by close combat instructors at STC Lochailort.

(NMS)

2. Death's Head cap badge designed by the officers of No.4 Commando, 1940, a short-lived emblem that did not receive official approval.

(NMS)

3. Military Cross awarded to Captain Hutchison Burt, for courage and leadership in No.4 Commando's D-Day assault on the Ouistreham gun battery.

(NMS)

4. Silver tray presented to Brigadier Lord Lovat on departing No.4 Commando to lead the Commando Brigade, 1943.

(THE HONOURABLE HUGH FRASER/NMS)

5. Lieutenant-Colonel Geoffrey Keyes, No.11 Commando, awarded the Victoria Cross for the 'Rommel Raid', 1941. This posthumous 1942 portrait is by Sydney Kendrick.

(JOSA YOUNG/NMS)

6. Flag captured at Anzio by men of 3 Troop of No.9 Commando and adorned by them with a tribute to the Scottish town of Rothesay, 1944.

(CLAN CAMERON MUSEUM/NMS)

7. Decorations of Stuart Chant, No.5 Commando, including the Military Cross for the St Nazaire Raid, with maps he used in training at STC Lochailort.

(THE HONOURABLE IAN CHANT-SEMPILL/NMS)

8. Silk map and No.11 Commando black cap hackle preserved by Lance Corporal Leslie Stables (on right of the photograph) in captivity after the 'Rommel Raid', 1941.

(ROYAL SCOTS REGIMENTAL MUSEUM/NMS)

9. Watercolour of Commando training at Achnacarry 1943, one of a series by Maurice Chauvet, a corporal in the Free French Commando Troop the 1er Compagnie Fusilier Marin.

(COURTESY OF THE COUNCIL OF THE NATIONAL ARMY MUSEUM, LONDON)

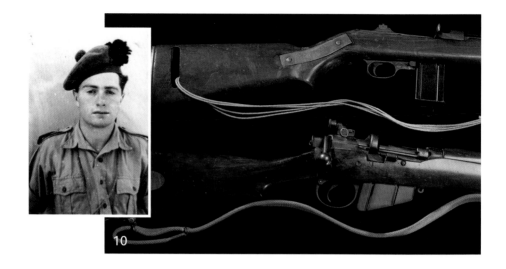

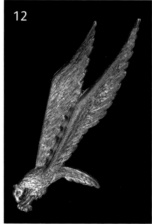

10. Weapons used by Tommy Macpherson on SOE service in France and Italy, 1944-45. The repair to the M1 carbine (top) followed damage in a parachute drop. Macpherson's earlier Commando training took him to STC Lochailort and the Isle of Arran.

(NMS)

11. Badge given to Mrs Barbara Salmon by a Czechoslovak soldier arriving at Mallaig station for paramilitary training in SOE's Group A schools, 1941.

(NMS)

12. Polish parachutist's qualification badge as worn by *Cichociemni* volunteers and men of the 1st Independent Polish Parachute Brigade.

(NMS)

13. Sword made in the foundry at SOE's Inverlair Lodge establishment as a gift for commanding officer Major Aonghais Fyffe, 1944.

(MR A. FYFFE/NMS)

14. British decoration awarded to training instructor Captain Antoni Pospieszalski, for an SOE operation in occupied Poland,1944-45. His SOE service began with the paramilitary course at Inverlochy Castle.

(NMS)

* * *

With such a steady traffic of British and foreign students, instructors and observers, and such a range of operational purposes, security was a high priority matter at the Group A schools. To ensure its integrity, security control was not exercised within the command structure of the Arisaig group but was administered externally by Intelligence Corps personnel of 49 Field Security Section of the Army's Scottish Command. This arrangement would later lead to some minor tension over 'outsider' interference. Non-commissioned officers from 49 FSS were billeted at Arisaig House to monitor the various houses and reported back to their own commanding officer, initially Major Gavin Brown based at Fort William. All communication emanating from inside No.1 Protected Area was censored as a matter of course, letters at an office in Glasgow, telephone calls through a special unit at the Post Office in Fort William.[78] Elaborate arrangements ensured the censorship and outward disguise of mail sent out from the Special Training Schools. The security detachments also monitored the arrival and departure of students and their movements outside the schools while they were in training.

One security benefit of the area chosen for the schools was that there were small railway stations between Lochailort and Mallaig at the villages of Arisaig and Morar, and a request halt at Beasdale where the line intersected the road at a gated level crossing close to Arisaig House. Security officer Lieutenant A. A. (Aonghais) Fyffe recalled: 'This was the ideal spot where a request halt would allow troops to be set down, with no one to see them but the solitary station porter, who also manned the level crossing.'[79]

But the principal security concern was less to do with the curiosity of local people and more about the requirement to prevent staff and students and other military personnel knowing too much about what was happening outside their own immediate sphere of concern, comparing information and making deductions.

In preventing loose talk and unnecessary observation the security arrangements were evidently successful. While teaching at Garramor and Camusdarach, Lieutenant Ernest Van Maurik only ever visited Group A headquarters at Arisaig House and, briefly, when there was a staff shortage there, Inverie House. He had heard something of the lodge at Swordland, and knew of Traigh House and others only as being connected with SOE activity, but did not ask further and was told no more.[80] Outside the SOE loop, in as much as there was one, instructing staff at the Special Training Centre Lochailort were by no means informed as to what was happening further up the Road to the Isles. Fieldcraft instructor Sergeant Angus MacKinnon wondered about it, but knew little: 'As far as I knew it was nothing to do with us. And we saw these lorries closed in going in a lot, and we couldn't fathom out who they were. We heard it was foreigners.'[81]

Despite having authorised the requisition processes and being responsible for security at the SOE schools, senior commanders of the Army in Scotland knew little of what was being done within their realm. In 1945 General Sir Andrew Thorne, the officer commanding the Army's Scottish Command, admitted to Colonel Jack Wilson, SOE's head of Norwegian Section and former head of training, that despite having been the most senior soldier in Scotland 'even he could not make out what we were doing in Arisaig'.[82]

In September 1941 an SOE staff officer working at the holding school for Spanish Section was ordered to a new appointment in relation to the Arisaig schools. This was Lieutenant Aonghais Fyffe who, during 1940 and early 1941, served with 49 Field Security section at Fort William and so was already familiar with the Group A schools. In February 1941 he had been asked by his commanding officer, Major Gavin Brown, to identify a property in the area suitable for a high-security military establishment of an undisclosed nature. Fyffe knew Lochaber well and after inspecting other possibilities recommended Inverlair Lodge, a house on the Braes of Lochaber near Loch Treig, well to the east of Spean Bridge. Inverlair lay outside No.1 Protected Area, but was guarded naturally by the River Spean which separated the house from the Spean Bridge to Kingussie road. The bridge leading over the Spean to Inverlair could easily be controlled. The railway passed close by to the north, with Tulloch station close at hand, so troop and supply movements would be simple. Inverlair Lodge and offices were the property of the British Aluminium Company, whose nearby Loch Laggan dam provided hydro-electric power for the aluminium refinement process.

After making his recommendation about the suitability of Inverlair, Fyffe heard no more about the matter and left the highlands when his job changed suddenly in April 1941. He had been recommended to SOE by his superiors, and in a brief meeting with Brigadier Colin Gubbins on the platform of Fort William railway station he was commissioned into the organisation on the spot. Now, after five months of applying his knowledge of Spanish to the benefit of SOE's Spanish Section in London, Lieutenant Fyffe was on his way back in the highlands with rather surprising orders. Inverlair Lodge had been requisitioned as per his suggestion, for the use of SOE, and he himself was being put in command of the new establishment. Its purpose concerned the other Special Training Schools and the overall security of SOE, in relation to which a potentially serious weakness had been identified.

Inherent in any training and selection process worth the name is the rejection of a proportion of candidates. Even if the Group A schools were turning down no more than 20 per cent of their students, that still represented some 500 personnel rejected over the course of the Group's existence. Given the overall approach to security, whereby most students at the Arisaig schools would have nothing more than vague understanding and assumptions about what it was they were being trained for, this was not necessarily a problem. However, across the Training Section of SOE as a whole, and including the organisation's operational holding schools, students could be identified at any stage as unsuitable mentally or physically for operations. The knowledge they had been allowed to accrue, even awareness of those people they had trained alongside, could be construed to compromise security. There were cases therefore where it was considered unsafe to return rejected students to normal army or civilian life, at least in the short term until the operations for which they were originally being prepared had been carried out or superseded.

Inverlair was conceived therefore as a place to send those individuals who had fallen out of the training process and were considered, often through no fault of their own, to be a temporary security risk. It was not a prison, nor was it a straightforward internment centre, although internment was certainly its business. It was a place where personnel in this category could be kept isolated, busy, and unaware that this was the impasse they had reached. Personnel sent for periods at Inverlair came from across several Country Sections of SOE operating in Europe, including individuals from Yugoslavia, Poland and Estonia, with a concentration of individuals and small parties rejected from Belgian and Danish Sections. Some used their own names, others the alias by which they were known within SOE. Only some 70 individuals were sent there in total and an average stay was of four to six months in duration.[83]

Individuals held for such a length of time had to be given something useful to do, preferably something that they could see to be useful themselves. The role given to them was to make Inverlair a workshop for the rest of SOE's training establishments. A small foundry was created where metal discarded from the various aluminium works around Lochaber was fashioned into training and operational tools. The Inverlair establishment produced targets and other parts for firing ranges and assault courses, and equipment such as climbing gear and boat hooks. In addition to the commanding officer and security personnel, there were only three permanent staff at Inverlair: two Italians and one Belgian removed from the SOE stream just as the others. One of the former, Lance Corporal Purisiol, was a skilled engineer; he produced the most sophisticated work from the foundry, including a small collapsible steel bow with aluminium tipped arrows ordered as a prototype by Captain Eric Sykes.

From the summer of 1943 the great project was to create an assault course and firing range on site. This was intended to train non-commissioned officers from Military Intelligence who had been selected to form liaison teams that would operate with Special Forces detachments in France following D-Day.[84] Major Fyffe (as he had been promoted) designed the assault course on the lines of the one at Garramor, and directed construction of an elaborate firing range complete with a 'street' of nearly 100 yards length lined with false building façades, pop-up and moving targets. Until the end of the year, intakes of the external trainees went over the courses and through fieldcraft work and extended exercises in the mountains of the Nevis Range to the south-west of Inverlair.[85] By February 1944 Inverlair was marked for closure, its purpose served as SOE turned to concentrate on deploying the *Overlord*-related operations. As a parting gift, Major Fyffe was presented with a handsome two-handed cross-hilt sword made in the Inverlair foundry by Purisiol. On his final day Fyffe relaxed the stringent security which had operated throughout to agree to Company Sergeant-Major Alexander Thomson's request that a group photograph be taken of the Inverlair staff in front of the Lodge.

* * *

Major Fyffe's responsibilities extended beyond his command duties at Inverlair Lodge. Working from his Inverlair base he was placed in charge of security at all SOE's Special Training Schools in Scotland, a job that entailed regular visits to the Group A complex at Arisaig. From early 1942 his jurisdiction extended to the east, when SOE opened up three new establishments in a different district of the highlands. This was 'Group 26', a complex of three properties in the forests of Rothiemurchus and Abernethy in Strathspey on the north-west side of the Cairngorm mountains.[86] Drumintoul was a substantial Victorian shooting lodge, part of the Rothiemurchus estate owned by Colonel John Grant of Rothiemurchus.[87] Glenmore Lodge, an establishment overlooking Loch Morlich, was the property of the Forestry Commission.[88] To the north towards Nethy Bridge was the secluded Forest Lodge, part of the Seafield estate, a timber-clad shooting lodge of 1880. These three buildings were requisitioned to form a training and holding centre for a company of selected men organised by SOE's Norwegian Section.[89]

SOE interest in Norway followed on from MI(R)'s earlier concentration on activity in that country, and developed alongside ongoing activity by the Secret Intelligence Service, all concerned with the strategic and industrial significance of Norway in the German war effort. After the Allied evacuation from Norway in May 1940, thousands of Norwegian seamen and other exiles made their way to the United Kingdom. Many were concentrated in Scotland, first of all at Hamilton, Lanarkshire, then in a reception camp at Dumfries. By spring 1941 more than 1300 men were formed into units of the Norwegian Brigade, training and contributing to the defence of Britain, but formally part of the Royal Norwegian Army and dedicated to their country's liberation. Yet although a pool of manpower was developing in Scotland and a resistance movement *Milorg* was organising in Norway itself, SOE's work took time to develop.

In September 1940 Captain Martin Linge of the Royal Norwegian Army was recruited by SOE in London. Linge had been wounded during the German invasion of his country and joined the Allied evacuation to escape the occupation. He came into the orbit of the newly-formed Norwegian Section by virtue of earlier acquaintance with one of the Section's two British staff officers, Royal Navy Lieutenant J. L. Chaworth-Musters, who had been based in Bergen when the Germans attacked. In his British exile, Captain Linge became the crucial link whose abilities and leadership allowed the process of selecting and training Norwegians for SOE service to be stepped up.[90] Choosing candidates from among Norwegians already in the United Kingdom, and from independent parties that were frequently arriving in Scottish ports in small-boats after completing the dangerous crossing of the North Sea, a company of trained men began to be formed.

Meantime, SOE was aware that the Directorate of Combined Operations was planning its first sizeable Commando raid on the coast of Norway. Captain Linge and a small detachment of Norwegian soldiers were lent to the operation to aid contact with civilians and add to the political value of the raid. After a few weeks of special training in Scotland, probably at the Group A schools at Arisaig rather than with the Commandos, Linge's party participated in the first attack on the Lofoten Islands of March 1941.[91] Although the Norwegian government in exile in London was unimpressed by the lack of consultation from the British over the Lofotens raid, the fact that Norwegians had been in action back in their own country was a fillip for Norwegian Section and its recruitment effort. One acquisition to the unit made shortly afterwards was Joachim Rønneberg, recently arrived in Shetland by small-boat, who was impressed by Linge and his assurance that a return to Norway on active service would not be far off.[92]

Now bearing the official title 'Norwegian Independent Company No.1', and with its members no longer civilians but soldiers enrolled into the Royal Norwegian Army, the SOE-backed unit was first based between establishments at Stodham Park, Liss in Hampshire and Fawley Court near Henley-on-Thames. The first training parties went through the Group A paramilitary course at Meoble Lodge, the Beaulieu Finishing schools and parachute instruction at Ringway. As was the practice at Group A for regular foreign intakes, Rønneberg was attached to the Arisaig staff to oversee the Norwegian training at Meoble.

Further plans for Commando raids on Norway were being hatched during 1941 that offered opportunity for the new Norwegian unit's involvement. The decision was taken to seek a more suitable and secure base than Henley-on-Thames where battle training could be conducted. Captain Linge, Lieutenant Chaworth-Musters and Lieutenant-Colonel Jack Wilson (appointed SOE's head of training in May 1941) searched the highlands for something suitable and settled on the three shooting lodges below the Cairngorms, well beyond the end of the public road to Coylumbridge. In contrast to the gentler landscapes of Hampshire and populous Henley-on-Thames, here was mountainous terrain somewhat similar to that of Norway, a large area of wild and relatively empty ground with few people to observe or obstruct what was going on.

Before the move was finalised, personnel from the Norwegian Independent Company participated in the second major Commando action in Norway, the Vågsøy Raid of December 1941. This operation had two serious repercussions for the SOE unit. The first was the loss of Captain Linge, killed in action leading an attack on German headquarters at Måløy during the raid. The second was that its effects exacerbated the rather uncomfortable relationship that had grown between SOE and Combined Operations on the one hand, and the Norwegian Army and its government in London on the other. German reprisals against civilians not only upset the Norwegian government in a straightforward sense, but aggravated its fear of being presented and perceived at home as a puppet of the British. There was unhappiness too from the *Milorg* resistance organisation within Norway which had not been consulted about British raiding plans and their possible effects on its clandestine activities.

Unease over the official reaction to Vågsøy led to disciplinary problems for SOE in the short term when three groups then in training for small sabotage missions demanded assurances that their operations had Norwegian government approval. As a security measure the teams concerned were temporarily interned in the Arisaig district. A minor exodus by discontented elements from the Norwegian Independent Company followed.[93] Fortunately, discord within and around the Company was largely resolved in the first months of 1942. Organisational changes made within SOE and the Norwegian military command structure established better communication and closer liaison between the two interests and with *Milorg* in Norway. Overall strategy and operations were planned through an Anglo-Norwegian Collaboration Committee in London. At Group 26 in the Cairngorms, although tensions about British policy and intentions did not disappear entirely, a potential crisis was averted and the Independent Company was able to get on with preparing for operations relieved of doubt about Norwegian sanction for its activities.[94] Stung by the loss of its founder and inspirational leader, the Company organised a memorial service for Captain Martin Linge at Aviemore. They further honoured his memory by adopting the unofficial title by which it has since been known, 'Kompani Linge' – the Linge Company.[95]

With Lieutenant-Colonel Jack Wilson placed in overall control of Norwegian Section at the beginning of 1942, the Group 26 establishments came first under the immediate command of Major Charles Hampton, who had formerly been a staff officer at the Independent Company holding centre at Achdalieu. A Norwegian liaison officer was also attached to the Group 26 staff reporting directly to Captain Leif Tronstad, the staff officer at Norwegian High Command responsible for Linge Company operations. Drumintoul Lodge was the headquarters and administrative centre, with Glenmore Lodge and Forest Lodge providing accommodation and training facilities. The staff of each establishment was almost entirely Norwegian, many of them brought back to the United Kingdom after the two Commando raids on the Lofotens, although the British staff contingent at Drumintoul grew over time. In 1943 the capacity of Glenmore Lodge was increased by the construction of log barracks by Newfoundland Forestry Unit personnel based at nearby Abernethy camp, allowing Linge Company to vacate Forest Lodge.[96]

Unlike the Group A schools' role as a station in the peripatetic training process, the Group 26 establishments served as Linge Company's permanent base. Training was concentrated there, although not exclusively. The Company conducted exercises in other parts of Scotland and continued to make use of other SOE training facilities, including the Group A schools to the west. Linge Company became the principal customers for the para-naval school at Tarbet on Loch Nevis, served by accommodation at Swordland nearby on the shore of Loch Morar. In early 1943 a typical soldier of Linge Company at Group 26 was still likely to have passed through the extended training process between Stodham Park, Meoble and Ringway. There is some evidence that the 1st Independent Polish Parachute Brigade made their pre-parachute training schools in Fife available to the Norwegians in order to aid their preparations and help ease pressure on SOE's centres at Ringway.[97] Finishing training at one of the Beaulieu schools gave instruction in such required skills as 'how to act behind German lines', 'how to make contact' and 'cover stories', and gave information about German politics and Gestapo methods. A wireless signals course at Thame Park, Oxfordshire was the final step before the student joined the Linge Company in the highlands.

At the Group 26 base, training continued on an ongoing basis as the men waited to be deployed on operations. Preparation for specific missions aside, the Linge men were kept busy with a flexible programme that refined the individual training received thus far and prepared the men, many of whom had little or no military experience, to operate as a military unit themselves as well as set-up and run resistance forces on formal military lines. Full use of the Cairngorm terrain and climate was made to develop reconnaissance skills and assessment of ground, camouflage and general tactics for operations. Some ski training was conducted in the winter of 1943/44, principally concerned with patrol tactics since most men of the Company had the ability to ski in any case. Specialist courses covered such subjects as boat-handling, mines, home-made weapons, propaganda, street-fighting and industrial sabotage.[98] Firing ranges and a length of railway tracks for mock demolitions appeared. The men practiced street-fighting among timber buildings specially constructed at Glenmore Lodge. These they creatively augmented with street signs such as 'Judas Stredet' and 'Quislings Torv', reflecting the Company's feelings about the collaborationist government in Norway led by Vidkun Quisling.[99]

One Linge Company sergeant, Paal Wergeland, remembered the frustration of training for months towards operations that were then cancelled: 'In war there is always much waiting, waiting, waiting.'[100] But if the men were trained hard, and felt a natural anxious impatience about their own and their country's future, life at Group 26 was not without compensations, as recorded by 2nd Lieutenant Knut Haukelid:

> We lived a good, tiring, open-air life. There were quantities of roe deer and stags in the mountains, and the rivers were full of salmon. Because of the war there were few who had leisure to profit legitimately from these good things, and the Scottish authorities were ready to turn a blind eye to our expeditions to get meat and fish for the camp. The British soldiers' rations were comparatively slender for the big Norwegian lads, and without extras from the mountains and rivers we should have lived much less well than we did. We ourselves, however, set a limit on our shooting; not more than five stags might be shot in one week. One of the boys was unfortunate; he was caught deer-stalking by a landowner and had to fork out a five pounds' fine for poaching.
>
> The object of the life was clear. We were to learn to fend for ourselves, like the men of ancient Sparta.[101]

To help maintain morale, SOE prepared secret briefings about successful missions and announced gallantry decorations to Linge Company men, all prepared in written reports which were read out to the assembled Company and then marked for destruction. To inspire and reassure the men that Norway endorsed their work to the very highest level, King

Haakon VII of Norway and his son Crown Prince Olav, Chief of Defence in the Norwegian government, visited Group 26 on more than one occasion and watched demonstrations of the Company's training programme. On return from operations in Norway Linge men would often be called for personal interview with their King, concerned to learn all he could about the condition of his people.

The Linge men had little contact with other military personnel in the area, even though Norwegians were serving nearby with 52nd (Lowland) Division and the Commando Mountain and Snow Warfare Training Centre was operating on the other side of the mountains. In March 1943 there was some unease that a new Independent Parachute Company, formed from the Norwegian Brigade and based temporarily at Grantown-on-Spey, was ski training on the hills immediately above Glenmore, one of the few places where sufficient snow lay that winter. In light of the scarcity of snow SOE gave permission for this, but the paratroopers were also practising field-firing just opposite Glenmore Lodge itself. The politics of the situation were delicate, but in light of the security risks Norwegian Section politely suggested an alternative arrangement might work better in future.[102]

A measure of contact with the local civilian population was however permitted. A tea room in nearby Grantown-on-Spey was a favoured spot, and Sergeant Paal Wergeland recalled enjoying days of leave in Nethy Bridge and Kingussie, and ceilidh dances at Grantown-on-Spey when not saving up leave for weekend trips to Edinburgh or longer visits to London. Local fraternisation was in itself a useful means of monitoring rumours and identifying security weaknesses, since civilians in regular contact with the Norwegians in their midst could be asked to report inappropriate behaviour without need for any detailed explanations. Major Fyffe was impressed that despite the considerable freedom of movement and association enjoyed by Linge Company men, there were no cases of careless talk from among their number.[103]

Linge Company had occasional opportunity to repay the hospitality it enjoyed by making itself useful locally. In October 1942 a party of recreational climbers suffered an accident on the Shelter Stone crag above Loch Avon in the midst of the Cairngorms. A midnight request from the police for military assistance from Glenmore Lodge was answered promptly and a rescue party organised. Two climbers were discovered safe, and the body of a third was recovered from the crag, a 'notable marching and climbing feat' that earned the admiration of those civilians present and enhanced the local reputation of the mysterious Norwegian soldiers at Glenmore.[104] By contrast, after numerous complaints about dogs kept at Glenmore Lodge, in May 1943 the Company received a bill from local estate keeper John MacDonald for the market value of five sheep destroyed by their dogs, actually huskies acquired for experiments in training with sled dogs. The bill, and the attention drawn by the dogs to the Company's activities, was enough for Lieutenant-Colonel Wilson to direct that the experiment with sled dogs be discontinued.[105]

On extended training schemes Linge Company ranged further afield than the immediate Cairngorm environment. Mock attacks included advances through Strathspey to capture coastal artillery emplacements near Fort George, Ardersier, and schemes along Deeside to the east of the Cairngorms to attack airfields in the vicinity of Aberdeen. Long marches over hard terrain preceded sabotage exercises at the British Aluminium Company's generating plant at Foyers on Loch Ness and larger plant near Fort William.[106] Late in 1943 security officer Major Fyffe had the opportunity to help organise and observe one of Linge Company's operation rehearsals, a scheme involving a night landing from Loch Linnhe onto the coast of Ardgour and an advance over mountainous country to the south shore of Loch Eil. The objective was a night attack on three ammunition depot ships lying in the loch which would be carried out by three sabotage teams in small-boats.

Fyffe was deeply impressed by the speed and discipline shown by the Linge men, but no more so than the Royal Navy officer commanding the Motor Launch (ML) which brought them down Loch Linnhe at the outset to land in relays by small-boat at Inversanda:

> He asked what kind of troops these commandos were – he had met them before but they were usually noisy, clattered about his deck, and slapped the water noisily as they pulled away from the ML. He hadn't heard a word spoken since our lot came aboard – 'What kind of chaps are these?' I explained that they were just very highly trained and indoctrinated to the hilt in security. He then asked if we would mind if he might be allowed to use an Aldis lamp to see just where the boat had got to. Tommy and I agreed and he swept the waters from ship along the supposed route to the shore; but there was nothing above the water. He then did pick out the boat just about

to pull away from the rocky shore as the last of the third party were melting into the countryside behind. He was clearly astonished by the speed of the transfers ship to shore and by the total silence of the entire operation; his crew seemed equally mystified.

Likewise surprised was the commander of the three vessels in Loch Eil on the other side of the Ardgour hills, which were quickly subdued in the concluding attack. Major Fyffe found that this officer's exasperation at the result was tempered a little by his admiration for Linge Company's performance:

It was a first-rate operation and I had to explain away the attack to the naval officer in charge the following day; he had, of course, not been forewarned by his superiors and was understandably peeved at the success of our groups and the complete failure of the ships' guards in all three instances. But we parted good friends and he complimented us on the efficiency of the operation, swearing we would never get a second chance to repeat the exercise with the same success.[107]

The strength of Linge Company fluctuated around a little over 200 officers and men at any one time.[108] The Company recruited a total of 530 candidates for service between August 1940 and May 1945. One hundred and sixty of these men were rejected during the training process and returned to their units within the Norwegian forces. At Group 26 there was considerable throughput of personnel. Teams and individuals departed on operational service, returned to Scotland at the conclusion of their missions, and men of the resistance arrived from Norway for training. Much of this traffic of men and supplies was conducted by a flotilla of whale-catchers and fishing vessels based in the Shetland Isles. The clandestine ferrying of personnel and materials across the North Sea by Norwegian fisherman employed by SOE has become known to posterity as 'The Shetland Bus'.[109]
Formally the 'Norwegian Independent Naval Unit', the Shetland Bus was not the only route in or out. Sea crossings were also undertaken by 30/54 Motor Torpedo Boat Flotilla of the Royal Norwegian Navy based at Lerwick, and other vessels operated by the British Secret Intelligence Service. On occasion men landed from submarines of the Royal Norwegian Navy based at Dundee. More frequently, men were dropped by parachute directly into Norway, a hazardous operation for air crews flying

at night and parachutists required to land in mountainous country. These operations were the work of Special Duty flights from RAF squadrons, including Catalina sea-planes flown from Woodhaven on the Firth of Tay by Norwegian airmen of the Royal Air Force.[110] After operations the men might be picked up again by boat, or they might take the overland escape journey to the Swedish border when necessary, a hazardous and exhausting trip over testing terrain.

The Shetland-based Independent Naval Unit was nevertheless a vital shuttle for the Linge Company, who shared its services with other operatives of Norwegian Section and the Norwegians' own intelligence service. The Shetland Bus was in fact instigated by the British Secret Intelligence Service (SIS) who recruited volunteers from the crews of refugee fishing boats arriving in Shetland from Norway in the summer of 1940. By the winter of 1940/41, SOE was involved in introducing and retrieving resistance operatives from Norway by the same means, to such an extent that SIS felt there might be a security risk to its own intelligence-gathering work and resolved to establish a separate base at Peterhead on the Scottish mainland. Information gathered through co-operation between SIS and Norwegian intelligence and coast-watching stations in Norway maintained from Peterhead, brought notable successes in conventional and unconventional attacks on shipping in Norwegian waters.[111]

Meanwhile SOE's Shetland base had its headquarters at Flemington House near Lerwick. For security reasons the boat station moved to remote Lunna Voe in the summer of 1941, and in the autumn of 1942 extended to a new purpose-built slipway and accommodation at Scalloway. A further station operated on the Scottish mainland at Burghead on the Moray Firth during 1942-43. Accessible by rail, and more easily reached from Group 26 than Shetland, Burghead was a useful reserve base. Only five trips were launched from there, however. The Burghead operation closed down following the loss of its commandant, two officers and one seaman to a sailing accident in the Moray Firth, an incident into which police investigations were suppressed for security reasons.[112]

The boat crews of the Norwegian Independent Naval Unit were civilian volunteers in the direct employ of SOE. Only in 1944 were they eventually incorporated as a regular unit of the Royal Norwegian Navy. Security was stringent. Waiting before trips the crews were kept entirely separate from the men they were to carry, and there was no exchange of information while at sea. Approaches through enemy-patrolled coastal waters to drop men and cargoes, and rendezvous for collections in the opposite direction, carried considerable risks. Some crewmen of the Unit received SOE training at the Group A schools in order to equip them for encounters with the enemy.

A North Sea crossing in winter was hazardous at the best of times, and only in winter did the long hours of darkness allow the fishing boats to make their secret journeys unobserved by enemy aircraft and coastal patrols. Losses of vessels and their crews due to the weather and enemy air attack, the capture and even execution of crews and their SOE passengers, were all part of the life of the Shetland Bus link. The winter of 1942/43 was the most costly, with seven boats and 33 lives lost. The success rate of trips improved in the winter of 1943/44 when three fast submarine-chaser vessels supplied by the American OSS replaced the fishing boats. All told, in over 150 voyages the Shetland Bus carried 192 operational personnel and 383 tons of equipment to Norway, and extracted 73 agents and 373 refugees on return.[113]

Once delivered to Norway, Linge Company operations fell into different categories. The ongoing commitment was to provide support, organisation and communication for *Milorg*. Trained wireless operators were the lifeblood of the resistance organisation, and Linge Company men were one source of skills and equipment to instruct members of *Milorg* groups in how to continue the work after their own departure. Fifty-seven Linge men were specially trained as wireless operators for work of this kind.[114] Others, like Sergeant Wergeland despatched to the *Milorg* division operating in Vestlandet, went as weapons instructors and military organisers to pass on the skills learnt in SOE's schools. For immediate impact on the German occupying forces and the industrial assets at the enemy's disposal, Linge Company planned and carried out numerous acts of sabotage against shipping and technical targets.

As was to be expected with hazardous operations of this nature, the results of missions were mixed. One sizeable operation of winter 1942/43, codenamed *Carhampton*, was a plan to commandeer a merchant convoy in the Flekkefjord in southern Norway and bring it back to the United Kingdom. This was the concept of Captain Odd Starheim, one of the founder members of Linge Company. The whaler *Bødo*, lent by the Royal Navy and launched on this occasion from Aberdeen, landed a 40-strong force of Linge Company and Royal Norwegian Navy personnel close to the fjord. The first disaster to befall the operation was the loss of the *Bødo* on the return journey, sunk with only two survivors from a crew of 35 when it struck a mine.

Unaware of the fate of their ship the raiding party waited some weeks for a suitable target to arrive in the fjord; but when the opportunity came they failed to press home their surprise attack on four ships. With the enemy alerted to their presence, the raiders were forced into weeks of hiding in the mountains in severe weather conditions that demanded all the survival skills the men had developed in their training. A second objective was nevertheless identified and achieved: the capture of a coastal steamer which was taken at gunpoint by 16 men of the team, leaving the remainder of those still with the operation to be smuggled back to British shores in a fishing boat. The next day a German aircraft spotted the commandeered steamer and sank it; there were no survivors from its crew or the *Carhampton* men who had taken it. The failure of Operation *Carhampton* was a chilling example of how much could be lost for little apparent gain when planning and chance went awry in sabotage operations.[115]

By contrast, the local knowledge and abilities of the Linge Company men could produce substantial results at comparatively little cost. Lieutenant Peter Deinboll, a Linge officer, was the son of an engineer at the Orkla pyrites mines south-west of Trondheim. The traffic of pyrites, from which the Germans could manufacture sulphuric acid for industrial use, was considered a highly worthwhile target. During 1942 Deinboll twice led small teams in sabotage operations launched by sea from Shetland, which destroyed first the generating plant that powered the mine and its electric railway and, in a subsequent operation, disabled a 5000-ton ship in the Orkla river. After the second attack Deinboll and his two comrades had to make their escape on skis over the Swedish border, with the injured Deinboll forced to survive alone for a week in extreme temperatures by taking refuge in remote mountain huts. Two further attacks launched in 1943 and 1944 damaged the railway transport that moved the ore from the Orkla mines. At the loss of one man killed and a second captured, the Orkla operations put serious hindrance upon an important industrial asset for the enemy.[116]

SOE's other main objective in Norway was to undertake and support attacks on enemy shipping. The broken Norwegian coastline was a vital strategic asset to the German war effort, one whose importance grew after the German invasion of the Soviet Union in the summer of 1941. SOE-sponsored actions against shipping in harbour ran from minor attacks on dock installations and commercial vessels to audacious attempts to destroy capital ships of the German Navy. In October 1942 a daring plan to attack the battleship *Tirpitz* in the Trondheimfjord using 'Chariot' two-manned steered torpedoes came within a hair's breadth of success. The *Arthur*, a Shetland Bus fishing vessel towing Chariots, managed to enter the fjord undetected. On board the *Arthur* were Royal Navy divers trained in Scottish sea lochs and ready to steer the Chariots to their target. When the attack seemed set to succeed, a sudden pitch by the boat caused the Chariots to break loose and sink. In November 1943 a failed attempt against Bergen harbour employed 'Welman', electrically powered one-man submarines, one manned by Linge Company's Sergeant Pederson who was captured after his craft was hit by fire from an enemy minesweeper.[117]

During 1943 selected men from Linge Company went from Group 26 back to the west highlands to undergo specialist training in ship sabotage from small craft at the Tarbet and Swordland Group A schools. In the relatively calm stretch of Loch Morar and rougher sea waters of Loch Nevis, they learned to handle kayaks and 'folbot' folding canoes and how to approach their targets and place 'limpet' magnetic bombs on their hulls. In autumn 1943 and spring 1944, eight kayak operations code-named *Vestige* were attempted against shipping in Norwegian harbours, two of which were successful. In the first, in September 1943, a team of three Linge Company men landed near Gulen. When conditions were right Sergeant Ragner Ulstein paddled out in his kayak under cover of darkness, stowing three 'limpets' between his legs. Undetected he placed his charges successfully on the *Hertmut*, a large refrigerated cargo vessel with a torpedo boat escort. The team withdrew and watched the resulting explosion. The damage done to the *Hertmut* put it into months of repairs and the sabotage team escaped successfully.[118]

But among the many operations undertaken by Linge Company, its greatest success, the feat for which it has been celebrated above all its many achievements, was the 'Heavy Water Raid', a sabotage attack on the Norsk-Hydro industrial plant at Vemork in the Rjukan valley of Telemark. The target was Norway's stock of deuterium oxide (D_2O), the 'heavy water' that was a chemical by-product of the Vemork plant's hydrogen electrolysis process and a substance that was arduous to produce. Before the discovery of uranium enrichment, heavy water was the key to the process of modifying atomic chain reaction. The Allies knew German scientists had uranium at their disposal and had been working on a nuclear reactor. With a workable supply of heavy water, it was possible that Germany might be able to beat the United States in research towards harnessing atomic energy. For the Allies, potential German realisation of atomic power for electricity generation was reason enough for concern; the dread prospect was that in the future it might conceivably arm Hitler's Germany with an atomic bomb.

Early in 1942 the Allies learned from British and Norwegian intelligence sources that much attention was being paid to increasing the production of heavy water at the Vemork plant. There was no clear information that work on a bomb was at hand, nor that production of a bomb in the short term was likely, but American nuclear scientists were especially anxious at these latest developments in Norway. The British government felt that no chance could be taken, however remote the possibility of a German bomb, and gave instruction that Vemork must be destroyed. One important information source was Professor Captain Leif Tronstad, who before arriving in the United Kingdom and serving with the Norwegian High Command had been a prominent figure in the early days of resistance organisation in Norway. Tronstad was also one of his country's leading nuclear scientists, and he knew much about the Vemork installation and its operation. A second was Einar Skinnarland, who lived and worked in the Rjukan valley and had contacts at Vemork. Skinnarland escaped Norway with Linge Company's Odd Starheim in March 1942. He quickly received training as a radio operator and was parachuted back into the Rjukan area within a matter of days, returning to work as if nothing had happened.

Conventional air bombing was ruled out at first. Rjukan was at the extreme range of British bomber aircraft, which to reach Vemork would have to fly by night over mountainous terrain and in risky weather conditions. Even if bombers were fortunate enough to evade German air defences and reach their target, Vemork was naturally protected by the deep Rjukan valley, and the heavy water plant itself was known to be deep within the basement of an eight-storey reinforced concrete building.[119] Instead, SOE was asked to prepare the way for an ambitious attack to be planned and carried out by Combined Operations Command, where assault parties of Royal Engineers from 1st Airborne Division would land in two Horsa gliders to attack the plant. The key to Vemork was the ability to operate on the Hardangervidda, a vast upland plateau of featureless winter snows that abuts the Rjukan valley. Linge Company's training in the Cairngorms of Scotland gave some approximation to the conditions they would face on the Hardangervidda. A team of four Linge men was selected to parachute into the area, guide the gliders in to landing zones on the Hardangervidda and lead the attackers to Vemork. First they briefed the Royal Engineer glider teams, who trained for the raid in the mountains of north Wales and also visited the Scottish highlands to view the Lochaber hydroelectric installations that could inform their destruction of the Vemork plant.[120]

The Linge Company team, code-named *Grouse*, included Sergeant Claus Helberg who was born and raised in Rjukan, and radio operator Fenrik (2nd Lieutenant) Knut Haugland, also born in Rjukan. Haugland's recruitment into Linge Company was influenced, he believes, by a boyhood background in the Scouting movement, an interest he shared with Lieutenant-Colonel Wilson who interviewed him as head of Norwegian Section.[121] The *Grouse* team jumped onto the Hardangervidda on 18 October 1942. Forced to endure fierce snowstorms and complete a strength-sapping ski journey over 45 km to the drop zone, they were ready to receive the gliders on the night of 19 November. The *Grouse* men briefly heard the engines of the Halifax bombers towing their gliders, but no more. The airborne attack plan, Operation *Freshman*, was a disaster. In deteriorating weather conditions, the bombers and their glider loads failed to find the drop zone. Heading for home, the tow rope pulling one glider snapped, sending it crashing into a mountainside. The second Halifax crashed shortly afterwards, killing the crew. Its glider came down against a mountain. Those of the Airborne Royal Engineers who survived the crash of the two gliders were interrogated and summarily executed in accordance with Hitler's Führer Order issued only weeks earlier.

Vemork stood intact, its German defenders alerted by the failure of *Freshman* to the Allies' intention to destroy it. Security measures around the plant were heightened. The *Grouse* team remained in operation in the vicinity however, and SOE was now given the chance to organise a sabotage raid of its own, a plan originally urged by Leif Tronstad. Tronstad and Wilson arrived at the Group 26 centre in Scotland to select and brief a second Linge Company team to parachute onto the Hardangervidda, rendezvous with the original *Grouse* party (renamed *Swallow* for this second operation), enter the plant and destroy the heavy water stocks with explosives. The second team, code-named *Gunnerside*, would be led by Fenrik (2nd Lieutenant) Joachim Rønneberg who selected five of the Company's fittest men for the task.

The *Gunnerside* team left the highlands soon after to prepare for the specifics of the plan at Brickendonbury Manor, where a mock-up of the heavy water apparatus was prepared allowing the saboteurs to practice the demolition process until it became as second nature to them. They then went to another SOE establishment at Gaynes Hall, near St Neots, Cambridgeshire, to await suitable conditions for the mission. Rønneberg meantime had been busy acquiring the necessary ski and survival equipment from the stores of the Royal Norwegian Army at Dumfries and specialist retailers in London. The team's all-important mountaineering boots came from a supplier in the East Midlands, recommended to Rønneberg by a well-shod hill-walking party he had happened to notice while training in the Cairngorms.[122]

Out on the Hardangervidda winter fell hard, testing the men of the *Grouse/Swallow* team to the limits of endurance as they lived in remote mountain huts surviving on meagre rations and scarce fuel supplies. The *Gunnerside* parachute drop required settled weather and clear, moonlit conditions. Waiting for these lasted three months, a test of nerve in itself for the men out in the snows, and also for Rønneberg's team holed up at Gaynes Hall. In January 1943, after weather again forced postponement until the next full moon period, Rønneberg requested his team be relieved from anxious waiting and take the chance to conduct some extra training in rugged country, perhaps back at the Group A schools at Arisaig. By chance an SOE officer at Gaynes Hall, Major Dunlop MacKenzie, owned a remote property in the Portavadie area of Argyll down on the eastern shore of Loch Fyne. It was agreed that this posed no security risk and *Gunnerside* gratefully accepted MacKenzie's offer of the use of his house at Crispie and a cottage further down the coast at Stillaig Bay. They spent some weeks there, split between the two houses, training and waiting in isolation. Second Lieutenant Knut Haukelid found that time passed slowly:

> At our own request we were moved to a solitary place, where we waited for the next full moon. A little stone house with white window-frames on an island in the north of Scotland was placed at our disposal. We went for long walks on the moors and in the hills, shot

seal and stags. It was lonely, healthy and tedious. The winter was even wetter than it is in Vestlandet.[123]

The location was not in fact an island, but might easily have seemed so, reached by boat from Greenock to Rothesay on the Isle of Bute and then back to the mainland by Tighnabruaich.[124]

On 16 February 1943 conditions were finally acceptable to drop *Gunnerside* on the Hardangervidda; but a storm blew up shortly after they landed and it took days of labouring through blizzard conditions to make the rendezvous with *Swallow*. Thereafter, the operation went entirely according to plan. Using insider information and a detailed reconnaissance of the plant perimeter carried out by Sergeant Helberg, an unguarded way into Vemork was identified. The normal access route into the plant was a suspension bridge spanning the Rjukan valley, a deep narrow gorge at this point. The bridge was heavily guarded. To bypass it the saboteurs would scramble down the gorge in the dark of night, cross the Maane River, and scale the 600-foot rock face on the other side, a feat apparently discounted by the German garrison as unlikely to the point of being impossible.

The attack was made on the night of 27/28 February. The combined team approached the area on skis and negotiated the gorge without major difficulty. They breached the perimeter of the plant with bolt cutters and crossed an open yard without incident. While a covering party waited and watched the movement of sentries, the demolition team entered the heavy water building through a service duct. A night watchman, and the plant foreman who arrived shortly afterwards, had to be held at gunpoint. The saboteurs placed plastic explosive charges with 30-second fuses on the electrolytic cells and retreated; the two Vemork workers were released in time to get clear. The saboteurs were still inside the plant perimeter when the charges exploded, a small explosion that did not initially trigger a reaction from the guard. By the time sirens sounded and the German garrison down the road to Rjukan was roused into action, the saboteurs were reversing their climb through the gorge. Undetected, they recovered their skis and equipment left on approach and made for safety on the Hardangervidda. For those of the two Linge Company teams not detailed to remain in Norway to work with *Milorg*, safety meant a punishing 250-mile journey on skis to the Swedish border, avoiding a massive German search effort all the way.

Without the firing of a single shot inside the plant, or the loss of a single life, Norwegian or German, Linge Company's attack on Vemork destroyed the entire stock of heavy water and put the apparatus that made it out of action. The success of the raid rested on good planning, rigorous training, and the abilities of the men involved to survive, navigate and operate in remote and testing mountain country. The risks were high and both teams avoided the bad luck that tipped many other sabotage operations into failure. Before departure from Scotland, the *Gunnerside* men were informed of the fate of those captured in the failure of *Freshman*, and each man was issued with a suicide pill in case of capture.[125] Mindful of possible reprisals, the team wore British uniforms, left British papers behind them and took care to emphasise their British origins to the two Vemork workers they encountered. Although security at Rjukan was tightened and curfews imposed, the German occupiers took no harrowing retribution on this occasion.[126]

The successful sabotage of February 1943 was not, however, the end of the heavy water story. Repairs to the damaged electrolysis plant were conducted as a top priority and production began again less than two months later. Before the end of the year, Vemork was added to targets for 'Flying Fortress' bombers of the US Army Air Force which had begun launching mass daylight bombing raids against industrial installations in Norway. Vemork was attacked from the air on 16 November 1943. Though little harm was done to the small stock of heavy water that had built up since production resumed in May, the plant itself was badly damaged. Twenty-one Norwegians were killed, exactly the kind of damage that the Norwegian government in London deplored and that the earlier sabotage raid was designed to avoid. A further 18 Norwegian civilians lost their lives on the night of 19 February 1944, when a three-man *Milorg* team, led by Linge Company's 2nd Lieutenant Haukelid, bombed and sank a ferry on Lake Tinn that was carrying what remained of the Vemork heavy water on its way to Germany.

Nevertheless, the sabotage raid at Vemork was perhaps SOE's single most outstanding success of the war. According to Colin Gubbins it finally and firmly established SOE's position in the eyes of the British government and the military Chiefs of Staff, lending it greater political clout in all its dealings thereafter.[127] Vemork made Norwegian national heroes of the men of *Grouse* and *Gunnerside*, all of whom received gallantry decorations, and it established Linge Company's place in popular memory of

Norway's resistance against enemy occupation. The story of the attack on the heavy water plant has been told many times, in film as well as in print; first in a highly accurate documentary film *Kampen om tungtvannet* produced in Norway in 1948, and then given the Hollywood adaptation treatment in 1965 as *The Heroes of Telemark* starring Kirk Douglas and Richard Harris.[128]

On the fiftieth anniversary of the attack a monument to the saboteurs was unveiled outside the old power station at Vemork, today housing the Norsk Industriarbeider Museum with its exhibition about the wartime heavy water raids.[129] In Scotland a monument to Linge Company was unveiled in 1973, raised on behalf of the people of Badenoch in sight of the Company's former base at Glenmore Lodge. This simple stone standing above the shore of Loch Morlich commemorates all the men of the Company, including 57 who lost their lives. The monument remains a place of pilgrimage for many Norwegian visitors to Scotland today, together with the memorial unveiled at Scalloway in 2003 in tribute to the men of the Shetland Bus.[130]

* * *

As in SOE's other training schools in Scotland, activity at the Group 26 complex began to wind down from early 1944 when training efforts gave way to deployment in the field for priority operations in support of the forthcoming *Overlord* landings in France. Despite being vacated by Linge Company in October 1943, Forest Lodge had a final extension to its military life when it briefly housed a rather different intake of Norwegians, this time Norwegian-Americans from the United States. Since April 1943 the Office of Strategic Services had been recruiting its own 'Operational Groups' ('OG's'), units of uniformed soldiers trained to parachute behind enemy lines, attack targets and bring resistance into the open. These were sizeable commando-style units comprising four officers and between 35 and 40 men, including wireless operators.

The population profile of the United States meant that OSS could recruit first and second generation immigrants from European countries under German occupation, ideally possessing the language skills that would allow them to operate in their 'home' countries. Many Americans of Norwegian descent were brought in to the Operational Groups by way of a US Army infantry unit, the 99th Infantry Battalion, which was recruited from centres of Scandinavian settlement in Minnesota. Men selected for the Norwegian OG units, or 'Norwegian Special Operations Group' as the units became, trained first at OSS establishments in Virginia and Maryland including 'Area B', the Greentop camp area also used by the American *Jedburghs*, and 'Area F', the former Congressional Country Club near Washington DC, where they encountered Major William Fairbairn in the unlikely setting of a luxury golf resort. Put through a highly demanding commando-style training programme nonetheless, 84 men and twelve officers departed for the United Kingdom in December 1943.[131]

Although Norway had faded somewhat in the run of OSS priorities since the Norwegian Operational Groups were first recruited, sabotage operations against Norwegian industrial targets were still being contemplated early in 1944 as the United States remained intent on contributing to the liberation of that country. Forest Lodge was chosen to be the temporary holding centre in the United Kingdom for all the reasons that made the surrounding district secure and useful for paramilitary and ski training, and for its resemblance to Norwegian terrain. However, the Norwegian Special Operations Group were at Forest Lodge for only a matter of weeks while they waited for the construction of a camp of their own in a new highland base among the Monadhliath mountains, outliers of the main Cairngorm range well to the west of the Group 26 establishments. Reached by estate track from Strath Errick to the east of Loch Ness, the now derelict Stronelairg Lodge sits between Glen Fechlin and Glen Markie in an expanse of empty hill country. Giving a certain circular quality to this account of highland special training centres, this last of the Victorian shooting lodges to be taken over for special operations purposes was the property of Lord Lovat, he who had helped trigger the first requisition at Inverailort back in May 1940.

American money was spent to create a custom-built hutted camp between Stronelairg and nearby Killin Lodge where the men could be accommodated and trained. Assault courses and firing ranges were constructed along the lines of those first developed at Lochailort, including another Fairbairn/Sykes-style reflex shooting range, and a street fighting zone. Within striking distance the old railway line between Spean Bridge and Fort Augustus provided a target for mock demolitions.[132] Although the Norwegians' administration (based in the nearby hamlet of White Bridge) had the resources to allow the units largely to fend for themselves in their temporary home, exercises across the wider area took the OG units east into the Cairngorms and over to the west highlands. For boat training they visited the SOE schools at Swordland and Tarbet.[133]

Between January and May 1944, the Special Operations Group trained around Stronelairg in expectation of missions in Norway. However, support for the *Overlord* landings and subsequent Allied advance took priority. Planning towards raids on Norwegian industrial targets came to nothing for lack of transportation, as all available military resources were dedicated to the greater effort shortly to come in France.[134] After a further short period spent training at SOE's former Preliminary establishment at Brockhall Manor in Northamptonshire, the units deployed behind German lines in France. Following up the insertion of *Jedburgh* units, they added self-sufficient striking power to Maquis resistance forces attacking communications, roads and railways.

The role of the OSS Operational Groups in France after D-Day was broadly similar to the Special Air Service units inserted by the British. Although entirely outside the control of SOE, SAS activity merits further mention here because of its multi-national character and its period of training in Scotland in advance of D-Day. For the purposes of the *Overlord* invasion, the two small SAS units that had been operating in the Mediterranean theatre were recalled to the United Kingdom and expanded into a multi-national brigade of the British Army's 1st Airborne Division. The SAS Brigade combined the two British raiding regiments returned from Italy with units of French and Belgian paratroopers and a signals squadron. The original idea behind expanding the SAS in this way was to deploy it as a force of conventional paratroopers air-dropped immediately behind the German front line, a change of purpose sufficient to prompt the resignation of Lieutenant-Colonel Bill Stirling from command of 2nd SAS. As a long-standing exponent of small-scale raiding, Stirling felt the guerrilla warfare attributes of the SAS were being squandered. In the event, the manner in which the Brigade actually came to be used in France, in small teams working from self-sufficient bases deep inside enemy-held territory, proved to be much as he would have urged.

Training for the new Brigade began in Scotland, at Comrie outside Perth and at a small camp at Ceres in Fife in November 1943.[135] In early spring 1944 the entire force assembled in Ayrshire in the south-west, a location which offered proximity to RAF Prestwick for parachute training and easy access to the rugged country of the Ayrshire hills for endurance exercises. 1st SAS were based at Darvel, 2nd SAS at Monkton near

Prestwick, the French paratroopers of 3rd and 4th SAS were at Auchinleck and Galston, with the Belgian squadron nearby at Loudoun Castle.[136] For the benefit of the Belgians, Inverlochy Castle in Lochaber had briefly been reactivated as a special training centre during December 1943. The Inverlochy course proceeded along the usual guerrilla warfare lines as previously experienced there by the Poles, with the extremes of December weather adding to the test. One Belgian paratrooper, Josy Déom, later recalled the Inverlochy assault course as the hardest encountered by the Belgian exiles in their years in the United Kingdom. Other features of the course included long route marches conducted in absolute silence known as marches 'mouths shut', and 'blind dropping' where groups were taken in a covered lorry to an unknown location and left there to identify their position on the map in order to find their way back.[137]

For selected men of the Norwegian Special Operations Group, conclusion of active service in France meant an opportunity at last to carry out missions in Norway. This was Operation *Rype*, a series of attacks mounted on the Nordland railway between Narvik and Trondheim. Before departure, the men selected for *Rype* returned to Scotland in December 1944 for further training. Taking command at this point was Colonel William E. Colby, who later became Director of the CIA under President Nixon:

> I quickly moved them to the Scottish Highlands where they could toughen up with long treks in the mountains and refresh their ability to shoot and ski. The area had the benefit of also being fifty miles north of the nearest American military police post and among sympathetic Scots who could understand the effect of their national drink on the soldiers let out only on Saturday night. We even survived a field exercise when, living off the land, we shot and roasted one of the royal deer from the preserve around Balmoral Castle, the King's highland retreat.[138]

Headquarters for these training (and poaching) expeditions was Dalnaglar Castle, an extravagant highland estate house in Glenshee on the eastern side of the Cairngorms. The small town of Blairgowrie 15 miles to the south was the venue for the Saturday evening carousals. Once again it was the possibility of snow and open country for ski patrol work that brought special operations troops to the Cairngorm range. The Operation *Rype* parachute drops and sabotage attacks for which they were preparing began in March 1945 and, despite problems with the air drops, proved effective in helping to prevent German troops in northern Norway moving south to reinforce the defence of Germany.[139] The strategic value of these actions aside, the insertion of 100 or so Americans for Operation *Rype* was enough to ensure a visible uniformed US Army presence in Norway before the German capitulation and participation in the disarming of the German garrison thereafter, something of a political coup for OSS.[140]

*　*　*

For SOE the operations supporting and following *Overlord* were far from the end of its contribution to the Allied war effort. But beyond D-Day, SOE's own training and holding establishments in Scotland reduced down to little more than care and maintenance. Group A closed entirely in December 1944; what remained of its function was taken on by the various specialist training establishments in the south of England and the operational holding schools of the Country Sections.[141] Group 26 remained in existence until the official disbanding of Linge Company in June 1945, by which time the few men remaining who were not already on active service in Norway had proceeded home to take part in their country's un-opposed liberation and the formal recognition that followed.[142]

Special Operations Executive was a complex organisation with a global reach. As well as operations launched from the United Kingdom, SOE supported resistance networks from its headquarters in Cairo, from bases in the Mediterranean and in the Far East which developed their own training administrations. SOE missions in neutral countries extended its influence still further. This brief account of its training schools in the Scottish highlands can only hint at the extent of SOE's work with resistance movements worldwide. Nevertheless, the paramilitary training schools were part of the system that helped resistance movements and exiled armies deliver substantial harassment to enemy forces in the occupied countries of north-west Europe. Resistance warfare did not itself liberate Europe along the lines of MI(R)'s fondest hopes in early 1940. But in placing growing pressure on German occupying forces, in helping to pave the way for D-Day and hampering the flow of enemy supplies and reinforcements to the Normandy front line in June 1944, SOE more than proved its worth.

At the end of the war in Europe the Supreme Commander of the Allied

Expeditionary Force, US General Eisenhower, wrote to Major-General Colin Gubbins to acknowledge the contribution of Special Forces Head-quarters:

> In no previous war and in no other theatre during this war, have resis-tance forces been so closely harnessed to the main military effort.
>
> While no final assessment of the operational value of resistance action has yet been completed, I consider that the disruption of enemy rail communications, the harassing of German road moves and the continual and increasing strain placed on the German war economy and internal security services throughout occupied Europe by the organised forces of resistance played a very considerable part in our complete and final victory .... Particular credit must be due to those responsible for communications with occupied territory. I am also aware of the care with which each individual country was studied and organised, and of the excellent work carried out in training, documenting, briefing and despatching agents ....[143]

Harder to quantify was the moral value of SOE's support over five years to the peoples of conquered nations. Underground armies con-fronting the daunting forces of enemy occupation might on occasion have felt frustration and anxiety over the manner and extent of the help extended by their British allies, but overall, and from the first, they received through Special Operations Executive and its partners the promise of the means to resist, and through it the indelible gift of hope. As Major-General Gubbins expressed it in his introduction to Knut Haukelid's published account of the heavy water raids in Norway: 'It was in the answer to the cry for arms to continue the fight that SOE had its being and its fulfilment, that the peoples could fling off the yoke from their necks and fight as free men again and, though tortured and oppressed, hold up their heads in pride in the face of their enemy before victory was won – and afterwards.'[144]

For the first Polish paratroopers at Inverlochy, for the multi-national students of the Group A schools in Arisaig, Morar and Knoydart, for American OSS personnel both there in the west highlands and in the Monadhliath mountains, and for the Norwegian Linge Company in its Cairngorms bases, the experience of training in the highlands of Scotland was a valuable weapon to carry forward into the highly dangerous active service for which they volunteered. And the highland connection ran further. For almost all who took part in covert operations in north-west Europe, whether they set foot in the Scottish hills or no, the guerrilla warfare training that was an essential feature of their priming owed something to the principles worked up at the Special Training Centre Lochailort and adapted by SOE into its schools in the highlands and elsewhere.

NOTES TO PART THREE

1. Interview with Patrick John Howarth, Imperial War Museum Sound Archive, 8976 Reel 1, 1996. Source: BBC Radio 4, 'Set Europe Ablaze'. Captain Howarth served with SOE headquarters in London and as a representative of the organisation's Polish-Czech Section at SOE Headquarters in Cairo. Jimmy Young was Major J. T. Young, Commandant of SOE's Group A training schools with headquarters at Arisaig House.

2. B. Pimlott (ed.): *The Second World War Diary of Hugh Dalton* (London: Jonathan Cape, 1962), p. 62.

3. The complex evolution of SOE is described in the early chapters of W. Mackenzie: *The Secret History of SOE: The Special Operations Executive 1940-45* (London: St Ermin's Press, 2000). Until the departure of the 'Electra House' element, the organisation was known by its constituent sections SO1 (propaganda) and SO2 (the Section D/MI(R) element). For simplicity the term 'Special Operations Executive' (SOE) is used here throughout.

4. C. Gubbins: 'Resistance Movements in the War', *Journal of the Royal United Services Institution* [RUSI Journal], vol. XCIII, May 1948, no. 570, pp. 210-23.

5. Ibid., p. 211.

6 'History of Training Section of SOE, 1940-45, compiled by Major G M Forty, London, September 1945', Special Operations Executive records, National Archives, Kew, HS8/435.

7. Ibid.

8. The original instructing staff at Brickendonbury included Kim Philby, famously revealed after the war as a Soviet spy.

9. A. Carswell: *For Your Freedom and Ours. Poland, Scotland and the Second World War* (Edinburgh: National Museums of Scotland, 1993), p. 5.

10. 'Polish Training. VIth Bureau Wireless training 1940', Special Operations Executive records, National Archives, Kew, HS4/185. Strawiński was killed in a training accident in Italy in 1944.

11. Quoted in W. Markert: *Na Drodze Do Arnhem. Historia 4. Brygady Kadrowej Strzelcó, Oficyna Wydawnicza 'Ajaks'* (Pruszków, 2000), p. 51. Translation courtesy of Magdalena Kanik.

12. G. Cholewczyński: *Poles Apart. The Polish Airborne at the Battle of Arnhem* (London: Greenhill Books, *c.*1993), p. 46.

13. 'STC Inverlochy W/Establishment, 12.6.41', located in file 'Inverlochy (Polish Students), 1941', Special Operations Executive records, National Archives, Kew, HS8/369.

14. 'Syllabus of Instruction for Polish Officers, Allied Wing, STC', in file 'Inverlochy (Polish Students), 1941', and file 'Polish Training. VIth Bureau Wireless training 1940', Special Operations Executive records, National Archives, Kew, HS8/369, HS4/185.

15. Archives of the Polish Institute and Sikorski Museum, London, A.V̄.20/88.

16. Markert: op. cit., p. 53.

17. J. Tucholski: *Cichociemni* (Warsaw: Institut Wydawniczy Pax, 1984), pp. 74-76.

18. Quoted in Markert: op. cit., p. 54. Advice about the etymology of the term courtesy of Magdalena Kanik.

19. War Office instructions given to Major Mackworth-Praed on his assumption of command at Inverlochy on 11 August 1941 were at pains to stress that it was a British Army Training Centre and not the exclusive preserve of Polish forces or SOE. 'Inverlochy (Polish Students), 1941', Special Operations Executive records, National Archives, Kew, HS8/369.

20. K. Barbarski: '1st Polish Independent Parachute Brigade, 1941-47 (2)', *Military Illustrated Past and Present*, no. 13, June/July 1988, pp. 12-20.

21. Cholewczyński: op. cit., p. 50.

22. D. Henderson (ed.): *The Lion and the Eagle. Polish Second World War Veterans in Scotland* (Dunfermline: Cualaan Press, 2001), pp. 130-32.

23. I. Valentine: *Station 43. Audley End House and SOE's Polish Section* (Stroud: Sutton House Publishing, 2004), foreword.

24. *SOE Syllabus: Lessons in Ungentlemanly Warfare, World War II* (London: Public Record Office, 2001), pp. 2-11.

25. P. Wilkinson and J. Astley: *Gubbins and SOE* (London: Leo Cooper, 1993), p. 85.

26. Colonel J. S. Wilson CMG CBE: 'Memoirs of a Varied Life', unpublished memoir kindly made available to the National War Museum by Lord Wilson of Tillyhorn KT GCMG and Brigadier J. S. Wilson, p. 70.

27. Ibid., p. 71.

28. 'History of Training Section of SOE, 1940-45, compiled by Major G. M. Forty, London, September 1945': Special Operations Executive records, National Archives, Kew, HS8/435.

29. Then the property of Mr Clive F. Bowman of Wellington College. Some of the Bowman family were in residence, taking refuge from the danger of aerial bombing in London. See D. Harrison (ed.): 'Special Operations Executive. Para-Military Training in Scotland during World War 2', unpublished booklet, *c.*2000. Information about the ownership of these and other properties is from Valuation Rolls in public records held by the National Archives of Scotland, Edinburgh.

30. Lord Brocket was a member of the Anglo-German Fellowship, a circle of aristo-

crats and business figures who sought to maintain friendly commercial and political relations with their counterparts in Nazi Germany in the late 1930s.

31. Minister's Letter to George Wicks MP, 30 December 1941, in file 'Organisation & Administration. Property', Special Operations Executive records, National Archives, Kew, HS8/337.

32. Letter of Lieutenant-General R. C. Firebrace, Commander-in-Chief, Scottish Command, to the Under Secretary of State, MI5, 18 December 1940, from the papers of Major A. A. Fyffe. The initial intention was to give Protected Place status to Achdalieu, Achnacarry, Torcastle and Glenfinnan house in addition, but these properties, which had been requisitioned as holding centres for the Independent Companies, were deleted from the list.

33. Security memorandum of Major Gavin Brown, Intelligence Corps, December 1940. From the papers of Major A. A. Fyffe.

34. Pimlott: op. cit., p. 134.

35. See 'History of Training Section of SOE, 1940-45, compiled by Major G. M. Forty ....': op. cit., pp. 23-29.

36. Ibid.

37. P. Dourlein: *Inside North Pole. A secret agent's story* (F. Renier and A. Cliff, trans.) (London: Kimber, 1953). Dourlein was later captured as a consequence of German Intelligence's penetration of Dutch Section's radio traffic. The kilted instructor is likely to have been Major J. T. Young.

38. Mackenzie: op. cit., pp. 331-32.

39. This was the first use of the 'SAS' title later adopted by David Stirling's desert raiding force.

40. M. Newnham: *Prelude to Glory. The Story of the Creation of Britain's Parachute Army* (London: Sampson Low, Marston & Co., 1947), pp. 24-30.

41. 'History of Training Section of SOE, 1940-45, compiled by Major G. M. Forty ....': op. cit., p. 3. Forty's official history contains a reference to an SOE archive document 'Syllabus of STC Loch Ailort', but this early written syllabus does not appear to have survived later 'weeding' of SOE administrative files or the fire which destroyed a large portion of SOE records in late 1945. The following account of the Group A syllabus is based on Forty's official history. The fullest record of SOE training, the syllabus of Special Training School 103 in Canada is transcribed as *SOE Syllabus: Lessons in Ungentlemanly Warfare, World War II*, Public Record Office, London, 2001.

42. G. Langelaan: *Knights of the Floating Silk* (London: Hutchinson, n.d.), pp. 61-74. A possible identification of the unnamed Japanese instructor is Gintaro Mizuhara, a naturalised British subject who was a music hall entertainer before the war (information courtesy of Mr Peter Brunning).

43. Unpublished memoir made available to the National War Museum by Lieutenant-Colonel E. H. Van Maurik OBE, pp. 51-79.

44. Film interview with Lieutenant-Colonel E. H. Van Maurik OBE recorded for the 'Commando Country' exhibition, National War Museum, 2006.

45. Van Maurik memoir: op. cit., p. 63.

46. Interview with Mr C. S. Hudson, National War Museum, March 2002.

47. S. Hudson: *Undercover Operator. An SOE Agent's Experiences in France & the Far East* (Barnsley: Leo Cooper, 2003), p. 12.

48. S. King: *'Jacqueline', Pioneer Heroine of the Resistance* (London: Arms & Armour, 1989). Rudellat received the MBE and the Croix de guerre.

49. Under this name she was commissioned into the First Aid Nursing Yeomanry, the usual cover for SOE's female staff and operational officers.

50. N. Wake: *The autobiography of the woman the Gestapo called the White Mouse* (South Melbourne: Macmillan, 1985), p. 105.

51. The word 'Maquis', a Corsican term meaning 'scrub', referred to the manner in which these groups took to living in woods and remote country to avoid the labour draft.

52. Wake: op. cit.

53. S. Ottaway: *Violette Szabo, The Life That I Have* (Barnsley: Pen & Sword Military, 2006), pp. 50-51.

54. Others held officer rank in the Women's Auxiliary Air Force.

55. SOE personnel file, National Archives, Kew HS9/1435.

56. Van Maurik memoir: op. cit., pp. 77-78.

57. The badge is now in the collection of the National War Museum, M.2006.22.

58. Later General Antonin Petràk. Course statistics from his 'Czechoslovak-British Reminiscences 50 years after the war' in D. Harrison: op. cit., pp. 36-42.

59. The Czech lands of Bohemia and Moravia were under direct German occupation. Under German pressure Slovakia declared independence before the German invasion of March 1939, and its puppet government existed as a client state of the German Reich.

60. The book is now in the collection of the Imperial War Museum Department of Documents, Misc, 2734. I am grateful to Dr Paul Millar, Honorary Consul-General of the Czech Republic, Edinburgh, for identifying the signatories. The following account of Operation *Anthropoid* derives from C. MacDonald: *The Killing of SS Obergruppenführer Reinhard Heydrich* (Macmillan, 1989).

61. Van Maurik film interview: op. cit. Captain Alfgar Hesketh-Pritchard was head of SOE's Czechoslovak section.

62. In fact a sub-section within Scandinavian Section until early 1942.

63. C. Cruickshank: *SOE in Scandinavia* (Oxford: Oxford University Press, 1986), pp. 142-68.

64. M. Langley: *Anders Lassen VC, MC of the SAS* (London: New English Library, 1988), pp. 47-48.

65. P. Kemp: *No Colours or Crest* (London: Cassell, 1958), pp. 45-46.

66. Information supplied by Mr Duncan Stuart, SOE Adviser, Foreign & Commonwealth Office, 2002. Report quoted in D. Botting: *The Saga of the Ring of Bright Water. The Enigma of Gavin Maxwell* (Glasgow: Neil Wilson Publishing, 2000), p. 53.

67. Botting: op. cit., p. 58. Yvonne Rudellat recounted a similar Maxwell anecdote to her biographer: see S. King: op. cit., p. 103.

68. P. Wilkinson and J. Astley: op. cit., p. 95.

69. W. Irwin: *The Jedburghs, The Secret History of the Allied Special Forces, France, 1944* (New York: Public Affairs), pp. 47-50.

70. There is little evidence to support various assertions for the etymology of the *Jedburgh* teams, of which one of the more spurious is that the *Jedburgh* code-name reflected the ancient heritage of small-scale warring along the Anglo-Scottish border. See F. MacKay: *Overture to Overlord, Special Operations in Preparation for D-Day* (Barnsley: Pen & Sword Military, 2005), pp. 146-47.

71. N. West: *Secret War. The Story of SOE, Britain's Wartime Sabotage Organisation* (London: Hodder and Stoughton, 1992), pp. 231-32.

72. Irwin: op. cit., pp. 40-41.

73. D. Stafford: *Camp X. SOE and the American Connection* (London: Viking, 1987), p. 71.

74. Imperial War Museum Photograph Archive, HU82537-HU82555.

75. This and previous quotation: W. Morgan: *Spies and saboteurs. An account of their selection and training* (London: Gollancz, 1955), pp. 131-32.

76. D. Harrison: op. cit., p. 59.

77. The card is now in the collection of the National War Museum, M.2006.11. Information from Mr Jean C. Guiet in a letter to the National War Museum, April 2006. See also D. Harrison: op. cit., p. 59.

78. Major A. A. Fyffe: 'Group 26 at Aviemore. Special Training School of the Norwegian Section of SOE. To organise resistance in Norway'. Unpublished typescript made available to the National War Museum by Major Fyffe's son, Mr A. Fyffe.

79. Major A. A. Fyffe: 'The Protected Area of Western Scotland and its Military Occupation from 1940', in Harrison: op. cit.

80. Van Maurik memoir: op. cit., p. 65.

81. Angus MacKinnon, transcript of National War Museum recorded interview, April 2002.

82. Wilson memoir: op. cit., p. 71.

83. Information from papers of Major A. A. Fyffe made available to the National War Museum by his son, Mr A. Fyffe.

84. These detachments were still another element of Special Forces headquarters' planned activities behind enemy lines in support of *Overlord*. They were intended to ensure meaningful communications between local resistance groups and Allied forces.

85. Major A. A. Fyffe, in Harrison: op. cit., p. 32.

86. Each of SOE's Special Training Schools and related establishments was given a number. The Group A schools were numbered and sub-numbered STS 21-STS 25.

87. The proprietor's son, Captain John Grant of Rothiemurchus, Lovat Scouts, was then serving on the staff of STC Lochailort.

88. This should not be confused with the present Glenmore Lodge, a modern building nearby which houses the Scottish National Outdoor Training Centre. The old Glenmore Lodge is today the Cairngorm Lodge Youth Hostel (Loch Morlich).

89. This first functioned as the core of 'Scandinavian Section' which developed sub-sections for Sweden and Denmark. From 1 January 1942 Norwegian Section became a Country Section in its own right.

90. E. Haavardsholm: *Martin Linge – min morfar* (Oslo: Forlaget Oktober, 2005).

91. 'History of Norwegian Section, Appendix B: A Short History of "the Linge Company"': Special Operations Executive records, National Archives, Kew, HS7/175. Commando leader Brigadier John Durnford-Slater's memoir records meeting Linge and his men for the first time aboard HMS *Princess Beatrix* en route to the operation via Scapa Flow. J. Durnford-Slater: *Commando. Memoirs of a Fighting Commando in World War Two* (London: Greenhill Books, 1991), pp. 44-45.

92. J. Rønneberg: 'The Linge Company and the British', in P. Salmon (ed.): *Britain and Norway in the Second World War* (London: HMSO, c.1995), pp. 152-57.

93. Rønneberg: op. cit., p. 154.

94. Paper by Major Hjelles and Hampton to the Anglo-Norwegian Joint Committee, April 1942, and 'Report from STS 26' by Lieutenant Chaworth-Musters, June 1942, Norges Hjemmefrontmuseum (Norway's Resistance Museum), Oslo, archive collection 1c/3 and 1a/10.

95. After the war the Norwegian government formally recognised the Kompani Linge title and granted permission for those men of the unit still serving in the Royal Norwegian Army to wear a shoulder flash bearing the name.

96. 'History of Norwegian Section 1940-45', Special Operations Executive records, National Archives, Kew, HS7/174.

97. Cholewczyński (in op. cit., p. 46) describes a silver cigarette box presented by Norwegian paratroopers returned from a raid in Norway to Colonel Sosabowski, commanding officer of the Independent Polish Parachute Brigade.

98. 'Spesial utdannelsen ved STS', February 1943, Norges Hjemmefrontmuseum (Norway's Resistance Museum), Oslo, archive collection 1a/53.

99. The timber buildings appear in photographs of Glenmore Lodge held by the Norges Hjemmefrontmuseum (Norway's Resistance Museum), Oslo.

100. Interview with Mr Paal Wergeland, Lingeklubben, Oslo, April 2006.

101. K. Haukelid: *Skis Against the Atom* (London: William Kimber, 1954), p. 57.

102. Memo from Lieut.-Col. J. S. Wilson to Captain Tronstad, 6 March 1943, Norges Hjemmefrontmuseum (Norway's Resistance Museum), Oslo, archive colln. 5-31.

103. The one case of this kind which Major Fyffe had to deal with involved a Royal Air Force pilot stationed at Kinloss who spoke in a public house about an operational flight to Norway. Major A. A. Fyffe, 'Group 26 at Aviemore ....': op. cit.

104. 'Report on Rescue party organised by Norwegian Unit, Drumintoul Lodge, Aviemore, for rescue of climbers in danger near Shelter Stone, Cairn Gorm Mountains' to Inverness-shire County Police, 3 October 1942, Norges Hjemmefrontmuseum (Norway's Resistance Museum), Oslo, archive collection.

105. Memo, Lieut.-Col. Wilson to Captain Tronstad, 25 May 1943, Norges Hjemmefrontmuseum (Norway's Resistance Museum), Oslo, archive collection 1a/36.

106. Interview with Mr Paal Wergeland, Lingeklubben, Oslo, April 2006, and Fyffe 'Group 26 at Aviemore ....': op. cit.

107. Major A. A. Fyffe, 'Group 26 at Aviemore ....': op. cit.

108. 'History of Norwegian Section, Appendix B: A Short History of "the Linge Company"', op. cit. A roll of the Company for 11 March 1944 gives a total of 219 on the active list. Norges Hjemmefrontmuseum (Norway's Resistance Museum), Oslo, archive collection, FOIV box 165.

109. 'The Shetland Bus' moniker became the title of the classic if rather censored account of the service written by Lieutenant-Commander David Howarth, who ran one of the service's stations at Lunna Voe. D. Howarth: *The Shetland Bus* (London: Thomas Nelson and Sons, 1951). See also T. Sørvaag: *Shetland Bus* (Lerwick: *Shetland Times*, 2002).

110. No.1477 (Norwegian) Flight, absorbed in May 1943 into 333 (Norwegian) Squadron Royal Air Force. The bulk of Special Duty flights were flown by 138 (Special Duty) Squadron Royal Air Force (originally No.1419 Flight) based at RAF Tempsford in Bedfordshire. See M. Seaman: 'Special Duty Operations in Norway', in P. Salmon (ed.): op. cit., pp. 167-75.

111. See O. Envig: 'MEDEA' and the Spies of Peterhead: A top secret wartime history' in *Mains'l Haul, Journal of Pacific Maritime History*, 40:3&4, 2004, pp. 42-61. Also M. Lein: *Spioner I Eget Land, Norske radiooperatører I Secret Service, Kompani Linge, XU, Milorg og sovjetisk tjeneste 1940-45* (Oslo: Genesis, 2003).

112. Major A. A. Fyffe, 'Group 26 at Aviemore ....': op. cit.

113. Sørvaag: op.cit., pp. 22-24.

114. 'History of Norwegian Section, Appendix B: A Short History of "the Linge Company"', op. cit.

115. 'Operation CARHAMPTON' files 1942-45, Special Operations Executive records (Group C, Scandinavia), National Archives, Kew, HS2/180-183; and C. Cruickshank: *SOE in Scandanavia* (Oxford: Oxford University Press, 1986), pp. 108-13.

116. 'Operation Granard 1942-43' file, Special Operations Executive records (Group C, Scandinavia), National Archives, Kew, HS2/194; and C. Cruickshank: op. cit., pp. 192-98. Deinboll was killed in the loss of an aircraft carrying a mission to the Oslo area in November 1944.

117. For Chariot torpedoes and Welman submarines, and their working up in Scottish sea lochs, see W. Fell: *The Sea our Shield* (London: Cassell, 1966); see also P. Mitchell: *Chariots of the Sea. The Story of Britain's Human Torpedoes during the Second World War* (Huddersfield: Richard Netherwood, 1998).

118. 'Operation VESTIGE' files, Special Operations Executive records, National Archives, Kew, HS2/208-210; and C. Cruickshank: op. cit., pp. 119-20.

119. P. Dahl: *Heavy Water and the Wartime Race for Nuclear Energy* (Bristol: Institute of Physics Publishing, 1999), pp. 191-92.

120. R. Wiggan: *Operation Freshman. The Rjukan Heavy Water Raid 1942* (William Kimber, 1986), p. 41.

121. Interview with Mr Knut Haugland, Lingeklubben, Oslo, April 2006.

122. R. Mears: *The Real Heroes of Telemark* (London: Hodder & Stoughton, 1996), pp. 120-21.

THE ROAD TO THE ISLES

123. Haukelid: op. cit., p. 68.

124. Mr Joachim Rønneberg confirmed the details of *Gunnerside*'s stay in Argyll in an interview with the *Dunoon Observer*, 27 March 2003.

125. Haukelid: op. cit., pp. 62-67.

126. By contrast, in April 1942 after two Linge Company men were apprehended by the Gestapo in the coastal village of Televåg, the village was destroyed, the inhabitants deported and 18 Norwegian civilians already in detention were executed.

127. C. Gubbins: 'SOE and the co-ordination of Regular and Irregular War', in M. Elliott-Bateman (ed.): *The Fourth Dimension of Warfare* (Manchester University Press, 1970), pp. 83-110.

128. *Kampen om tungtvannet*, Hero-Film, 1948. *The Heroes of Telemark*, Columbia Pictures, 1965.

129. Almost nothing now remains of the electrolysis building, demolished after the air bombing, but the suspension bridge remains and the saboteurs' route through the gorge can be observed.

130. A substantial Norwegian history of Linge Company covers all its operations in Norway and gives a detailed account of the Group 26 schools. See F. Bind: *Kompani Linge* (Oslo: Gyldendal Norsk Forlag, 1948), 2 volumes.

131. B. Heimark: *The OSS Norwegian Special Operations Group in World War II* (Praeger, Westport, Conn., 1994), pp. 7-14.

132. The short-lived Invergarry and Fort Augustus Railway closed to passenger traffic in 1933. The line was revived for military use during the war, finally closing in 1946.

133. MacKay: op. cit., p. 111.

134. West: op. cit., pp. 236-38.

135. MacKay: op. cit., pp. 178-79.

136. Ibid: pp. 180-81. See also R. Ford: *The Fire from the Forest. The SAS Brigade in France, 1944* (London: Cassell, 2003).

137. Quoted in G. de Pierpont and A. Lefèvre: *Historique des regiments parachutiste, SAS Commando et para-commando Belges* (Brussels: Groupe Go, 1977), pp. 35-39. Information about the Squadron's time in Scotland courtesy of M. Paul Marquet of the Belgian SAS Regimental Association.

138. W. Colby: *Honourable Men. My Life in the CIA* (London, Hutchison, 1978), p. 45.

139. The airdrops were carried out by US Army Air Force B-24 Liberators of 'Carpetbagger' Special Duty Squadrons using Scottish staging bases at RAF Leuchars and Kinloss.

140. Heimark: op. cit., pp. 62-64. Dalnaglar was the property of Williamson Brothers of Milton of Balgonie, Fife.

141. 'History of Training Section of SOE, 1940-45, which was compiled by Major G. M. Forty ....': op. cit., p. 24.

142. 'History of Norwegian Section, Appendix B: A Short History of "the Linge Company"': op. cit.

143. Quoted in Foot, MRD: *SOE in France: An Account of the Work of the British Special Operations Executive in France 1940-44* (London: Frank Cass, 2004), pp. 387-88.

144. Haukelid: op. cit., pp. 29-30.

PART FOUR

The Men from the Boys
HIGHLAND FIELDCRAFT

> Birch, bracken and bog, moor, mountain and moss, a scene both soft
> and harsh, bright and dim, flashing in rare sunshine and drenched in
> steady rain but always fresh, the Rough Bounds were good for soldiers
> in training, and indeed good for anybody anyway.

SUCH WERE THE reflections of 2nd Lieutenant Arthur Kellas late in 1940 at
the end of six months in Lochaber with his Independent Company.[1] 'Good
for anybody anyway' was a sentiment acknowledging the benefits of the
outdoor life over and above the imperatives of war. An essential element in
Commando training in its various forms was that it was a moral as well as
a physical test, a measure of individual character. Hard training in rough
country was intended to discriminate between the soldier who was fit for
special service and the soldier who was not; not just in terms of physical
fitness and strength, which could be attained, but in terms of the inner
qualities of each man. The training programmes were structured to give
every candidate the opportunity to develop and meet the standard required
in the time allowed. Inherent in the approach was the idea that training in
this way was character-building in itself. Just as Kellas expressed it, this
was an idea of individual development that might apply in any military
context. It could, and would, be seen to apply in civilian life as well.

One trend that emerges from a study of the wartime special training
centres in the Scottish highlands is how over the course of five years they
became a little less 'special' than they were at the outset. In the Commandos in particular the numbers of men and scale of organisation involved
from 1942 onwards made 'special training' a mass participation activity,
still something extraordinary but rather less exclusive than in the formative years. Although the earliest essays in training for special service troops
were highly innovative, they did not evolve in isolation thereafter. While
progress was patchy and might have been better realised, fresh thinking

was being applied to tactical training across the British Army, demanding higher standards of fitness, initiative and adaptability from all soldiers.[2] This might not have taken them to the lengths of exertion and resource-fulness demanded by the Commando training regimes, but it did take them off the parade ground and rifle range and out into open country all over the United Kingdom.

Even the Royal Navy was in on the act, and not only with its Royal Marine and Royal Naval Commandos. The continuity between the methods of the Army regime at the Special Training Centre Lochailort and that operated by its Royal Navy successors at HMS *Lochailort* from late summer 1942 was based on a coherent, if rather unsophisticated, philo-sophy. The premise was that a spell of Commando-style training could work as a vehicle for young cadets to accelerate them towards the stan-dards required to become naval officers in Combined Operations and to reach them quickly. The training itself need have nothing much to do with the specifics of the job the cadets were being groomed for; the idea was to take the raw material of cadet-ratings and make men of them. By encour-aging self-reliance and initiative, the making of officers could follow.

This was the same idea that in May 1943 led the Army's Directorate of Military Training to open the Highland Fieldcraft Training Centre, an establishment whose form owed a good deal to the models previously established for special service purposes but with a particular function and approach of its own. Just as the Royal Navy's interest in Lochailort pro-ceeded from an urgent need for officers to command landing craft in forthcoming amphibious operations, so the growing prospect of a Second Front in north-west Europe and the consequent expansion of the Army demanded greater numbers of junior officers than were at its disposal. With this imperative, long-standing concerns about the high rate of re-jection among candidates coming forward for officer training became urgent.

One element within the problem gave cause for optimism about finding a remedy. The 25%-plus failure rate among Officer Cadet Training Units included a significant number of potential officers who were not being rejected by the War Office Selection Board as outright unsuitable, but were thought not yet ready, lacking the maturity to fulfil the leader-ship role at that time. With further training and experience it was felt these 'Not Yets' might present themselves successfully in future. There was, how-ever, no structured means whereby their development could be influenced by anything other than time once the men concerned returned to the ranks of their original units.

To address the vexed question of these 'Not Yets' lost to the officer corps, the Army looked outside the military field for expert advice. The Army's Adjutant General, General Sir Ronald Forbes Adam, took the problem to the eminent educationalist Dr Kurt Hahn, headmaster of Gordonstoun School. This unusual educational establishment near the Moray coast of north-east Scotland had for the duration of the war moved away from the strategically sensitive Moray Firth to Plas Dinam, Merionethshire, Wales. Hahn created Gordonstoun in 1934 on the model of his first progressive school in Germany, located at Salem near the Bodensee, after pressure from the Nazi authorities led him to leave the country of his birth.

Hahn's educational philosophy rested on the development of the whole person. Gordonstoun's curriculum expanded beyond academic work and games in the traditional sense to provide teaching and activities designed to build responsibility, confidence and the ability to work with others in each individual pupil. The backdrop to Hahn's approach was provided by the waters and mountains of north-east Scotland where pupils were introduced to the challenges of sea and land-based adventure activities. Hahn extended his work beyond the walls of the school through the 'County Badge' scheme, intended to give young people across the whole country opportunity to participate in structured activity of this kind, including short residential courses.

The approach from the Adjutant-General was not the first time Dr Hahn had been able to contribute his thoughts on education to the war effort. The previous year he began the first 'Outward Bound' courses for young merchant seamen. These represented a meeting of minds between Hahn and one of his powerful backers Lawrence Holt, chairman of the Blue Funnel Shipping Line. Hahn wished to perpetuate the idea behind the lapsed County Badge scheme by running a sailing school for young people at Aberdovey. Holt had long been involved in sea cadet training and in 1941 he was concerned that young men joining the wartime Merchant Navy lacked experience of the kind Hahn's methods might offer.[3] During the Battle of the Atlantic, in the all too common situation where merchant ships were torpedoed by submarines and their crews forced into lifeboats or into the water, younger seamen were proving less likely to survive than experienced older hands. With Holt's backing, Hahn devised the Outward

Bound courses based on traditional sailing skills to promote resourceful-ness, know-how and resolve in younger seamen.[4]

The Army's problem with its potential officers was not one of survival, not at least at that stage, but it was similarly concerned with measures that might enhance maturity and capability in young servicemen. Dr Hahn's courses for the Merchant Navy already included expeditions on land, and he suggested something similar might usefully be done for the Army. The Adjutant General consequently asked his Director of Military Training, Major-General John Whitaker, to set up training centres along Outward Bound lines for the benefit of the 'Not Yet' potential officers. Looking for a combination of mountains and water, Whitaker first sought a suitable venue in the west highlands but found the area so replete with high-security special training centres and Royal Navy installations that he turned instead to the expanses of the Cairngorms. A hutted camp built for the Canadian Forestry Corps at Torwood in Glenfeshie to the west side of the range was vacant. To create the necessary capacity, 52nd (Lowland) Division's Mountain and Snow Warfare School was ejected from a second camp in the glen and also from Glenfeshie Lodge which was to be the new training centre's headquarters and officers' mess. Glenfeshie was a long way from the sea, but testing mountain country it had in abundance.[5]

To set up 'No.1 Leadership Development Training Centre' Whitaker summoned the services of Lieutenant-Colonel T. G. P. Corbett, 2nd Baron Rowallan, an officer with experience of adventure training both in military and civilian life. Lord Rowallan had been wounded and decorated for gallantry during the First World War. In April 1939 he took command of 6th Battalion Royal Scots Fusiliers in his native Ayrshire, a new Terri-torial Army unit that he built up and in 1940 led into active service in France. Rowallan was also a leading light in the Boy Scout movement in Scotland, and in 1945 was to be appointed to its highest office as Chief Scout of the British Commonwealth.

Since early 1941 Lord Rowallan had been in command of a Young Soldiers Battalion in Scotland. This was one of the Army's training units for boys over 16 years old who were too young to be enlisted into the ranks of the field army. Taking over an unruly battalion of what he described as 'young keelies' with a propensity for petty crime, Rowallan sought to apply a combination of consistent military discipline with training and guidance that, other than in cases beyond the pale, could unlock the individual potential in his young charges. His Scouting-inspired approach was sufficiently successful to see what had been an almost ungovernable collection of disadvantaged urban youth develop sufficient competence and responsibility to be asked to provide demonstration platoons for the Special Training Centre Lochailort, despite initial doubts expressed by its commandant:

> But when the course finished my boys had made a tremendous impression, and there was no longer any question about drawing demonstration platoons from our boys. We insisted that nobody should go there who had an entry on his conduct sheet in the last three months, and this we just managed and no more. As they approached manhood our boys became very fit, and were able to run the others off their feet. Before we knew what was happening we were made the enemy in exercises.[6]

For his new task in Glenfeshie Lord Rowallan first assembled a cadre of instructors at the War Office's Advanced Handling and Field Training Centre at Llanberis, Wales. His chosen chief instructor Major W. E. Williamson and other mountain warfare specialists were seconded from the 52nd (Lowland) Division establishment whose erstwhile Glenfeshie premises the new centre was to occupy. A visit to Glenfeshie left Rowallan greatly encouraged: 'Here was ample silence in which the human spirit could expand and develop, where the sense of awareness could become keen and subtle.'

He settled on the name Highland Fieldcraft Training Centre (HFTC) as one sufficiently vague on security grounds but that captured the essence of what was to be done.[7] Glenfeshie would do well for most of the year, but since the teaching of skiing or winter warfare was not the principal part of the Centre's purpose a second Scottish location was identified to allow the work to continue and escape the snows that might come to block the road into the glen from Kincraig. Winter quarters would therefore be on the shores of Loch Ewe in the distant north-west of Scotland, at the village of Poolewe in Wester Ross.

The staff and first intake of 120 students assembled in Glenfeshie at the end of May 1943 for a ten-week long course. The candidates had all shown officer potential in some form, whether by dint of education or other attributes. The defined aims of the course were eight-fold:

1. To recultivate the senses atrophied by civilisation
2. To develop self-reliance
3. To develop self-confidence
4. To develop resource
5. To develop the inquisitive mind
6. To develop adaptability
7. To give practice in leadership and administration
8. To quicken reaction to the unexpected[8]

The syllabus attempted to cover a huge range, from weapons training through fieldcraft, navigation and signalling to weather forecasting and botany. The course intensified gradually. In early weeks the students would remain in the vicinity of Glenfeshie for drill, instruction in infantry platoon weapons, hill-walking, demonstrations and practice in other subjects. After three weeks, five nights were spent in bivouac out in the hills, the students left to make the best of it with the natural materials and limited rations available to them. Following a short break of home leave in the middle of the course the students returned to apply the wisdom they had received thus far in exercises out in the field.

So followed weeks of river crossing and rope-bridge building, rock-climbing, rafting, tree-felling and a variety of navigation and endurance exercises. A typical challenge was Exercise 'Pass the Ammunition', a fiend-ish obstacle course over which heavy ammunition boxes had to be trans-ported intact. The course culminated in traditional Commando-fashion with a multiple-day scheme out in the hills. The students were already fam-iliar with the surrounding mountains, marching through the Cairngorm massif towards its highest point, the 4296-foot Ben Macdhui, and beyond, confronting tactical situations on their way. In their immediate stomping ground they became especially acquainted with the routes up to the flat and indeterminate tops of Mullach Clach a' Bhlair and Meall Dubhag immediately above their camp. Between them was the rocky rent of Coire Garbhlach where climbing, abseiling and 'scree-running' rapid descents of steep ground could be practised. Students might also be transported far to the west for exercises over terrain in Moidart, otherwise used by special service troops.

It might not have seemed a great comfort at the time, but HFTC students at least benefited from elementary advances in protective clothing that by 1943 had been introduced as part of the Army's efforts towards developing capability in mountain warfare. In addition to standard-issue kit including battle dress and boots, each student was issued with two pieces of specialist clothing, a windproof smock and a string vest.[9] The hooded smocks they owed to the work of Frank Smythe and other mountaineers advising the War Office. They gave protection from the winds that scourged the Cairngorms and were at least water resistant if not actually waterproof. For protection from rain the students still relied, as did other soldiers, on gas capes and groundsheets.

The string open-work vest concept was the particular contribution of the Scott Polar Research Institute at Cambridge University.[10] The garment's function was to moderate the effects of the contrasting bouts of exertion and inactivity that winter combat entailed. Worn under layers of other clothing, the vest drew hot air and condensation away from the body, dampness which could be allowed to escape at the neck after exertion so as not to turn cold. By keeping clothing fastened at the neck during periods of extended inactivity, the vest had the opposite effect and retained heat. This at least was the theory. HFTC students were given to applying sheets of newspaper between the vest and the next layer, to help seal in the heat generated by their own bodies.

String-vest clad or no, those who took the winter course at Poolewe had the lochs and hills of the north-west highlands at their service. The mountains above Loch Maree and Loch Torridon were the favoured venues, with assault boating on these waters part of the challenge. Further afield, the Isle of Skye served as the setting for extended exercises. The HFTC camp at Poolewe lay in an area on the western edge of the village behind the church. A short distance to the north, the house of Tournaig supplied the officers' mess. Respite and relative comfort was available to the students in the YMCA Hostel at Pool House.

Loch Ewe was an important assembly and reception point for Atlantic and Arctic convoys. On 26 February 1944 an HFTC exercise near the seacoast over to the west near Melvaig was interrupted by a request for assistance in a rescue effort. An American 'Liberty Ship', the *William H. Welch*, had foundered on the approach to Loch Ewe. In high winds HFTC staff and students used their new climbing abilities to help recover survivors from below dangerous cliffs and evacuate them from the shore by stretcher.

As was intended by their designers, the HFTC courses were a mixture of the exhausting and the exhilarating. The diary of Cadet Ronald Brash, who went through the Poolewe course in 1944, records the lows and highs of the experience and the youthful spirit of competition that sustained it. The following excerpt describes the completion of Exercise 'Torridon' in April 1944, the three-day scheme that was Poolewe's equivalent to Exercise 'Ben Macdhui' at Glenfeshie:

SUN 9: What a way to spend Easter! We climbed a 2300-foot mountain in 1½ hours without a break and during the day covered nearly 20 miles. I felt quite ill at one point but recovered after a brief rest. Our billets at Kinlochewe were small and we had to cook outside. This is acknowledged to be the worst day of the whole course.

MON 10: Away by 5.30 am for a final bash along the north shore of Loch Maree to Letterewe. 5 Platoon got there second and set up a new record in the time taken. We got back to camp about 4.30 only to find I had lost my map case. After dinner I borrowed a YMCA cycle and found the maps near Loch Kernsary.

TUE 11: Quite an easy day. In the afternoon a sort of Scavenger Hunt was held as an inter-platoon competition. 5 Platoon came second. Great praise was given to the Company by the Commandant and the Chief Instructor on Exercise Torridon.

WED 12: Free day. We had a full dress rehearsal of the Revue and it is coming on fine. The course is coming to a rapid conclusion as W.O.S.B. starts on Saturday.

THU 13: We had four small exercises, but after Torridon they seemed exceptionally tame. Now we all feel really fit. 5 Platoon has the reputation of being a 'bashing on' platoon, and is fiercely rivalling 6 – the acknowledged 'cream' platoon of the whole Company.[11]

'W.O.S.B.', the War Office Selection Board, was the test to which ostensibly all the Centre's work was directed, the point at which it would be decided whether its 'Not Yet' students had made enough progress to proceed to officer training. HFTC Instructor Major John Downton described the process:

Each course ran for ten weeks and at the end of the course a full Selection Board was convened at Glenfeshie itself, consisting of a President (a full Colonel), a Vice President (a Lieutenant-Colonel) and several officers drawn from various Selection Boards throughout the country. They were resident in the camp for four days and they followed the cadets through everything for these four days, including a two-day exercise. At the end of four days they announced the results. Thereby at the end of the time, after the twelfth course, we were getting steadily about 70% of the cadets through the course, which I suppose is a satisfactory number.[12]

Even for those who did not pass there was a feeling that the experience and their efforts had not been wasted. As one successful student put it, the purpose of the course was 'making 18½ year-olds into 22 year-olds in ten weeks' and in this it was perceived to succeed.[13] Lord Rowallan later recounted the comment of the Selection Board Chairman after a particularly successful Board: 'You may have succeeded in producing 80 per cent of officers, but more important, you have produced 100 per cent of men.'[14]

Its purpose served, the Centre closed in November 1944. That the experience had a more enduring effect on its students was indicated by the formation of an association for students and staff after the war. Societies of this kind are common to service organisations, keeping men who served and fought together in contact. For a short-lived training course whence students were scattered through myriad military units in different theatres of war, this was an unusually strong bond. In 1953 the Highland Fieldcraft Training Centre Association built a memorial cairn at Carnachuin in Glenfeshie to commemorate the students who trained there and at Poolewe and lost their lives during the war, including one fatality during training.[15] An equivalent plaque was unveiled in St Maelrubha's Church, Poolewe. Later the purpose and methods of the course were revisited by the peacetime Regular Army. From 1976 until 2002 the Royal Military Academy Sandhurst ran 'Rowallan Company', a training cadre set up to address a high failure rate among officer cadets coming before the Regular Commissions Board.

* * *

Rather different in purpose though it was, the hot-house growing of potential Army officers at the Highland Fieldcraft Training Centre was clearly an off-shoot of the special service training idea. The Commando influence was certainly there, one of the course's ingredients in with the Gordonstoun influence, Lord Rowallan's Scouting techniques, and an overt Christian ethos reflecting Rowallan's personal religious faith. The psychology was more subtle and training a little gentler than at such places as Lochailort and Achnacarry. With less emphasis on weeding out the unsuitable, the 'Returned to Unit' measure was applied only in cases of serious breach of discipline. The emphasis was on coaxing the best out of each individual student by encouragement, regulating the challenge according to his ability. Nevertheless, the focus on the individual, on the qualities of each man, was something that HFTC and the others had in common.

In the nature of its field exercises and other elements of its syllabus such as unarmed combat, demolitions and the approach to weapons training, HFTC borrowed heavily from its special service forebears. The remote mountain setting and consequent attention to fieldcraft, stalking and survival in hard country were of course integral to the HFTC function. Physical training included assault courses and an Achnacarry-style 'Death Slide' over the River Feshie. Training with standard infantry rifles began along conventional lines, but then extended into tactical training with other weapons 'to encourage observation and quick reaction. Hip-firing at appearing and disappearing targets in natural country, Pistol Stockade, "Haunted House" etc.'[16] The 'Haunted House' was of course another variation on the reflex shooting range idea pioneered by Fairbairn and Sykes.[17] Weapons used at HFTC included pistols and the Sten sub-machine gun, and students were introduced to handling explosives and setting booby traps. Lectures covered a variety of topics, but reference to special service operations was common. No.3 Course heard talks on 'The Chindits' and 'No.4 Commando at Dieppe', amongst others.

Beyond Lord Rowallan's earlier connection with the Special Training Centre Lochailort, the HFTC staff featured at least two staff instructors who previously taught there. Staff Sergeant Chisholm of the Lovat Scouts, formerly of STC Lochailort, was drafted in to teach fieldcraft.[18] Captain John Annand had also instructed at STC Lochailort. Annand was a holder of the Victoria Cross, the first Second World War recipient of Britain's highest gallantry decoration, awarded for his bravery in the withdrawal to the River Scheldt in Belgium in May 1940. Damage to his hearing led him to be seconded to training thereafter and he was on the Lochailort staff during early 1942.[19] Visiting lecturers at HFTC included the apparently ubiquitous Surgeon Commander George Murray Levick who described unlikely sources of protein to be found in mountain country and gave practical demonstrations of improvised field cooking.[20]

HFTC's connection to Gordonstoun, Outward Bound and the Scouting movement also throws up some interesting questions about the relationship between special service training and the development of outdoor education.

An influential figure at the HFTC was Major R. G. (Bobby) Chew who from January 1944 was Chief Instructor on the HFTC staff. Chew was a schoolmaster who began working with Dr Kurt Hahn at Salem and came with him from Germany to be a master at Gordonstoun. On Chew's recommendation Gordonstoun employed his old school friend, the explorer and STC Lochailort original Freddy Spencer Chapman. Like Lord Rowallan, Chew had experience of taking Young Soldier battalions to STC Lochailort and, as a mountaineer, he was also involved in the autumn and winter of 1942 with the Commando Mountain and Snow Warfare Training Centre at Braemar.[21] After the war Chew would return to Gordonstoun first as housemaster and later as headmaster. Over this time and under the patronage of former (and founding) pupil the Duke of Edinburgh, Gordonstoun's County Badge scheme was revived and promulgated as the Duke of Edinburgh Awards programme which flourishes today in merger with the Outward Bound Trust.

Another on the HFTC staff was Gordonstoun old boy Captain Adam Arnold-Brown who as warden of the first Outward Bound Mountain School at Eskdale in the Lake District became a figure in the post-war growth of Outward Bound into a national and international programme. The syllabus at Eskdale bore strong resemblance to that of HFTC, shorn of its purely military elements.[22] It is probably no surprise that certain individuals involved at HFTC, and indeed in wartime special service training elsewhere, found continuity after the war working in the field of structured outdoor recreation for young people. Polar explorer George Murray Levick was already active in this arena before the war with his Public Schools Exploring Society.[23] Post-war, the last commanding officer at STC Lochailort, Lieutenant-Colonel C. S. Howard, became warden of an Outward Bound school in Wales.[24] When in 1957 the Army decided to open its own Outward Bound school for young servicemen, the first commandant was the bagpipe-playing, broadsword-wielding former Commando officer Colonel Jack Churchill. Although the school was in Wales, first in Snowdonia then moving to Tywyn, Churchill brought a dash of Achnacarry to the proceedings by greeting student intakes from the train with a welcome on the pipes.[25]

There was continuity in place as well as in personnel. After the war, and from the late 1950s in particular, educational centres on Outward Bound lines mushroomed all across the country both through charitable and public provision. Naturally enough, many were located in coastal settings or mountainous country. In Scotland these included Glenmore Lodge, wartime home of the Norwegian Linge Company. In 1948 the Scottish Education Department leased the Glenmore premises from the Forestry Commission and opened it as the Scottish Centre of Outdoor Training, offering mountain-based courses to school groups.[26] In 1959 the Centre moved to purpose-built premises nearby, taking the name Glenmore Lodge with it. During the 1960s and 1970s educational authorities and charities established numerous camps and converted sizeable private properties to run as outdoor centres.[27] These included Achdalieu Lodge above Loch Eil, temporary home in the early 1940s to the Independent Companies, which today still functions as an Outward Bound centre.[28]

Such incidental connections aside, it is possible to view the evolution of special service training methods within the broader context of ideas about outdoor activity and its perceived benefits which gained in credence and popular participation during the first half of the twentieth century. In the British setting there were Lord Baden-Powell's Scout and Girl Guides Associations founded before the First World War and the Youth Hostel Association formed in 1930, markers amidst an unstructured growth in the popularity of cycling, camping, hill-walking and climbing. By the 1940s these ideas were infiltrating the corridors of power, tuned as they were to ambitions for the country's post-war reconstruction through a planned society, and so received government endorsement through enabling measures in the 1944 Education Act and 1945 Education (Scotland) Act. In Germany private ventures like the Salem school emerged alongside state support for adventure education in schools sponsored first in the Weimar Republic. These were picked up by the Nazis who were also applying related ideas to their own purposes through the Hitler Youth movement.[29]

A connection between the guiding principles of outdoor education for young people and wartime training centres that set out to teach guerrilla warfare did not sit entirely comfortably for those who sought personal and societal progress through education of this kind. If it was an aberration, however, it was not one of anyone's choosing. For Kurt Hahn and others like him, internationalism was one of the tenets to which their doctrine aspired. If war was on their mind, it was only in seeking to enhance progress towards preventing it. In 1937 Freddy Spencer Chapman was a master at Gordonstoun, heavily involved in the school's 'Moray Badge' local outreach scheme (from which the County Badge national programme sprung), when he wrote: 'It is because of the desire to test one's uttermost strength and to face danger that men are so easily led to war .... To live dangerously as a yachtsman, mountaineer, skier or even high jumper and rugger player removes and satisfies this urge.'[30] Three years later he was teaching guerrilla warfare at the Special Training Centre Lochailort and set fair for more than three years of fighting behind Japanese lines in Malaya.

Put to the regrettable requirements of warfare they may have been, but there remains the consideration that for many men who passed through the special training centres this was their first experience of an environment such as the Scottish highlands. As much in horror as in admiration, some from distant parts or from urban backgrounds marvelled that they could be in such a place and still be on their own country's soil. The Special Training Centre Lochailort might have started out in 1940 as the project of a small group of well-connected military officers, including two major Scottish landowners. But as the idea spread, and the throughput of trainees burgeoned, substantial numbers of men from all sorts of backgrounds had the opportunity to measure themselves against the challenge of an environment that had hitherto been largely an exclusive, aristocratic preserve.

After the interlude of war, the popularity of hill-walking, camping and mountaineering picked up once more and grew apace, bringing ever more people of different backgrounds out into country once set aside for those few permitted by the owners to shoot deer or grouse and catch fish. This was a trend that pre-dated the war, and one indeed which was temporarily inhibited by it. And yet the new military imperative of getting men out into the hills to make them fitter, better soldiers, and stronger, more developed individuals, was something that sat well with changing perceptions of what the Scottish landscape might be used for, and by whom. As an adjunct, clothing and equipment available and widely used for outdoor recreation in the two post-war decades included quantities of surplus material produced for the Army in wartime. These featured such tools as the Bergen rucksacks used by the Commandos, as well as the windproof smocks, if not the string vests, favoured at the Highland Fieldcraft Training Centre.

However it was viewed, the choice of the Scottish highlands as a location for special training centres was bound up with the concept that the challenge to be found there was one of a wilderness environment. To some extent this idea rested on an artificial construction, since much of the 'wilderness' in question was in reality a carefully husbanded landscape dedicated to the pursuit of field sports, its nature the consequence of land ownership patterns and economic development over previous centuries. The aristocratic figures who in 1940 recognised in their own and in their neighbours' highland estates a proper place for a particular kind of military training, had a good deal in common with those involved in formal outdoor education after the war. From either perspective the highland environment was viewed as a place of challenge, and so as an amenity.

This was a powerful strand in the ethos of outdoor education for the rest of the twentieth century and was a view that underpinned the explosive growth in outdoor leisure pursuits and adventure tourism which today supports a small industry of activity suppliers and clothing and equipment retailers. In the remoteness, the testing landscape and unpredictable weather, the highlands are a place for challenge and for pleasure and growth in overcoming it. In line with the environmentalist mores of the present day, and mindful of the sincerely-held love of the landscape that in a straightforward sense motivates those who visit the highlands for recreation, the limitations of the purely utilitarian view are now being scrutinised by the theorists of outdoor education.[31]

*   *   *

During the Second World War the guerrilla warfare specialists of MI(R), the Commandos and SOE did not come to the highlands of Scotland to play. Prevailing perceptions of the highland environment suggested one answer to fears proceeding from the military reverses of 1940: that British soldiers had somehow to renew themselves to meet an inexorable danger, that nature is noble but cruel and so by returning to a more natural state selected men might equip themselves with the ruthlessness and manly virtue that would be needed for the coming struggle. As the fortunes of war swung in Britain's favour during 1942, that hard-edged conviction was somewhat ameliorated and absorbed into more conventional military approaches, but it remained an accepted weapon in the armoury of British fighting forces thereafter.

Special service units of the British forces today have the opportunity to train in varied environments across the world, a pool of locations far greater than was available to their predecessors in the 1940s. Although the Scottish highlands are no longer the major context for their programmes, Commando training still takes place there today in the form of mountain training for units of 3 Commando Brigade Royal Marines. This is carried out over estate land in Lochaber and Argyll with the agreement of landowners, and is conducted in advance of regular winter deployments in Norway. In recent years the value of the Scottish training context has increased, as it affords preparation for operations in the mountains of Afghanistan and in the high ground along its border with Pakistan. The Scottish east-coast base of one regular Commando unit, 45 Commando Royal Marines at Condor in Angus, is within easy reach of the Cairngorms. A Joint Service Mountain Training Centre currently operates in Argyll, while other accommodation centres act as bases for Army and other service units wishing to conduct exercises over the Scottish hills.

Completing this book at a time when British forces are engaged in confrontation with guerrilla fighters in Afghanistan and Iraq, it is impossible to overlook reflections on the nature of irregular warfare and our attitudes towards it. Guerrilla training camps hidden in the mountains are not an image that carries positive connotations for western societies in the first decade of the twenty-first century, and yet something quite similar was happening here in Scotland during the 1940s. This is not to suggest a correlation between the Commandos or Special Operations Executive of the Second World War and such present-day forces as Iraqi militias or the fighters of the Taliban; nor a moral equivalence with terrorist groups operating inside the countries they seek to harm. Where guerrilla warfare is concerned, ethics operate in relativity and context, not in absolutes.

To Britain's wartime enemies, the Commandos were cut-throats and SOE-sponsored resistance fighters were terrorists. In the terms that we understand today, the denomination was unjust. Special service troops and resistance fighters did not target innocent civilians as a matter of policy; nor did they pursue the indiscriminate killing of enemy soldiers as an end in itself. Raiding and sabotage operations carried enormous risks and dire consequences in failure, but suicide missions they were not. And yet in the summer of 1940, elements within the British armed forces did self-consciously extend the limits of what they had previously held to be ethical in warfare because that was what seemed to be necessary in order to confront a greater evil, an irreconcilable and militarily powerful enemy who was at their gate.

With the Second World War over it was not long before British soldiers beheld the challenge of guerrilla warfare from the opposite perspective, given the role of pacifying territory in counter-insurgency operations. In the withdrawal from British imperial possessions across the world, and in the long conflict with the Provisional IRA in Northern Ireland, British soldiers were restored to the position of greater military strength but tasked with opposing armed irregulars fighting on ground they knew and enjoying some measure of local support. That Britain had come to the point of contemplating the application of similar methods on its own soil in 1940, and of fostering such capability in others in the following five years, did not generate any particular sympathy for an enemy engaging in warfare through irregular means. But it did perhaps bring a fuller understanding of how this type of warfare worked, and how it might be confronted.

It is commonly held that one of the most successful counter-insurgency campaigns ever fought was that conducted by British forces in Malaya between 1948 and 1960. The British senior officer directing operations in that campaign's most effective phase was General Sir Hugh Stockwell. Sir Hugh had seen much service against enemy forces, regular and irregular, since he left Scotland in 1941. It is nonetheless tempting to suggest here that he might have carried forward some rudimentary thoughts about the nature of guerrilla warfare that came to him as an Independent Company commanding officer in 1940, and from his time as commandant of the Special Training Centre Lochailort in 1940-41.[32] It is certainly true that at the end of the Second World War, British forces had an understanding of warfare of this kind far in advance of anything they brought into it.

* * *

The Second World War did not fall lightly on the United Kingdom. The country was left materially damaged, exhausted and bankrupt, all but divested of its imperial power, and with its population seeking to recover from countless personal tragedies. Yet retaining its territorial integrity intact throughout, mainland Britain avoided some of the worst of Europe's experiences, those wretched and divisive years of enemy occupation that blighted other nations. Among the men and women who came to the Scottish highlands to learn to fight were those who had tasted its bitterness first hand, their own countries overrun. Others were convinced in principle that the war situation demanded uncompromising action, or were attracted by the prospect of adventure and the status of belonging to a unit of selected men. Many simply wanted to get on with the war so as to get it won and finished and get back to their own lives as quickly as possible. They volunteered for special service with their eyes open.

In centuries past the Scottish highlands had known warfare of the most bitter kind. Its echoes in the training centres of the 1940s are not entirely easy to reconcile with the powerful popular memory of the Second World War that endures in Scotland, as it does throughout the United Kingdom. Fighting knives, assassination weapons and unarmed combat manuals do not sit entirely comfortably beside the ration books, unused gas masks and 1940s fashions that are the staples of what the 'Home Front' in Scotland is now commonly taken to have been about. That relatively innocuous things such as these have come to symbolise what happened in Scotland during the Second World War, almost to the exclusion of anything else, is of itself one of the luxuries of victory. Alongside them, the phenomenon of the special training centres is a sobering reminder of what fighting a major war entailed and how high the stakes really were.

The idea of the Commando soldier is one that was and is inseparable from the question of his training. It is not an idea that originated in Scotland, or one that by any means belongs there alone. But it is perhaps in the setting of the Scottish highlands that it may most readily be understood. In September 1952, on a hillside lying below the road between Spean Bridge and Achnacarry, in the presence of Lord Lovat and other members of the Commando Association, Queen Elizabeth the Queen Mother unveiled a memorial to the Commandos.

The monument was the work of Scottish sculptor Scott Sutherland, who in 1949 won an open design competition for the commission. Sutherland's sculpture of three Commandos was cast in bronze by H. H. Martyn & Co. of Cheltenham.[33] The Commando Memorial is a tremendously successful piece of art, one of the best-known and most visited public sculptures in Scotland. It is a highland landmark in itself, a place today of casual tourism, but still one of pilgrimage.

The three huge bronze figures of the Commando Memorial, clothed and equipped for a raid or an exercise, gaze resolutely out over the landscape across to the hills of the Nevis range and the Grey Corries. The scale and naturalistic style achieved by Sutherland express exactly the Commando idea, the spirit of extraordinary endeavour and sense of modernity that lay within the enterprise. The Memorial works above all by dint of its setting, standing in a place not where Commandos fought and died, but in the land over which they were made. Upon the stone base on which the three figures stand, a bronze tablet dedicates the monument to the memory of the officers and men of the Commandos who lost their lives during the Second World War. The inscription ends: 'THIS COUNTRY WAS THEIR TRAINING GROUND.'

NOTES TO PART FOUR

1. A. Kellas: *Down to Earth [or Another Bloody Cock-Up]. A parachute subaltern's story* (Edinburgh: Pentland Press, 1990), p. 63.
2. T. Harrison Place: *Training in the British Army 1940-44. From Dunkirk to D-Day* (London: Frank Cass, 2000).
3. J. Hogan: *Impelled into Experiences. The Story of the Outward Bound Schools* (Wakefield: Educational Productions, 1968), p. 33. Holt was chairman of the committee that oversaw the *Conway* training ship for boys.
4. The 'Outward Bound' title was a symbolic reference to a flag flown on ships soon to leave harbour.
5. 'History of the Highland Fieldcraft Training Centre', in booklet 'Commemorating the 50th anniversary of the Highland Fieldcraft Training Centre and Association 1943-1991', Highland Fieldcraft Training Centre Association records, National Museums Scotland, M.2003.7/schedule 3. Glenfeshie Lodge was the property of Sir George Macpherson-Grant, Bt.
6. Lord Rowallan: *The autobiography of Lord Rowallan, K.T.* (Edinburgh: Paul Harris, 1976), p. 118. The connection with STC Lochailort seems to have begun in spring 1942, making the commanding officer at the time Lieutenant-Colonel C. S. Howard.
7. Ibid, p. 122.
8. 'Basic Officer Training at H.F.T.C.', Highland Fieldcraft Training Centre Association records, National Museums Scotland, M.2003.7/ schedule1.The following information on course content derives from training programmes held under the same reference.

9. Examples issued at HFTC are in the collection of the National Museums Scotland, M.2003.8.1-2

10. During 1939 the Institute's G. C. L. Bertram and B. B. Roberts worked on the development of winter warfare clothing for the War Office. Bertram and Roberts tested their adaptation of the string vest concept by rigorous cycling around Cambridge. Their prototypes and other examples are in the museum collection of the Scott Polar Research Institute. See C. Bertram: *Antarctica, Cambridge, Conservation and Population, a biologist's story* (Petworth: Bertram, 1987), pp. 74-75.

11. 'Diary kept by Cadet R. W. Brash, Highland Fieldcraft Training Centre, Course 7 (Poolewe, 14 February to 24 April 1944), Highland Fieldcraft Training Centre Association records, National Museums Scotland, M.2003.7/schedule 1.

12. Statement of Lieutenant-Colonel John Downton to the National War Museum, April 2002.

13. Interview with Mr John Morrison, HFTC Association, National War Museum, February 2006.

14. Colonel E. Rait-Kerr quoted in Rowallan: op. cit., p.129.

15. Cadet R. V. Milnes died of pneumonia during an exercise on the Isle of Skye.

16. 'Basic Officer Training at H.F.T.C.', Highland Fieldcraft Training Centre Association records, National Museums Scotland, M.2003.7/schedule 1.

17. The reflex range set up in a ruined house is described in A. Arnold Brown: *Unfolding Character. The impact of Gordonstoun* (London: Routledge & Kegan Paul, London, 1962), pp. 78-79.

18. Ibid., p. 99.

19. Interview with Leslie Thornton, Imperial War Museum Sound Archive, 10421, Reel 11, 1988.

20. Ibid., p. 80.

21. Papers of Lieutenant-Colonel R. G. Chew in the possession of his son Mr Tony Chew. Chew was simultaneously involved with training Light Scout Car Companies at Ballantrae House, Ayrshire. These were 'sonic deception' units that used sound recordings to confuse the enemy about the movement of military forces and locations of engagement. In the Normandy campaign they served as 'R Force' under 21st Army Group. Lieutenant-Colonel Chew was decorated for service in Norway in 1945.

22. Brochure 'Outward Bound Mountain School', Highland Fieldcraft Training Centre Association records, National Museums Scotland, M.2003.7/schedule 4/2. Prior to service at HFTC Arnold-Brown served with 4/5th Battalion Royal Scots Fusiliers, training in mountain warfare in the Cairngorms as part of 52nd (Lowland) Division.

23. In 1947 the Society was renamed 'British Schools Exploring Society'.

24. Lt. Col. A. F. Austen MBE BEM: 'The Special Training Centre Lochailort, Inverness-shire, A Personal Memoir', Royal Signals Museum Archive, Ref. 936.4, p. 41.

25. B. Lane: *Military Mountaineering* (Cumbria: Hayloft, 2000), p. 43.

26. C. Loader: *Cairngorm Adventure at Glenmore Lodge, Scottish Centre of Out-*

door Training (Edinburgh: William Brown, 1952), p. 18. See also H. Lorimer: 'Telling Small Stories: spaces of knowledge and the practice of geography', *Transactions of the Institute of British Geographers*, volume 28, 2, 2003, pp. 197-217.

27. P. Higgins: 'Outdoor Education in Scotland', in *Journal of Adventure Education and Outdoor Learning*, 2 (2), 2002, pp. 149-68.

28. Achadalieu was acquired in 1964 by the Dulverton Trust and was run as a Youth Training Centre. From 1977 the Outward Bound Trust took over the running of the establishment of what is now the Outward Bound Centre Loch Eil. M. Tomlinson: *An Act of Faith. The Dulverton Trust 1949 to 1989* (London: Dulverton Trust, 1989).

29. T. Parker & K. Meldrum: *Outdoor Education* (London: Dent, 1973), pp. 39-43.

30. Quoted in R. Barker: *One Man's Jungle. A Biography of F. Spencer Chapman* (London: Chatto & Windus, 1975), pp. 159-60. Reprinted by permission of The Random House Group Ltd.

31. Higgins: op. cit.

32. For an account of his career see J. Riley: *The Life & Campaigns of General Hughie Stockwell. From Norway through Burma to Suez* (Barnsley: Pen & Sword Military, 2006).

33. Scott Sutherland was then Head of Sculpture at Duncan of Jordanstone School of Art, Dundee. Among his other work is the Black Watch Memorial on the northern outskirts of Dundee. Information about Scott Sutherland's life and work courtesy of Mr Alastair R. Ross. See also J. Whitaker: *The Best. A history of H. H. Martyn & Co., carvers in wood, stone and marble* .... (Falmouth: Whitaker, 1985).

Indexes

INDEX OF COUNTRIES AND
ASSOCIATED LOCATIONS

INDEX OF REGIMENTS, ORGANISATIONS AND MILITARY OPERATIONS

(SOE = Special Operations Executive)